Spirit Animals of the Star Signs

Power Animals of the Zodiac

AUTHOR: Grace Gabriella Puskas

✧

Please visit my Youtube Channel the *Dream & Spirit Weaver* for FREE educational videos, wisdom sharings, and spiritual/holistic/esoteric teachings.
(https://www.youtube.com/@TheDreamSpiritWeaver)

✧

Contents

Chapter 21: Self-Evolution & Completion…   **264**

Background to the Author

A lot of my personal journey has been shared in Chapters 1 and 21. But, one thing I would like to say is that my spiritual journey began very naturally and organically, in 2012, leading up to the Time Shift and Galactic Center Alignment. I started to naturally be pulled away from all the distractions I had once known; alcohol, partying, promiscuity- an overpowering sex drive, drugs, food, t.v. film, connections and friendships that served my toxic ways, and a lack of self-discipline. I instead began to fast regularly and consciously, in addition to giving up sex, drugs, all processed and unhealthy foods (I was already vegetarian by this time), tobacco, and even hallucinogens that had once aligned me with my Higher Self. I began to realize all of these were a distraction, and true "enlightenment" could be received through conscious fasting and celibacy alone. Fasting and celibacy, abstaining from sexual interaction and release, were also the route to my psychic gifts and intuitive, precognitive, and extrasensory powers. It was a tricky time and I spent a lot of time in isolation, also parting ways with a soulmate I shared a deep soul bond with, as well as a highly charged and passionate sex life, which was all I had known for quite a few years. Close to the 2012 Winter solstice, I started to have an intense increase in OBE's, astral projection, lucid dreaming, and multidimensional dream encounters. Waking life felt like I was, quite literally, awakening from a dream.

On December 21st exactly, I had a very real and powerful shamanic rebirth. I felt and saw myself leave my physical body, witnessing myself as a light being on another plane, in another dimension, and in another world. Telepathy, clairvoyance, clairsentience, clairaudience, deeply evolved empathy, psychic powers, and spiritual perception were already the norm for me by then, but they increased afterwards. Since the 2012 timeline shift, astral, spiritual, and psychic phenomena have expanded to new levels. I began working more consciously with my spiritual gifts, finally enrolling in a number of holistic and complementary courses in 2013. In 2014, after being guided to leave the security of my job (full story in 'Listening to the Signs of the Universe: *A Personal Story of Synchronicity…*'), I found and entered the Local Legend National Writing Competition, and won. At the same time I met with former BBC Dragon Den's Star, Rachel Elnaugh, once calculated business woman now turned Divine Feminine- Gaia Advocate- Sister Shaman Warrioress of Truth (true energy!), who saw my heart and spirit. She recorded my blueprint poem 'A Message from Source,' which I channeled during the 2012 power portal, professionally for FREE, further opening me up to a world of opportunities.

My full list of credentials and experience: Reiki Master Teacher/Healer, Herbalist, Dream therapist, Chi Kung practitioner, Crystal therapist, Reflexologist, Aromatherapist, and soon to be Past Life Regression therapist (estimated qualification date: end of 2023). I am also a spiritual teacher, guide, empathic counselor, astrologer, psychic, channel, wordsmith, and author, with much experience in sound healing, speaking, and co-creative collaborations. I'm a visionary poet who likes to transcend comfort zones by leaving behind a fear timeline, and moving towards a timeline of LOVE. Unity consciousness, authentic and conscious spirituality, holistic health, and healing planetary consciousness as well as Mother Earth, beautiful Gaia, are my main life goals and service. I am a Medicine Woman and free-flow Musician.

For anyone interested in my personal astrology, to gain a bit of insight into my personality and psyche; I am a *Pisces Sun, Taurus Rising*, and *Cancer Moon*. I am a *Life Path 11*, the *Master Intuitive & Illuminator*, and have my *North Node in Capricorn*. My *Venus is in Pisces* while my

Mars is in Aquarius, also having a *Grand Water Trine* and *Grand Earth Trine* in my birth chart. This is incredibly rare! I was born on March 14th 1992 in Sunset Boulevard, Los Angeles California. Grace Gabriella is my birth name.

Introduction

Spirit animals, which are also known as power animals, are an intrinsic part of the human journey. From tribal aboriginal cultures to native ancestral communities, people who have been open to the spiritual and sacred nature of life have been open to spirit animal contact & communication. Spirit animals act as messengers; they are here to communicate deeper truths, wisdom, insight, and meanings. They do so through the spiritual and astral planes, the subtle dimensions of consciousness.

The realm of the invisible and unseen is always accessible, yet not everyone opens their eyes and hearts to this reality. Unlimited potential and awareness into our eternal and multidimensional natures are available to us. Every human is given opportunities for spiritual growth, enlightenment, and soul-evolution. Are you ready?

Spirit animals are the animals that show themselves when we are vibrating high enough for connection, communication, and contact. They can come to us in dreams, through visions, through our higher selves in meditation or soul-journeying, or through the use of spiritual and shamanic healing modalities. If you're vibrating high enough, with a clean and pure channel (mind, body, & spirit), you may even communicate with them on a daily basis…

Spirit animals appear when the third eye is open. Our hearts and higher selves must be open to the reality of unlimited potential, higher consciousness, and the astral & soul planes to receive their wisdom. Like a circuit, if we are closed off- either through fear, ignorance, or other limiting and self-sabotaging mindsets, belief systems, or behaviors, we will be closed off to their power. Our inner light will turn off. And thus, the magic of this interconnected spiritual universe will equally diminish. The beauty of the spirit world is available for every human, and I want to make this clear.

When I was younger, I always remember intuitively feeling that I was different. Topics I wanted to discuss didn't interest my friends or family, and so I became closed off to 3D distractions and activities. I put myself in *Hermit mode* and connected to the dream, astral, spiritual, and multidimensional quantum planes and worlds on a daily basis. Yes, I explored my shadow self too. Shadow work integration is essential to every shaman. I essentially evolved to such a high frequency, simultaneously removing all poisons, pollutants, chaos, drama, addictions, and chemicals at the same time, that spirit animal contact became normal. I am the sort of woman who sees people's auras, reads people's minds, and can tell what star sign someone is within a few moments of meeting someone! This is very real to a lot of people nowadays, especially people who have done the inner work, and have further healed their wounds, trauma, and past life karmas.

If this applies to you or if you're more of a beginner, this book is the most comprehensive guide on spirit animals and the zodiac star signs you will find. I wrote this while traveling South America in 2022, and it took me many long days, weeks, and months to complete. From the sacred Mayan lands of Mexico to the mountainous rainforests of Monteverde, Costa Rica; all the way to Ecuador and the Amazon jungle… I am graciously proud to present to you, **Spirit Animals of the Star Signs**: *Power Animals of the Zodiac*.

In divine grace and oneness ✦

Chapter 1: Spirit/Power Animals

Spirit Animals: *The Essence*

Spirit animals are spiritual guides that have walked alongside mankind since the start of our earth journey. They exist above and beyond the physical plane, and therefore we must raise our vibration and cleanse our pineal glands to be able to connect with them. I am sorry to say that consuming lots of alcohol, pharmaceutical drugs, chemicals, processed foods, and other intoxicants, like artificial sweeteners- or repetitively using harmful chemical-infused hair, skin, and hygiene products, will decrease your ability to see and interact with the spiritual planes and dimensions. A 3 day fast or water cleanse is recommended, if you're not already on a pure or shamanic path and are seeking to connect with your animal helpers in ceremony. Detox, cleanse, and purify. (You can consult the *Frog spirit* for help in this area!)

Regardless, your frequency needs to be on some level of purity and purification. Water cleanses, meditation elevates and expands your awareness, and nature can clear and activate. Setting the intention is good enough in some cases, and you can of course read this book as a self-help tool for wisdom acquisition and deeper personal discovery.

So there are two aspects to the information presented in this book:

1. Self-knowledge and self-awareness expand; this book is a spiritual self-development guide for uncovering the hidden messages, meanings, and mysteries of the spirit animal queen/kingdoms.
2. You can use this as a shamanic tool for physical healing and self-alignment… You may want to actively and directly connect to your spirit and power animals, and, thus, I have included a simple yet powerful exercise that can help you do so.

If you are operating at a high enough frequency, it is easier to tune into the wisdom and insights from the spirit worlds. Your spirit animal guides and helpers exist just an internal shift or intention away from this physical-material plane. All you need to do is call on them for guidance. They are here to show us a more beautiful, interconnected, and divine world- a world where there's no separation or fear, as we realize we are all *One*. Self-realization transforms to self-actualization with the help of our spirit animal guides. Great healing occurs, and we also recognize how there is more to life than the 3D realm and world. Higher consciousness is activated through their assistance, which flows down and in turn activates memory, buried wisdom, higher truth, instincts, primality, the Higher Self, imaginative gifts, creative genius, profound intuition, discernment, higher mental reasoning, empathy, emotional intelligence, and anything else you can think of.

The purpose of Spirit Animal contact and communication:

- They offer unique insight, guidance, direction, and wisdom into your life purpose.
- They steer you onto self-alignment and the right path, simultaneously helping you to overcome self-destructive and self-limiting cycles.
- Addictions, codependency, substance abuse, greed, lust, negative self-talk, and anything else that puts out your light + disconnects you from your Higher Self is released.
- You can discover the repressed and rejected parts of yourself that need integration. Shadow work is available and accessible through spirit animal learning, communication, and self-discovery.
- You can also integrate and harmonize your light and shadow attributes. This allows you to become a whole, integrated, and complete being.
- Spirit animals assist you in making sense of your past, transitioning from your lunar South Node (the things you are supposed to outgrow) to your Lunar North Node (what you are working towards, embodying, and becoming… your future self).
- They show us our true potential, infinite possibilities, multidimensionality, and our divine essence. Spirit animal guides offer us insight into the subtle realms, where we are able to see through the veil of illusion and connect to Source.

Animals visit us through the astral realms when we are in tune with our soul self, connected to our spirit body, Source, the divine, the Great Spirit, God; whichever higher power you believe in. Spirituality is not religion, and this is something I want to make clear. Although you can be religious and still find resonance in these chapters. We all have a soul regardless of our beliefs, and the spiritual dimensions of being and Self are available to every human. You may already be connecting to some of your spirit animals through astral projection, lucid or shamanic dreaming, and transcendental meditation. It's important that you know that each animal carries a specific and unique set of symbolism. Consciously opening yourself up to these realms requires discernment, and wisdom.

For example, you wouldn't connect to the energy of the Tiger if you wanted to access visionary or psychic gifts! The tiger spirit represents primal instincts, physical vitality, and matters of self-protection and courage linked to the earthly realm. Simultaneously you wouldn't seek inspiration from the Horse spirit if you were looking to expand your dreaming capabilities; you'd look to the Lizard for this.

This is why knowing the exact energetic qualities of each animal is important. You have a set of personal power animals based on your star sign. However, you can connect to every single animal for guidance, insight, and inspiration. There are, in fact, certain qualities and energies "missing" in each of us, which signifies that there will be animals that aren't your personal spirit animals who can help you. They help you integrate what you are missing. (These are covered in each Star Sign chapter.)

Working With Your Power Animals (Keys to navigating this book)

The beauty with the animal realm is that the human journey can be found and represented in the entire animal queen/kingdom species. Every spirit animal has an astral body- every animal has an aura. There are different terms and expressions within the spiritual community for spirit animals, but the general consensus is that they provide us with a *medicine*. This medicine is non-visible and subtle, it's energetic, yet it eventually travels into the physical world based on the inner work we do. You can find a resonance in any or all of the animals mentioned in this book, even though they may not be your zodiac sign's traditional animals.

When looking at the animals you need to work with for integration, remember that they are the qualities and attributes you are missing. This is almost always to do with:-

1. Your planetary ruler, which has its own astral influences.
2. Whether you embody more feminine or masculine energy.
3. Which element you belong to, so whether you are born of fire, earth, air, or water.

A quick example to make sense of this… Aries, the first sign ruled by *Mars*, the planet of war, aggression, action, competition, life force, and vitality, is masculine by nature. Fire is masculine and Mars is a masculine planet, therefore they are one of the most hotheaded and impulsive, yet equally willful and passionate, signs of the zodiac. One of the spirit animals Aries needs to work with for wholeness, inner harmony, and integration is the *Swan*. The Swan is a gentle spirit animal that symbolizes emotional intelligence, purity, sensitivity, harmony, and a love of peace. These are totally opposite characteristics to the Aries personality.

If we look at the last and final sign, Pisces, a complete opposite to Aries; Pisces has many spirit animals that symbolize visionary, psychic, spiritual, gentle, and emotionally serene and intelligent gifts… because these are their strengths. Yet, Pisces can lack the warrior-like and fiery spirit of Aries, and therefore doesn't have many personal animals in the first selection of spirit animals: *Instinctive & Primal Spirit Animals*. What Aries has, Pisces lacks. And what Pisces embodies and specializes in, Aries lacks. Generally speaking, Aries is a master of physical instincts and sexual vitality while Pisces is a master of tuning into the Higher Self and soul planes. They are complete opposites in astrology. (Aries is the first sign known as the 'Child' while Pisces is the last sign known as the 'Old Soul!')

Each star sign takes a little from their opposing signs, or the signs that are of different elements. Below are some other key points you should know to make the most of this book.

1.   Fire and air signs are masculine, while earth and water are feminine

If you want inspiration and find a particular spark of attraction in a sign different to your own, you can look up the spirit animals of the sign to see what you might be missing. *Why are they so charming/bright while I'm so introspective and mellow?* (A question usually spoken by earth and water signs...) *Or why are they so emotionally intelligent and calm when I'm so impatient and impulsive?!* (A question asked by fire and air signs.)

2.   Each star sign has an opposite you can look to for harmony and balance

Every star sign has an opposite that, astrologically speaking, you're supposed to find balance with. Through your opposite sign's traits and strengths you can discover yourself on a deeper level, also find balance, wholeness, and unity within. The combinations are as follows: Aries and Libra, Taurus and Scorpio, Gemini and Sagittarius, Cancer and Capricorn, Leo and Aquarius, and Virgo and Pisces.

3.   Remember that there is more to astrology than your Sun Sign…

Astrology speaks of all the planets or planetary placements influencing your personality, internal desires, emotions, motivations, etc. You should find out your Sun, Moon, Venus, and Rising signs to find the most accurate descriptions of your spiritual essence. The Sun, Moon, Venus, and Rising signs are the primary planetary placements, although you can consult *all* the planets and the corresponding spirit animal meanings, for a completely holistic account. A great free online resource that will tell you your Natal/birth chart planetary placements is Cafe Astrology. It's free, easy to navigate, and clearly shows you what planets fall in which signs. *Here is the link!* You will need to know your birth time, place, and date of birth.

Listening to the Signs of the Universe *(A Personal Story of Synchronicity…)*

Sacred space is essential for any intended contact and communication. Outside of dreams and astral travel, lucid dreaming, and astral projection, the first time I received direct contact from one of my personal power animals, the *Owl*, was through a *Shamanic Journey* "workshop" I was invited to. A long story short- and I'm sharing this because I believe it provides a beautiful example of life's synchronicities when we awaken to our higher purpose and soul calling; I left my last societal job in 2014. I was working as a sales assistant at Holland & Barrett. I loved learning about superfoods and herbal supplements, and that was the sole reason I took the job (over any other). Over a short period of time I knew it wasn't serving me. I felt suppressed, limited, and out of alignment, and the moment I made the decision to leave to trust in the universe, and my Higher Self, life changed. It changed in miraculous ways.

The very day I chose to hand my notice in there was an Owl exhibition right outside my workplace. That's right, a *gathering of owls* were present right outside, on the *day* I chose to listen to my Higher Self and put complete faith and trust in the Great Spirit. *Wow.* (It still brings me awe to this day…)

That decision led me to attending the Olympia Mind, Body, & Spirit show, in London, which I couldn't attend due to not being able to get the weekend off work. It was a real moment of Love VS fear, and I chose love. Something inside me knew I had to attend this weekend; I couldn't explain it logically, of course, but I knew intuitively that I was supposed to go to this MBS show/festival. I ended up buying a Watkins MBS magazine that led me to the Local Legend National Spiritual Writing Competition, which I entered and won. This sparked the start of my journey as a philosophical author and poet. I also met the amazing Rachel Elnaugh, previous BBC Dragon's Den Star turned 'spiritual business mentor and evolutionary.' She saw my spirit, despite me being a shy and humble girl in my early twenties, with no previous famous or business connections, and recorded my evolutionary blueprint poem, *A Message from Source*, for FREE. All professionally with a beautiful sacred geometric art back piece. I also connected with many wonderful courageous star seeds and light warriors in my generation, who introduced me to the spiritual community scene in London (which ended up changing my life forever).

All of this- alignment with my true destiny, from *one conscious choice*. And the owls were there to reassure me…

Oh yes, the shamanic journeying event. This was organized by Rachel Elnaugh and a shamanic practitioner friend of hers. I received my powerful ancestral awakening shamanic journey by her side (she now owns a budding eco-village in the Lake District and has recently left the corporate world to become MP for the Freedom Alliance in Derbyshire), receiving medicine and direct guidance into my life path and soul purpose from the Owl spirit. The owl turned out to be one of my personal spirit animals, as I discovered the next year from another powerful shaman called Hazel, during my Spirit Animal Medicine Wheel Journey. (Legit.)

A Sacred Space (for Spirit Animal contact)

Here is a simple and "fool-proof" exercise to connect to your spirit animal guides & helpers.

You will need:-

- A tribal or shamanic drumming track. This serves as a *heartbeat*. Tribal or shamanic drumming creates the vibration of a universal heartbeat, which activates primal impulses and higher spiritual vibrations.
- A sacred and quiet space; somewhere you won't be disturbed and can really go within to connect to the divine spirit. You will need minimal to no external distractions. You should make yourself feel comfortable too, which requires…
- Comforting blankets, pillows, and cushions; natural lighting- use natural sun or moonlight as best as possible, or candles, an eco-lamp, or darkness. Also, some sage, palo santo, (organic) herbal incense, or resin like frankincense. Cleanse your auric field, which is also known as an electromagnetic energy field (the scientific name).
- To set your intention. Your intentions can be to connect to the astral realm for spiritual wisdom to shine through. Or you might already know of your spirit animals and wish to call on them directly for guidance. If you don't know or don't currently have a personal connection with any of them, set the intention for a personal animal spirit to come through.
- You might want to do a day fast and cleanse, especially if you're intending to perform this in the evening or at nighttime. Cleansing your system with purified water, soothing herbs, and light fruits are ideal and recommended. 3 days would actually be the best option, but one day will suffice. If you're someone who truly finds it hard to fast, only eat high in life force and living foods- organic foods like fresh salads, vegetable soup, and raw nuts and seeds. You want to be as "light" and pure as possible because you are a channel for subtle and spiritual energies to flow through.

Close your eyes, take some deep breaths, and start to feel chi- universal life force energy flow through the cells of your body. Spend a few moments focusing on your breathing and the flow of chi inside and around you. Take a moment to notice the pulse of energy over your heart; through your palms, and circulating up and down your spine, to the top of your head.

Once you feel calm and peaceful within, merge your heartbeat with the drumming. Remember that the drum is the heartbeat, a universal primal and spiritual pulse that connects you to the quantum field. It is this universal heartbeat that aligns you with your spirit body, and the astral realm where spirit animal communication is possible. Synchronize your breathing to this heartbeat for a while.

Now, focus your intention on speaking with your spirit animal. This all takes place on the astral planes, the ether, and the spiritual realms. Set your intention of connecting with your spirit animal, first taking a few moments to think about the qualities of the animal. Make a mental note of its symbolism and strengths. Meditate and reflect for a while on the essence and energetic associations of the animal. You can also picture its aura and white light streaming through its auric field… If you are unaware of which animal you would like to connect with, set an intention for higher wisdom to come through. You can also have a picture in front of you for inspiration.

Now tune into the frequency of the animal's medicine. Visualize its natural habitat. Picture being submerged in its natural place, such as a rainforest, the ocean, a cave, lake, waterfall, mountain, or jungle. You will know which one is correct based on your intuitive feeling, so listen to your gut feeling where your instincts lie. Start to take some deep breaths and still your mind...

Feel your awareness merging with nothingness, with the silence and space of the infinite. This is the home of the Great Spirit, and of the spirit animal realm. Spirit Animals are guardians of the astral and ether. They act as messengers to the Great Spirit and the divine, and want to guide and lovingly assist you. There is nothing to fear. You are protected and held in a gentle and benevolent embrace. Merge your mind with this infinite source field, the spaces in between all you know and let your mind drift and wander, as you stay connected to your body.

Once again, feel the life force pulsate between your palms, and momentarily visualize a loving light surrounding your heart, and the top of your head by your crown. It's in silence and emptiness where sound and space arise.

Once you are in a space of surrender, trust, and pure openness, allow your animal guide to come in. Picture it traveling towards you, infusing your energy field with light and wisdom. It is bringing you insight, direction, and connection. Take note of where this animal connects with you. For example, an owl will touch you on your Third Eye… and Eagle will shine its light through your crown… There are animals who will surround you and others will rest gently in your heart; some you will see etherally in the faint distance, and others will appear more vividly as if they are right by your side, or on top of you. Your journey is unique.

Make your intentions known: actively ask for help. Project feelings of love and harmony, openness, and receptivity. You are open to receive the love and insight that wishes to be shown to you. Be vulnerable while remaining strong in your light and truth simultaneously. Observe as the animal's medicine trickles down or up into your being. Be patient, be still, and be receptive. Always remember that there is only love in this realm, no harm can come to you. Embrace all the sensations and warm and tingling feelings, and let the animal work its magic.

You can stay in this space for as long as it feels right or comfortable. If you start to get a little nervous, as the sensations can be quite intense, also overwhelming you with unconditional love; say the mantra or affirmation, *"All is love. I am divinely guided and protected."* Remember to send your gratitude and appreciation to your spirit animal helper. Come out of this energetic space slowly and still connected to the feelings, astral insights, and sensations received… Your auric field is still receiving the Higher Self and soul guidance and wisdom, through the ether and your astral/spiritual body.

Once you repeat this process, it will seem easier and easier to perform. It will get to the stage where your power animals are by your side in everyday waking life! You may call on them effortlessly, or see glimpses of them during day-to-day activities. You may start to connect with them in dreams, which we explore more in the final chapter.

The main 35 Spirit Animals have been grouped into the following:-

- Instinctive & Primal
- Emotionally Intelligent
- Wise & Insightful
- Down-to-Earth & Grounding
- 'Higher Self'
- Spiritual & Evolved
- Creative & Inspirational

Chapter 2: Instinctive & Primal Spirit Animals

We are the animals that best represent your instincts,
Your primal nature, the inner fire and self-respect.
We are courageous, bold, and highly independent;
Other animals know not to mess with us- we're the ones who live with intent.

Our physical vitality, passion, and life force,
Allow us to be respected, perhaps sometimes feared, but never ignored…
We are a symbol of sexuality, survival, and everything connected to basic need;
We can teach you what it truly means to establish strong roots, self-love, and security.

Lion

The lion is a majestic and regal power animal symbolizing courage and devotion. This noble animal is courageous, fiercely protective of loved ones, self-expressive and confident. The lion spirit is a symbol for family, community and brotherhood. Deep bonds run through the connections in a lion and lioness tribe, so if this is your power spirit animal you have a strong calling towards community and family bonds. Lions are the kings and queens among many animal species, in the physical realm. They are relaxed and content to be themselves and do not live in fear of others. This is why they have the symbolism of being courageous and supremely confident. They're playful, charming, dignified, and full of pride... A lion will protect themselves and others in their family or community, also risking their lives for those they love or care for. Non-shamanic related symbolism of the lion includes the *Lion of Judah*, representing Emperor Haile Selassie as linked to Rastafari culture. In this culture and spiritual tradition they see the lion as a symbol of nobility, strength, devotion to the divine and spirit, kinship, and self-sovereignty. In astrology, the lion is the glyph (astrological symbol) of Leo, the 'heart of the zodiac;' the loyal and loving fire sign with qualities including benevolence, kindness, generosity, playfulness, optimism, creative life force, courage, nobility, social grace and charm, and a big spirit. So you can see the link here.

You will often find lions lazing around in the Sun, as they love their rest and sleep. Yet they're also incredibly courageous, bold and determined- they're fiercely protective, which links to the energetic qualities of teaching, educating, and inspiring others. A healthy balance of rest, play, and work is prevalent through this spirit animal. If you resonate with this animal, you have an evolved sense of self-worth, self-esteem, personal authority, and self-empowerment. Self-autonomy too. You are a divine, majestic, sensual, soulful and intuitive person. Potent instincts and physical vitality are available to you, yet you don't lack heart or sensitivity. Lions are very compassionate and empathic, sensitive and emotionally intelligent. They may be fierce protectors with a dominant side, however they experience and show real love, loyalty, gentleness, and companionship. You are likely playful, energetic, romantic, intimacy loving, affectionate, and highly companionable! You crave social bonds and connection and use your potent instincts and intelligence to create success in your life. Those with the lion spirit by their side tend to be victorious. There's strong will power, ambition, and motivation; a link to the Sun and dominant solar energy allows for enhanced personal authority and ambition linking to the intellectual realm & planes. Intellectual and psychological driving forces are strong. Being so charming and playful allows you to find yourself and develop your own truth through intimacy and authentic, deep, bonds.

The lion spirit brings pride, self-assertiveness, intelligence, and confidence to express your views and feelings. There is nothing timid or shy about this spirit animal. Further, creative life force, inspirational and devotional qualities, innovation and originality, and charisma and integrity are available to you. The lion is a call to self-leadership. You may experience sensations of an ethereal and energetic crown of gold and jewels sitting on your head, by or near your Crown chakra. The lion helps to align you with the qualities of the Heart and Crown chakras simultaneously. It amplifies your desire to heal yourself and thus step into leadership positions so you can be a wayshower or teacher. Overcoming wounds, traumas, and past pains linked to how willing and open you are to family, love, and community and kinship/friendship bonds is a key additional symbol of the lion. Emotional vulnerability, companionability factors and intimacy are tied into self-empowerment, self-expression, and creativity and talents. You should see the close bonds in your life, including community and kindred spirit bonds, as catalysts to self-healing and personal development.

Anything to be mindful of?

If the Lion is your spirit animal, you need to be mindful of the following shadow traits or follies:-

- False pride, egocentricity, and arrogance; being center-stage all the time, and therefore not knowing when to be humble, modest, or a team-player
- Aggression and psychological, physical, spiritual, or emotional violence
- Bullyish and tyrannical tendencies… seeking to control, over-power, or oppress others
- A lack of motivation and stepping away from your true calling (you must learn to balance your desire for rest with work, service, and your legacy or destiny!)

Panther

The panther is a powerful and sensual symbol of astral wisdom and magic, the shadow self and realm, sensuality, subtle and fine-tuned perception, ether and spirit, emotional depth and intelligence, instincts, psychic gifts, and spiritual powers. The panther represents darkness, and thus all the qualities linked to the moon and astral realm. People with this spirit animal tend to be deep, mysterious, very sensual and mystically-inclined, and gifted in the realms of prophecy. They possess prophetic vision and seer-like qualities. The panther is a symbol of personal power and magnetism, self-sovereignty, and a deep and ancestral cord to the astral and spiritual realms. You may find yourself receiving intuitive glimpses and insights through your higher mind, or through instincts and bodily wisdom. The panther is sensual and majestic. Their instincts are on a whole new level, and just watching them move gracefully and bathed in a surreal type of sensuality can be a mystical experience. The panther spirit evokes raw emotions, primal desires, and motivations and to heal from ancestral, karmic, and family wounds & pain. Overcoming trauma is associated with this power animal. People with this spirit animal aren't afraid to 'go deep' and explore the wounds of the past, then turning the pain and wisdom found into self-knowledge, higher powers, and self-alignment. You can integrate your Higher Self through the panther's energy.

The panther teaches you the power of being honest with yourself. Emotional vulnerability, honesty, wisdom, intelligence, and empathy are all expanded and amplified. Through one eye gaze, the panther's medicine can penetrate your soul, transporting you to the depths of soul & spirit. There's a deeply transformative and alchemical quality to the panther. A soul connection including a deeper connection with the universe and cosmic forces is available. The more you work with the panther, the more you will feel "at home" with the universe and with nature. Your senses will develop. Extrasensory gifts and divine abilities will evolve too. Clairsentience, clairaudience, and clairvoyance are all available with this powerful and sensual animal, as are psychic gifts and telepathic powers. Telepathy is using non-verbal communication to communicate, which relies on advanced instincts, compassion, and intentions of interconnectedness and unity. The panther is not only instinctive and psychic with spiritual powers, but also caring, sensitive, and empathic- they're capable of deep displays of love, loyalty, and devotion. Through such an evolved emotional and spiritual frequency you can seek out life's deeper meaning, creating an ethereal cord to the astral planes where wisdom is found. Simultaneously, intimacy, true love, soulmate love, and self-love can be discovered and embodied.

A final meaning and message of the panther spirit is the link this sensitive and self-aware animal has to dreams. Being so in tune with the unseen and hidden realms of emotions, feelings, instincts, subtle impressions, and feminine energy and qualities allows those with this power/spirit animal to access the realm of dreams and multidimensionality; sometimes quite effortlessly. You may find yourself slipping in and out of dreamspace at will, or entering transcendental meditation states quite easily. A lot of insight, knowledge of the self, healing imagery, symbolism, and intuitive guidance are available to you in dreams. There's a bridge between your subconscious mind and consciousness- whereas many people find a disconnect here, you can alternate between the two. Subtle perception is available when you feel comfort in the dark, in darkness, and in the shadow realms. Shamanic essence is often explored and developed through the panther spirit animal. Feminine wisdom and qualities can be developed and integrated, such as nurturance, caring, sensitivity, empathy, receptivity, selflessness, and unconditional love.

Anything to be mindful of?

If the Panther is your spirit animal, you need to be mindful of the following shadow traits or follies:-

- Getting lost in darkness, depression, despair, or low moods and melancholy
- Finding so much comfort in the dream, astral, or spiritual worlds that you feel disconnected from others and society
- A fear of intimacy or romance- relying on excessive solitude
- Alternating between the extremes: codependency vs supreme self-sovereignty & independence

I am the Lion, with great heart and pride;
My connection to the sun allows me to truly shine.
I'm courageous, brave, and love to lead,
I am a symbol of strength- yet I love my sleep!
You can often find me lazing around, relaxed and content,
I balance achieving my goals and leading the pride with a
healthy natural rest.

Confident beyond belief, I always achieve
and as a symbol of brotherhood and true community,
I will always protect my family and live up to my duty.

I am the Panther, feeling comfort in the dark,
I do not fear the places others usually find hard.
Content being alone for the unknown is my home;
the places most are scared to wonder- I feel free to roam.

My coat is bathed in mystery and sensuality...
the ancients believed my energy is linked to divine sexuality.
My eyes penetrate deep into your being, you can tell me no lies
for I see beneath the surface and sense the things you try to hide.
The solitary path is my nature and my pleasure,
In my independence is where I discover life's true many treasures.

Crocodile

The crocodile (sometimes referred to the alligator power animal, you can use the crocodile symbolism for the alligator as well), is a symbol of primal power and inner strength. The crocodile is very much linked to your emotions, instincts, inner feelings, and the realm of emotions and physical senses. Instincts linked intimate relationships and how you respond, react, and feel within them is a main meaning of the crocodile spirit. If you resonate with the crocodile, you have heightened senses and psychic abilities, psychic powers, and incredibly physical vitality. Your instincts may arise from primal desires, a strong libido, and sexual needs and motivations. Animal instincts are strong in those with this spirit animal. The crocodile enhances your ability to be in tune with your surroundings. The element connection here is water. Water is connected to emotions, the hidden and subconscious realm of feelings, astral insights, and feminine energy. Subconscious connection too. Crocodiles are animals of both water and earth, so you likely feel comfort in the realm of primal instincts and desires just as you do in the physical and material realm. You get your security and comfort from the environments you find yourself in, from the earth and physical foundations & structures. Passion, courage, fierce determination, self-preservation and protective qualities are all enhanced with the crocodile. Not only does this primal animal represent instincts and physical strength and vitality, but it also symbolizes nurturing and sensitivity. Both sensitivity and self-awareness are available in vast measures with the crocodile.

Getting in touch with your feelings and emotions are very important if this is your power animal, or if you resonate in any way. The crocodile allows you to explore the past, accessing memories of past experiences. These memories are rooted in emotions and related to childhood, family, and ancestral cords of knowledge. Issues in childhood or 'parent wounds' can come to the surface. This animal helps to bring the subconscious to conscious light. For example, if you have a mother wound- a core wound unresolved from childhood regarding your connection (or lack of connection) to your mother, the crocodile will help you access it. Awareness can shine around the painful memories and repressed emotions associated with your past. The same applies to having a father-wound. Psychic and spiritual powers and abilities of perception link to the water element, so this is where this symbolism comes from. Courage and fearlessness to succeed in business, professional partnerships, and life also expands into love and intimacy. You can use the strong sense of inner strength and courage to address core wounds, family problems, and imbalances or distortions from your youth.

This is a great power animal to have if you suffer from low libido or a lack of sexual vitality and confidence. The crocodile assists in increasing passion, and can help you address the ways in which you express this passion. Do note, however, sexuality as a theme for self-discovery in relation to the crocodile is more physical, (somewhat) lusty, and purely primal. It's an "animal instincts" type of sexual style. Feelings of intimacy and connection come through physical sensations and pleasure, not through more romantic, gentle, sensual, or tantric expressions of sexual desire and need. If you know anything about astrology, the crocodile symbolism relates to more of a 'Mars sexuality' than a 'Venus sexuality.'

Anything to be mindful of?

If the Crocodile is your spirit animal, you need to be mindful of the following shadow traits or follies:-

- Aggression, psychological and emotional violence, and a desire to intimate and control others
- Emotional and sexual repression; repressing your feelings and true inner desires & needs
- Pushing down core wounds, not addressing trauma or painful memories
- Sexual repression and low/lack of libido, or excessive lusty and primal tendencies…

Horse

This is one of the more serene and beautiful (inner beauty) primal power animals. The horse is a symbol of sexuality, willpower, primal desires, physical vitality, and instincts. Horses carry a lot of personal power and loving, affectionate, and beautiful energy. They are wise, empathic, sensitive, compassionate, and loyal. They are devoted in love and highly companionable. Horses are the ultimate type of 'spiritual and primal' love. Passion is immense- if this is your power animal, you are extremely passionate with a strong sex drive. You love intimacy, love, romance, and physical pleasure. Yet you're also very sweet, nurturing, and sensitive. Spiritual and devotional love is strong in those with the horse spirit animal. Free will is yours too. Personal power and authority are amplified, while opportunities increase and flow in abundance when you embody the horse's medicine. The message is to not become fearful or stagnant. Empower yourself sexually, sensually, and in terms of the resources in your life. You're a very sensual and intuitive creature if the horse is your spirit animal. Ambition, aspirations, hopes, goals and dreams are all available for access, as are 'level ups.' Primal instincts and vitality are very strong, and combining these with purity- intentions for peace, cooperation, harmony, unity, selflessness and love, etc.- can create a lot of prosperity in your life. You should re-find your confidence, because you have a lot of talents and deeply buried personal power! Self-authority has evolved too.

A secondary key meaning and symbolism of the horse is freedom, travel, and movement. You likely love adventure and taking regular or sporadic outings, trips, and travel breaks. The horse is actually similar to the Centaur, in spirit, which is Sagittarius' astrological glyph/symbol. A lot of Sagittarius' qualities can be related to the horse spirit; a love of culture, learning, and community; a love of higher education and philosophy… The Centaur symbolizes primal instincts and sexual life force, but the dual aspect to this creature is the Archer (also Sagittarius' glyph). The Archer reaches for the stars and is concerned with higher truths, spiritual ideals, and ideologies. So all of this can be applied to the horse as a power animal. If this is your spirit animal, you have immense energy and genuine passion and zest for life. You may be sporty, blessed with good health and fine physical attributes, whilst possessing evolved inner strength. Sport, health, well-being, fitness, and adventure all come under the horse's symbolism. Also, due to the link to movement, there is a sense of journeying, i.e. taking a soul journey. Journeying and travel are not just limited to physical movement. The horse can show you how to travel dimensions, access spiritual and philosophical truths and ideals, and go on an inner journey, like to the inner realms of spirit. Multidimensional awareness is available with the horse spirit.

Liberation, self expression, and total freedom to be the self-autonomous individual that you are are a further meaning and message. The horse represents self-autonomy, self-sovereignty, and independence. But they equally need companions and community connections. The horse can therefore help you find balance in your life, a healthy balance between independence and healthy attachments. There's a sense of majesty and nobility associated with this spirit animal- horses are very graceful. Modest, noble, wise, perceptive, intelligent, nurturing, and intuitive, horses are the perfect symbol for merging and balancing your higher and lower self. Through the horse spirit, you can learn the true meaning of being both grounded, primal, and in tune with your instincts and libido, your sexual life force, and your spiritual divine self. This spirit animal is the epitome of passion. The message is to use this passion to establish strong and loving bonds in your life, hence why horses are so companionable and represent companionship and intimacy. Also, channeling inner passion into creative, educational, professional, intellectual, and artistic projects and pursuits. People with the horse spirit tend to have many interests, passions, and projects that take up their time. Although they are strongly independent, self-autonomous, and self-reliant, the horse also symbolizes community and teamwork. You attract the most success (and love and fortune) when you are being cooperative and playing well as part of a team. Unity consciousness is advised over any extreme 'lone-ranger' pursuits. Finally, fertility is linked to the horse. Your personal presence and power and your commitment to truth, honesty, and authenticity is what attracts the best opportunities and connections into your life. Always seek liberation and freedom while remaining down-to-earth, fertile, and aligned to your destiny.

Anything to be mindful of?

If the Horse is your spirit animal, you need to be mindful of the following shadow traits or follies:-

- Falling into extremes between physical instincts & bodily needs, and spiritual essence
- Allowing people to control you through limiting beliefs, preconditions, and fears
- Passing by opportunities… becoming so restless and frivolous that you either pass by significant soulmate and career bonds, or neglect commitments altogether!
- Restlessness and an excessive need for freedom and independence, which can lead to impulsiveness, irritability, aggression, and a lack of sensitivity, humility, and self-awareness

DREAM MESSAGE:

If you see a horse in your dreams, this is a sign that you need to explore your sexuality. A horse running freely through green or open horizons suggests you are in tune with your sexuality, liberated, and in a state of freedom; or you are working towards this. A horse in distress, stuck, trapped, stagnant, or blocked from movement in any way implies repression. You currently feel blocked and unable to express yourself sexually, and/or sensually. You likely have some wounds and repressed trauma to deal with…

One or more horses in your dream signifies you have choices in love- you have options! Alternatively, you are currently exploring polyamory or more tribal and open forms of love and sexual union, play, or intimacy. Stay open to self-reflection and contemplation, as it's in our wounds and suppressed shadow traits where great wisdom, light, and truth are found.

Wasp

The wasp is a unique spirit animal in that many people see this creature as annoying or even something to fear. But the wasp contributes to the great ecosystem of life. It helps the ecosystem function as a whole, it is part of the interconnected greater whole; and this makes the wasp essential to our survival as well, because it assists in the homeostasis of nature. The wasp teaches us how to overcome struggles and setbacks. It brings the teaching of hardships, and that life can truly 'sting.' Sometimes not everything is smooth sailing. In order to produce a magnificent result, we must first go through challenges, trials, and tribulations. There's a divine order and flow to things. Life involves duality, there is lightness and darkness in everything. Pain and suffering have a purpose, and struggle and temporary lack or setbacks lead to our growth and self-development. If we want to see the best finished result, i.e. a thriving, healthy, harmonious and self-sufficient ecosystem- Mother Earth functioning as a whole, we must first go through the evolution process. This is the ultimate message of the wasp animal.

Wasps are often overlooked and undervalued, and are further seen as annoying to many. This can teach you to value yourself first and foremost. Appreciate all you do, because there will be someone who sees (values, appreciates, recognizes) you! Wasps are similar to bees in the respect that they represent hard-work, perseverance, and determination. If this is your spirit animal, you likely work towards something diligently and with complete focus, determination, and desires to succeed. You're problem-solving, accomplished, high-flying, and concerned with how your actions can help or assist. This spirit animal implies service and helpfulness. An interesting fact: wasps help to keep insect populations down and thus help plant life, which in turn manifests as sustainability and the earth's perpetual survival. The message is that life may not always be joyous and easy, or peaceful, but every little act adds up. All actions and intentions are significant. If this is your power animal, you may be very concerned with the small details in life. Also, extremely practical, discerning, grounded, and modest. You do the work that needs to be done without a fuss and without demanding attention. A further symbolism is the beauty and abundance of the earth, and how you can tune into Mother Earth and her energies for abundance. Opportunities, connections, and self-expansion are available to you when you work in harmony with the earth (the natural world). This includes universal forces and energies like yin and yang.

There is a light and darkness within everything- every experience and emotion, sensation, or event. Your lesson from the wasp spirit is to accept, embrace, and learn through the pain. Even mistakes and deadends or u-turns can lead to wonderful beauty, victory, and connection in a future cycle or chapter. Always focus on the positive and find wisdom and solace in the growing pains.

Anything to be mindful of?

If the Wasp is your spirit animal, you need to be mindful of the following shadow traits or follies:-

- Not succumbing to pessimism or negative thinking when life "stings"
- A fear of failure; not giving up when there are challenges or setbacks
- Being mindful of motivation, creating plans, adhering to order and organization-structures, and respecting physical and practical foundations in your life
- Laziness and idleness… also irrational fears related to human interaction, intimacy, and connection.

I am the wasp, I am similar the beautiful bumble bee,
the creature many of you love- but not me.
I contribute just as much to planet earth's ecosystems,
So please don't hate me, even though my appearance is misleading.

I'm here to show you there is both light and darkness,
in every moment, so don't deny or repress!
Yes, life might sting, there can be setbacks and challenges
but these are the key to your growth… embodying the wisdom of
oneness and duality.

Chapter 3: Emotionally Intelligent Spirit Animals

We are the emotionally intelligent and serene spirit animals,
We bring peace, contemplation, and feelings of tranquility.
You begin to feel calm just from our presence,
Our sensuality and soulfulness spark a deep inner remembrance.

We are majestic, kind, gentle-hearted, and pure;
Intuitive, self-aware, incredibly instinctive, and evolved.
See, we bring the subtle perception, divine wisdom, and spirituality
and are here to teach you that life is not all about ego or a materialistic reality.

We feel, we bring purity, and we seek out authentic connections
knowing that nothing is as important as heart-centered, honest, relating.
We ask you to slow down, and to connect to psychic and spiritual gifts,
as there is a world of deeper meaning, divine truths, and timeless magic…

Dove

The dove is a symbol of purity and peace. People with the dove spirit animal tend to be peace loving and harmony seeking individuals. They choose unity, cooperation, harmony, and peace in every moment, and over chaos, conflict, or destruction (every time). Spiritual illumination, purity, faith, hope, angelic consciousness, serenity, and emotional intelligence are main meanings and symbolisms of the dove. A serenity and inner calmness is available through this power animal. The dove helps to show us just how important spiritual values and 'higher consciousness' themes are in daily life. It builds a bridge between the material and physical world and realm, and the divine and Great Spirit. Higher consciousness, spiritual ideals, morals and ethics, integrity, trust in the divine and a higher power, and everything related to the spiritual multidimensional realms are enhanced. The dove's medicine is calming, balancing, soothing, cleansing, and purifying, least to mention integrating. Referring back to the "bridge" mentioned, the dove spirit is the perfect animal for understanding how the lower self & higher self are interconnected. The heart is the central chakra or energy chakra. It is through the heart where we experience raw emotions, physical desires and sensations, instincts related to bodily wisdom, and primal needs and feelings (lower self/energy centers); and intuition, inspiration, subtle perception, self-expression, psychic visions and abilities, and everything linked to spiritual consciousness (higher energy centers). The heart emits powerful vibrations and ethereal energy that allows us to access emotional intelligence and empathy. As a symbol of ultimate peace, the dove can help you connect to your heart space. Emotional maturity, wisdom, and empathy are all increased.

Insight, wisdom, self-knowledge, inspiration, clarity, and spiritual powers are all available for integration. Manifestation powers and utilizing spiritual laws, like the law of attraction, can be learned through this animal. Illumination and enlightenment are other key messages, including self-realization and self-actualization. Self-realization is realizing wisdom, truth, and physical experiences through our interactions and daily lives. It can occur in both the subconscious and conscious realm. Self-actualization is integrating wisdom and understanding, and bringing it up into the light; into consciousness. It's actually living the truth or profound insight and realization. The dove inspires both of these things. If you resonate with this animal, you may find yourself embodying peace and harmony to inspire change, such as through helping others and the world transcend chaos, illusion, and destruction or darkness. Or you could simply influence positive change this way in your friendship, social, family, and professional circles. Immense calmness, peace of mind, serenity, and psychic and intuitive insight are present and inherent. Further, dove medicine provides a sense of detoxification, cleansing, and clearing; cleansing your aura of ignorance, fear, negativity, and illusion is possible, as is using the dove to assist in a physical cleanse or detoxification.

Meditation, mediumship, channeling, connecting to the angelic and spiritual realms, and tuning into your Higher Self can all be accomplished, and enhanced with the dove spirit. Alchemical transformation linked to purity and white light are equally attainable. Inner alchemy, inspiration, manifestation gifts, divine abilities, soul alignment, imaginative abilities, clairvoyance, clairsentience and clairaudience flow through the dove's auric field and energy. These are qualities often shown by people with the dove as their spirit animal. A key message is to align yourself with the mystical and faith-inspired qualities of universal trust, hope, and unconditional love. Another is to commit to more of a pure or clean path, eliminating toxins, junk food, addictions, and self-limiting or destructive cycles. Introspection and self-reflection including soul-searching can father be enhanced with the dove. Slowing down and connecting to your inner source, through the subconscious and subtle realms, can aid in multiple areas of life. Self-evolution is on the horizon. There's beauty, love, and harmony all around you, if you're willing to open your heart, connect to your soul and inner spiritual essence, and activate your Higher Self through your third eye; seeing with higher eyes.

Anything to be mindful of?

If the Dove is your spirit animal, you need to be mindful of the following shadow traits or follies:-

- People-pleasing, appeasing, and overly-compromisable tendencies
- Seeking to retain the peace at all costs, even at the expense of your own self-love & self-care
- Passive, self-sacrificing, and selfless tendencies *in excess...* try to balance these qualities with more dominant, forceful/direct, and "yang" attributes
- A lack of boundaries and becoming a doormat, pushover, or emotional dumping ground for others

I am the Deer, a way shower for your path,
I can offer you guidance, a direction aligned to your heart.
Steering you through toward the new so your spirit can soar;
as a symbol of strength, I can keep showing more.
Surfacing what's hidden and offering new ways,
I am your light and your strength when lost in the maze.
Purity, empathy, and integrity define me,
In nature we find our answers that lead to our best reality…

For I am the pathfinder, the light holder; the compassionate gentle force,
My sensitivity and psychic instincts continuously open new doors
to self-evolution, personal growth, higher awareness, and intuition-
I may be full of grace, yet my nurturing spirit contains valuable wisdom.

Deer

The deer represents a gentle and graceful spirit. The deer is a symbol of inner strength, instincts, and intuition. This gentle and benevolent spirit animal is compassionate and full of sensitivity and grace. They are caring, nurturing, devoted, affectionate, and loyal creatures. There's a very strong feminine energy associated with this animal. If this is your power animal, you have the ability to pick up on things below the surface. You're instinctive to the needs of others, and intuitive to the subtle energies from the hidden realms of feelings and emotions. You possess keen observation and perception skills and have fine tuned many psychological, emotional, and spiritual abilities. Yet, you also have heightened senses and physical instincts… Nobility, dignity, and integrity flow through you in great force. You are not the type of person to cheat, con, or play games. You value intimacy and connection, kinship and romantic and family bonds. Actually, you place supreme importance on companionships and loving bonds. Manipulation is not something you're prone to, nor is circulating or perpetuating BS, ignorance, or separation. Deers bring the message of connection, authenticity, platonic love, romance, family, friendship, and transparency. Due to such strong instincts, they possess advanced emotional intelligence. They are very evolved spiritually.

You like to radiate empathy and compassion, and people can sense you're modest with good morals. Integrity allows you to go through life smoothly and graceful, you project an air of respect. Pure-heartedness, peace, contentment, and feelings of security and safety are integrated. Passion and purpose are part of the deer's meaning and symbolism too. You may find yourself engaged in humanitarian, environmental, or charitable deeds. You're a believer in service, devotion, and living with purpose. You like to feel safe and secure in your physical environments, and you often bring feelings of protection and warmth to others. The deer is genuinely beautiful, inside and out. Feminine qualities are expanded. Your inner voice guides you through the lowest times and highest ones. When you speak, you're gentle yet ooze confidence. Your aura is shimmering and serene in a way that increases the vibration of the spaces you're in.

Innocence, purity of mind and thought, emotional maturity, emotional wisdom, spirituality, self-love, and universal love are other key symbols. Innocence and faith allow you to navigate life with your intuition intact, whilst allowing for self-protection. You resonate with deep friendships and are highly companionable; a soul mission or destiny might be part of your life's legacy. Your identity is tied into the compassionate and heart-centered connections in your life. This is not a superficial or 'lacking depth' spirit animal. Such potent instincts also allow for qualities like clairaudience and clairsentience- you may have telepathic abilities or be susceptible to psychic insights. The deer can act as a messenger of wisdom and subconscious insight from the spiritual realms. Another message is to seek out harmony and more authentic, deep, connections.

Express yourself creatively and imaginatively as well, as you likely have many unseen artistic talents. Your sensitivity can give birth to some extraordinary creations and revelations, if you should open yourself up to the universe's magic. Finally, the deer is 'at one' with nature and the natural world. Sacredness is a part of her teachings and symbolism. The deer projects a demeanor of caring, devotion, understanding, acceptance, and self-awareness. Sacred life force and essence can be understood through her wisdom and energy, while remaining grounded throughout all of life's situations can be embodied. Empathic, peaceful, and non-violent communication is an additional meaning of the deer spirit. A pure and innocent heart outwins any conflict.

Anything to be mindful of?

If the Deer is your spirit animal, you need to be mindful of the following shadow traits or follies:-

- Vulnerability and naivety; innocence that leads to 'idiot compassion' or letting others take advantage of you
- Being gullible, overly submissive or passive, and selfless to the point of loss or lack
- Self-criticism… Apply your evolved compassion and understanding to yourself too
- Kindness and generosity without pure intention- only give if it's sincere

I am the dolphin- I love to swim and play,
I have a special sonic radar that can travel through the waves…
You will always see me smiling, swimming happy and free;
I value love, friendship, joy and my community.
I can teach you how to live in tune with nature's patterns and rhythms
and how to use the creative life force to help manifest your visions!
Living in water is symbolic of feelings and emotions,
We use our voice for healing and breath is our devotion.

If you wish to experience the sheer joys of being, simply learn to breathe;
Breathing lets go of blocks to joy and allows for full release.
Some say us dolphins used to be human- advanced souls from another world,
yet if this is truth or divine imagination,
The sea is truly home.

Dolphin

The dolphin symbolizes playfulness, love, and harmony. This is a strong "community" spirit animal- those with this power animal have many friendships and social connections. They're big believers in community, kinship, friendships, and kindred spirits. Connections often serve as a reflection to the soul, so may likely be creative or rooted in some shared artistic or intellectual gift or vision. Harmony, diplomacy, and profound psychological and intellectual gifts come under the dolphin's meaning and medicine. They are empathic and sensitive, self-aware and deeply intelligent. Dolphins are a symbol of telepathy, a rare type of communication that implies being able to see through the veil of illusion. People who are capable of telepathic communication are in tune with subtle instincts and spiritual powers. They're highly perceptive with skilled observation. They're in tune with the realm of emotions and feelings, and are able to transcend the 3D limitations and restrictions of the physical world. This is all symbolized through the dolphin. Amazing intelligence combined with a strong connection to the watery realms of divinity, which includes the subconscious mind and ethereal energies; opens doorways to deeper levels of the self. The self and psyche come alive and burst with insight and vibrancy. So do the inner spirit and soul. Holistically, the dolphin spirit animal allows you to "get deep" with yourself and all the parts that make you whole. From amazing imaginative gifts to extraordinary visionary and spiritual insights, to profound creativity and artistic abilities to key intellect, the dolphin is a unique sea creature.

Water is symbolic of emotions, so virtually everything linked to the water elements is available for development and embody. You can evolve through empathy, emotional intelligence, and spiritual maturity. You can equally find strength and solace through higher mental gifts- attributes linked to the higher mind. Problem-solving, observational skills, analysis, logic, wit, decisiveness, discernment, and tuning into both instincts and potent intuition are readily available. The dolphin can assist you in accessing all of these! As a lover of community and kinship, intimate bonds and connections open doorways to deeper aspects of yourself; you can learn about your internal motivations and burning desires through the connections in your life. Others serve as a mirror to your soul & psyche. In this respect, the dolphin teaches you the art of *positive mirroring*, or *positive reflection*. The dolphin brings the vibration of inner calmness, peace, and serenity. You can learn self-mastery of emotions and mastery of communication, recognizing that there are more than the 5 physical senses. When you get in tune with the inner realms of feelings, instincts, and emotional empathy, you can start to see (and experience) the sacredness of life. This sacredness then enables deeper intimacy with self and the world around. *Extra*ordinary insight, imagination, and creativity are direct manifestations of the dolphin's spiritual symbolism. Compassion, nurturance, caring, generosity, sincerity, nobility, modesty, and intuition are some other key associations. If you resonate with this spirit animal, you likely have a calming and welcoming aura, projecting a friendly vibe. But you simultaneously radiate an openness to play, fun, and laughter! You love to socialize, create or participate in fun, and connect with like-minded and colorful individuals.

Furthermore, the dolphin is a powerful animal for balancing inner dualities. Real harmony of polar opposites or apparently "contradictory" characteristics can come about. For example, imagination vs intellect, intuition vs logic, instincts vs higher reasoning, and emotions vs intelligence… The dolphin spirit asks you to get in tune with your inner world. With sole reference to duality and oneness, you can find deeper truths and answers to life's questions through self-exploration and healing. Finding oneness in duality is a key pathway to this. Wisdom, higher guidance, divine revelations, prophetic visions, and astral insights are all linked to the dolphin power animal. The clear message is to master your speaking style, fine-tune communication, ascertain higher & ultimate truths, and evolve through authenticity and transparency. Your feelings serve as a gateway to your higher mind, and vice versa. Union of self is attainable.

Anything to be mindful of?

If the Dolphin is your spirit animal, you need to be mindful of the following shadow traits or follies:-

- Superiority and believing others to be psychologically or intellectually inferior to you
- Getting trapped in the past; unwilling to look through your emotions, feelings, and inner realm sensations
- Extreme solitude and independence vs extreme social desires… aim for balance & harmony
- Being overly adaptable to the point of losing yourself; losing touch of reality through diminished boundaries

Turtle

The turtle is a symbol of slowing down and becoming present and patient with ourselves. Life is a journey that requires patience. Wisdom, self-awareness, and increased positive qualities come with presence and self-awareness. If this is your spirit animal, you are not impulsive, irrational, overly zealous or electric at all. You take your time; you possess amazing observation and perceptive skills. You're spiritually in tune with evolved emotional intelligence, instincts, intuition, empathy, and nurturing instincts. Turtles feel most home in the sea, where they are free to swim and explore, gracefully and at their own pace. This symbolizes feeling comfort in the realm of the emotions, and ethereal, astral, subconscious, and spiritual dimensions and planes. Yet they're also free to walk on land, which signifies an earthly connection. Wisdom, a sense of security and grounding, and working with the energies and healing forces of Mother Earth are available to you. Humility, grace, strong virtue, sincerity, modesty, nobility and inner serenity are available in equal measure. Selflessness, inner calmness, and content with yourself and surrounding can also be integrated and mastered. Through learning the art of patience, you become more in tune with bodily wisdom and the sensation of the physical environments you surround yourself by. Through such strong emotional intelligence and physical instincts, you are able to pick up on subtle impressions, information, and hidden wisdom around you. This includes empathic gifts like feeling and sensing other people's internal state of affairs, or mind-reading. Sensitivity combined with compassion allows you to tune into the health and inner frequency of others, sensing a range of emotional, psychological, and spiritual underlying forces.

Trust in the divine life force and sacred essence of things. The turtle symbolizes cosmic energies, universal and sacred laws, and our connection to important life stages & cycles. This powerful but calm and humble water animal shows you how to reach your full potential, access creative and imaginative gifts, and connect to the spiritual and subconscious realms; through the link to divinity. Artistic, musical, and imaginative abilities can be expanded with the turtle. If this is your power animal, you may have frequent or sporadic strokes of creative genius. Or regularly meditate, engage in visualization, and connect to your higher mind (also known as the Higher Self) to receive flashes of insight & inspiration. This is a deeply inspirational, talented, and light-infused spirit animal to have, but not in a masculine, gregarious, or dominant way. The turtle brings a mystical and sensual form of inspirational energy- vibrations and self-knowledge rooted in sensuality, spirituality, and creative and magnetic life force. Further, you're able to access the big picture and prophetic or higher consciousness-themed visions. Ethereal energy enables you to see beyond the veil of illusion, while the link to the subconscious realm & mind opens portals to cosmic consciousness. On a physical level, the turtle's medicine grounds you. It's from a space of feeling secure and safe in your body and home that you can open yourself up to higher dimensions. Again, this animal is extremely wise, perceptive, and intuitive.

Other symbolism includes the feminine traits, caring, kindness, generosity, astral wisdom, spiritual perception, imaginative gifts, nurturance, receptivity, passivity and selflessness, and sacredness. Self-alignment and mastery of your emotions can be learned through trusting in a higher power, also through taking steps, regardless of how small, towards your purpose. A soul mission or specific type of service that helps others may be part of your life's legacy and unique destiny or personal path. The turtle sparks subtle yet powerful internal shifts, which equally stimulates inner alchemy. Through the powerful currents of the inner realms of being, you can find mental clarity, truth, greater vision, and holistic insight; you can see what your true goals & aspirations are, in alignment with your soul's plan. Longevity, tranquility, self-protection, steadfastness, perseverance, healing, and personal transformation are core qualities not yet covered. The turtle represents the need to retreat, a strong desire for home and family bonds. This can be actual (blood) family or soul family, the key is that you likely seek out strong foundations with loving & harmonious support systems. If there's no emotional warmth and peace, comforting and stabilizing environment, or feelings of being able to rest, retreat, and introspect; you won't stick around for too long. People with the turtle spirit crave a welcoming and spiritually-encompassing home environment. You require peace, harmony, and non-violence in the bonds you keep or choose to live with. *Home is within* too- it's important you find your sacred place inside, so you can reflect and positively mirror sensations of harmony and serenity. In addition, healing and working with healing powers of the universe are symbolic of the turtle's medicine.

A final message of the turtle is achieving success and victory through utmost integrity. Work hard, stay committed and devoted, and never cut corners. The turtle strongly advises against cheating in life, making choices that aren't aligned to integrity and righteous, pure, or "clean" intentions. I.e. playing dirty or embodying a con-like or scam energy can result in some serious negative repercussions. To win and become accomplished, live with grace and act with heart or soul. Keep your intentions pure and have supreme trust, patience, and faith that the universe is working in your favor.

Anything to be mindful of?

If the Turtle is your spirit animal, you need to be mindful of the following shadow traits or follies:-

- Retreating into yourself; isolation, loneliness, and separation
- Fear of intimacy, companionship, and connection… platonic or romantic
- Excessive reliance on emotions, instincts, and feelings over a lack of logic, rationality, and mental/intellectual gifts
- Become lost in fantasy, mysticism, addictions, or illusions!

Swan

The swan is a symbol of purity, grace, and true love. Companionship, soulmate bonds, and true love all come under the swan's realm of healing light and power. Swan represents deep peace and inner contentment. They radiate warmth, grace, serenity, calmness, and harmony. They are full of love, affection, and loyalty, and have a rare type of inner beauty. One feels safe, calm, protected, peaceful, and put at ease just from observing a swan. People with this spirit animals are highly companionable. Companionship and finding a soulmate on your wavelength is, in fact, very high up on your lifelong accomplishment list. You believe in true love, and you desire nothing more than to find a true love partnership. But first, you must find true love within. The swan calls for inner harmony and self-alignment before you can come together with your soulmate in this life. Eternal love, infinite potential, self-love, and self-care are other key meanings. Swans are poised and symbolize integrity, purity, nobility, sensuality, and inner majesty, and intimacy. Sensuality and positive impressions and inner sensations of intimacy ooze out of those with the swan spirit… You likely strongly embody your inner Shiva (Divine Masculine energy) and/or Shakti (Divine Feminine energy). You like dance, self-care, poetry, music, art, and nature. You're a big believer in natural beauty, and choose natural and organic forms of beauty, love, and intimacy over anything superficial. The swan spirit is very similar to the energy of Venus, the planet of love, beauty, pleasure, and female sexuality.

Emotional intelligence… emotional maturity… deep and evolved empathy… The realm of emotions and subtle feelings are brought to light. Humility, diplomacy, and compromise define you, and you see other's as a reflection to you. This means you're anti chaos, drama, and ignorance. Through seeking emotional bonds and deeper more authentic expressions of connection, you naturally gravitate from anything superficial and lacking depth. You can be a real BS and ignorance detector too! Manipulation, negative vibes, bad vibes and ill-intentions are all sensed on a deeper level. You're in tune with your soul, higher mind, and bodily instincts & wisdom. Through emotional intelligence and your desire for purity, you would usually always choose independence and solitude over anything that doesn't serve you or help you grow. The swan is a major self-evolution, self-mastery, and personal transformation and self-care animal to have by your side. The message is clear: live with grace and integrity, and don't be afraid to dive deep into your emotions, feelings, and psychic instincts and impressions. You tend to draw a lot of knowledge and insight from the subconscious and astral realm, whether you're conscious of it or not. You most likely have profound and vivid dreams, also being aware that there is a lot of symbolism to be found in dreams. Telepathy, clairvoyance, clairsentience, psychic gifts, clairaudience, and sensitivity to the emotions and feelings of others, including your physical environments, are all key to the swan.

The unseen and invisible realms and worlds are available, as your soul's true needs, desires, and shine. Your "soul shines!" With such a strong feminine and sensitive, spiritual, and serene energy comes increased self-awareness, and advanced powers of both empathy and subtle perception. When swans mate they mate for life, therefore a core message is how you can embark on your own journey of transformation to find your true kindred spirit. Finding harmony within is the first step to wholeness. Vulnerability, freedom to express your truth, feelings, desires, emotions and gifts, and realization that you are the creator of your destiny are part of the swan's magic.

Anything to be mindful of?

If the Swan is your spirit animal, you need to be mindful of the following shadow traits or follies:-

- People-pleasing, sacrificial, and overly passive tendencies
- Super-sensitivities and hyper-emotionalism
- Fear of intimacy, romance, or companionship, and fear of rejection or solitude
- Idealized belief systems of love, like "fairytale love," or becoming a hopeless romantic…

Chapter 4: Wise & Intuitive Spirit Animals

We are the intuitive and wise spirit animal helpers,
Some of us are intelligent problem-solvers whilst others bring the fun & color!
From being witty, sharp-minded, analytical and logical,
To observant, perceptive, quick-thinking, and intellectual;
We are the animals who can help you attune to Source
connecting your mind to the psychological realms with passion and life force.

We possess energy, vitality, keen insight, and multiple perspectives,
We are here to show you how to rise above the distractions to align with the collective.
Ancestral healing, ancient wisdom, clairsentience, and psychic gifts-
Look towards us if you're seeking higher guidance and alchemical mental magic.

Elephant

The elephant represents memory, ancient wisdom, and grounding. This beautiful creature is a symbol of royalty, our connection to the earth, and matriarchal values. Past life connections are realized through the elephant's ancient wisdom and memory. Family and friendship bonds are very significant with this spirit animal; if this is one of your power animals, you place supreme value and importance on the close and intimate bonds in your life, whether they be platonic, romantic, family or friendship. Elephants are loyal, nurturing, caring and sensitive animals. They're instinctive and very intuitive, receiving primal pulses and spiritual vibrations through the ground. They can sense energy and more subtle states of being, including information from the astral and ethereal realm, which links to feelings, subconscious messages, and emotions; through the earth. Intuition is one of their greatest gifts. Mother earth provides a direct link to higher consciousness and deeper insight. Ancestral wisdom can be brought to light, including memories and flashbacks of connections shared in previous lives. There's a sense of being able to see the past, present, and future with the elephant spirit. Some people may connect to the elephant spirit for past life recall, astral and dream activities, or to expand wisdom and self-awareness of ancient times. Instincts are powerful. Heightened sensitivity allows for a range of gifts linked to the subtle and emotional realms, and the intellectual one.

Empathy and compassion are very well-developed in those with this power animal. In fact, your deep-rooted sense of compassion is likely on a whole new level, and this is connected to the elephant being a symbol of matriarchy. Nobility, majesty, divine grace, an awareness of your soul's path or purpose, and seeing the true significance of soul connections are learned through the elephant. Patience, inner strength, and commitment can be developed. Patience is a virtue, the elephant teaches you to take in all of the information from your physical environments. Then, observe, rationalize, intuit, and discern… This can help you determine who is a friend or foe, what people's motivations are, and if you're on the right path. The key is to listen to the subtle signs of the universe, be receptive to the subtlety of life, as this is where portals to growth and self-awareness lie. Further, female elephants often raise and care for each other's children; there's a real sense of community, where they all live and help each other. The elephant spirit teaches that we must respect our kin, elders, teachers, and family. Our DNA contains memories of our royal and ancestral lineages too, whatever this may be to us specifically. For example, if you have felt strongly drawn to the healing arts, studying with an experienced, qualified, and authentic Reiki Master in this life, you might choose to complete your Reiki to Master Teacher level, thus becoming part of this lineage. The elephant teaches sacred lineage, quantum and metaphysical laws, and timeless truths in sync with our personal destinies and the type of services and legacy we are supposed to create. Also, inner wisdom, listening to your inner voice, and seeking out pathways of security, stability, and strong foundations & roots.

Being one with nature is another key symbolism, which leads to Higher Self alignment. Self-discovery, personal transformation, and forming close and intimate bonds that can lead to our self-evolution. Letting go of the past is key to the elephant's teachings as well. We must learn from the past, observing key patterns and cycles of wisdom & growth, and then let go. Keep the wisdom and memory, but let go of the pain of the past. Key qualities not yet mentioned that come with this compassionate, ancient, and majestic animal: resilience, self-protection, intelligence, empathy combined with intellect, longevity, motherly instincts, multidimensional wisdom, and longevity. If this is your power animal you are likely to have strong maternal and/or paternal instincts. Your sense of protecting and providing for loved ones is incredible, sometimes quite intense! But this stems from a deep need to nurture. You're caring, loyal, affectionate, sweet, and supremely compassionate. Your subconscious serves you well, acting as a memory-bank of virtually all memories throughout your life. You would be wise to develop key skills in perception, intelligence, and instinctual and intuitive awareness, because this can lead to establishing secure foundations and doorways to abundance. Finally, you're full of grace, gentle, and capable of evolved displays of empathy. You are beautiful inside and out.

Anything to be mindful of?

If the Elephant is your spirit animal, you need to be mindful of the following shadow traits or follies:-

- Hidden resentment, unexpressed anger, and emotional repression and avoidance
- Inability to let go of the past… getting stuck in the past
- Unwillingness to deal with sadness, grief, ancestral wounds, and trauma
- Blocks to reclaiming personal power and self-autonomy; you should learn to become more self-reliant whilst still nurturing family, intimate relationship, and emotional bonds

Cow

Although many humans still eat cows and are under the illusion that they are inferior in spirit and soul to dogs, cats, and other animals; the cow is a very special animal. The cow encourages wisdom and sacredness, it is respected by a significant number of communities and cultures across the world. Cows are sentient, self-aware, empathic, wise, beautiful, and incredibly compassionate. In fact, this is one of the most nurturing, kind, and gentle-hearted land creatures.

The spirit of the cow represents compassion and unconditional love. Also, forgiveness, which is largely due to the fact that this species has been murdered and tortured by humans for such a long time. Cows are sacred and help to show us the sacredness in life and self. All life is sacred, and we humans have a sacred, timeless, and eternal essence too. The cow spirit animal can teach us the importance of self-sovereignty and independence. Humans have largely abused the cow spirit, due to our reliance on their milk. This has created codependency and an unhealthy attachment. Yet, cows remain compassionate, loving and open- they are emotionally intelligent and clearly affectionate, when in the right setting (not be used or abused). The cow spirit is here to help us rise above the follies of codependency, regain our independence and self-sovereignty, and transcend the illusions & ignorances of the physical realm. Transcending the 3D and fear timeline is part of this. This further includes healing from toxic cycles, both toxic traits within, and the toxic cycles that manifest when a shadow trait or karmic cycle becomes unlearned. Something becomes karmic when we repeatedly fail to learn the lesson…

Thus, the cow is a symbol of higher consciousness. Are you ready to shift timelines? Karmic cycles and relationships keep us bound in toxicity, self-destruction, and negativity and separation. While true love bonds allow us to heal, grow, and evolve. True love is within. True love can be seen as the perfect combination of unconditional love and self-love, and once we establish this unity inside we can reflect it outwards. Despite all the abuse, suffering, and ill-treatment cows as a species are caused, they still choose to remain loving to us. This is a beautiful example and representation of the power of love. And, empathy, universal compassion and forgiveness, grace, and humility. Cows are wise, perceptive, very intelligent, intuitive, and empathic. They possess advanced and evolved emotional sensitivity- they are conscious, thoughtful, and considerate. The power of miracles can simultaneously be learned through the cow's medicine. The cow teaches both self-sufficiency and transcending codependency, and raising our vibrations to match a spiritual type of energy. This spirit animal values kindness, generosity, community, empathic self-awareness, and acts of humility and integrity. A further symbolism is how you can work on the land and directly with the land, with the forces of Mother Earth. This is a strong environmentalism spirit animal, so if it's one of yours you are likely suited to some volunteering, environmental, or farming role. Or, being part of a conscious and spiritual community where you work in harmony and sync with spiritual and ecological values. Healthy self-esteem in relation to becoming in control of our own resources, services, and talents, and self-autonomy can be learned and mastered through the cow.

Recognizing the sacredness of life, which is largely linked to the feminine and astral realms, the realm of subconscious insights, spiritual and ethereal wisdom, and psychic instincts & sensitivities; and further living by sacred laws and rules that govern our universe, can increase abundance in your life. Abundance, prosperity, monetary flow, and a perpetual stream of positive connections, well-being, love, and inner joy and contentment are part of the cow's message and meaning. Divine synchronicities come about when you live in alignment with your soul and inner source. Finally, the cow presents the wisdom that there is a choice of love or fear in every moment. Love VS fear… which one do you choose? The key to choosing the best timelines and future pathways is to stay connected to your Higher Self, further being aware of the spiritual and primal life force all around you (and within).

Anything to be mindful of?

If the Cow is your spirit animal, you need to be mindful of the following shadow traits or follies:-

- How the choices you make affect your future; timeline shifts related to the decisions made in the present moment
- Codependency, fears, anxieties, and illusions. Also, inflexibility and a rigid mindset
- Your own toxic traits and projecting them out into relationships and the world
- Controlling and intimidating or overly cold tendencies; be careful of losing touch with your inner sensitivity and empathic nature

Coyote

The coyote is an interesting spirit animal. This animal asks you to trust in the divine detours and setbacks of life, finding pearls of wisdom in your failures and mistakes. The message: embrace the parts of your life that have not gone to plan. You can find lasting wisdom, maturity, insight, self-respect, self-love, and future success in the difficult times of life, it is simply the times you've put your all into something and it hasn't gone as planned. The coyote helps you find self-acceptance combined with embodying a powerful intuition. Knowledge of a higher power is available, and people with this power animal tend to have incredible instincts. You can learn the true meaning of "everything happens for a reason" as well, recognizing the cyclic nature of being. Everything in existence has a natural cycle and organic growth progression. Self-evolution is a journey, whether it's the evolution of your cells and belief systems, or the evolution of the planet and universe as a whole. The coyote teaches timeless and sage-like wisdom. Wisdom of the ages, natural cycles of time and Gaia's (our planet's) evolution, and ancient knowledge can be found and seen. You may start to awaken to the realization that you have a spiritual or divine mission, or that you're connected to a higher power and angelic or holy forces. You might become aware of past lives and how some of the connections in your current life have key lessons and timeless teachings to ascertain.

Divine, benevolent, and spiritual forces and powers are strong with the coyote spirit. Yet, they are available and manifested in a very down-to-earth and grounded way. Celestial energy can be rooted within your body and higher mind. Higher dimensional awareness and the gifts & abilities that accompany them can be grounded into your physical, daily life, existence. Divine synchronicities are also strong with this power animal, so you are likely open to frequent "unexplainable encounters" that lead to either significant growth and abundance or deeper and more meaningful connections, collaborations, and partnerships. This is a big 'partnership and collaboration' spirit animal to have by your side, but first you need to master your own lessons and characteristics within. Also, develop your instinctual self-awareness. Intuition is linked to your higher mind (Higher Self, spiritual and divine forces) while instincts are rooted in bodily wisdom; the sensations and impressions you receive from physical environments and surroundings. The coyote is in tune with both of these. Some key themes associated with the coyote include: feeling disappointment before realizing success, seeing karmic or toxic partners/lovers before finding your soulmate, integrating your own inner yin and yang before you can enter into a true love partnership, going through your sadness and pain before living a blissful life, and experiencing poverty consciousness and lack before receiving abundance and prosperity. Sometimes you need to get deep with your feelings and true emotions, including grief, pain, trauma, past wounds or current ones, and recognize- fully accept- that you're not in the night place. You might be in a lower vibrational, toxic, karmic, or destructive and healthy cycle or relationship; you may have taken a wrong turn or detour a while back. Being totally honest with yourself about your current life cycle and situation is the first step towards healing and self-evolution.

Self-mastery is a powerful symbol of the coyote's medicine. Healing is a gateway to growth and inner harmony and balance, which manifests in a number of positive ways (and in all life areas). Failure can be a blessing. Failure is often the key step to divine revelation, and relationships that bring you wonderful satisfaction- deep friendship, kindness and honesty, true companionship, and joy and harmony. All the wonderful, high vibration, magical, warm & comforting, and colorful feelings and sensations that we humans are supposed to experience. A no can mean a yes, rejection may signify a different opening, and endings and stagnation can be the catalyst needed for doorways and true manifestation- beginnings that best serve your ultimate self. There's a divine plan. Finally, laughter is symbolic of the coyote's wisdom and medicine. You can find joy and moments for connection, also releasing blocked or trapped energy and emotions, through laughter. Laughter instantly raises your spirits, reminds you of the interconnected nature of all things, and can help you stay optimistic through the difficult times. Humor births humility, modesty, and integrity and ethics; when you feel connected to others and your highest joy, you're better able to stay optimistic and connected to your inner source of power and light. Any trauma bonding or unhealthy attachment you've unconsciously fallen into can be instantly released through laughing. Additionally, laughter is a medicine that eases stress, anxiety, and the tension that comes with working hard to pursue your goals. If you consider yourself a hard-worker who takes pride in their self-discipline and perseverance, determination, and willpower to succeed, the coyote can help you develop light-heartedness linked to laughter and self-expression.

One final thing, the coyote is symbolic in shamanism and Native American culture. The key themes here are shapeshifting and working in dreams, directly with the subconscious mind and multidimensional realms.

Anything to be mindful of?

If the Coyote is your spirit animal, you need to be mindful of the following shadow traits or follies:-

- Be careful of falling into depressive cycle, including mood swings, pessimistic thinking, and self-pity
- Don't close yourself off to the multidimensionality of life; there is hidden wisdom and divine insight/revelation in every human experience
- Taking life too seriously- not knowing how to 'lighten up!'
- Flexibility and adaptability… seeing through illusion and chaos through an open-mind & philosophical perspectives

Fox

The fox symbolizes agility and swiftness of mind, tuning into your mental abilities and intellect. This is a deeply intellectual spirit animal to have, possibly the most. The fox is sharp minded, witty, full of intelligence and innovative and inventive ideas, and a real problem-solver. They have key gifts in perception and observation, and usually use their brilliant mind to create prosperity and security in their lives. The meaning of the fox is tuning into your higher mind and mental powers for imaginative, intellectual, innovative, and creative manifestations and creations. You are likely resourceful and a master of manifestation. You're aware of metaphysical forces and universal laws, and have mastered the law of attraction and your own manifestation powers. The fox represents logic, keen insight, analytical gifts and abilities, wit, higher intelligence, sound judgment, and potent instincts. Foxes are very clever, so if this is your power animal you are too. There's a tendency to disconnect from the realm of emotions and feelings, relying solely on logic. This has both its advantages and disadvantages. Purely positive, it means you excel in business and situations that require a rational and non-emotional approach. The fox can help you separate your heart from what you know needs to be done, to "get things done" and achieve practical or physical success. It's not the spirit animal to call on for holistic living where a more integrated and gentle or compassionate energy is needed. It is the perfect animal, however, for tuning into the realm of higher reasoning, originality, and logic- the mental plane, where there is a vast amount of potential and new ideas waiting to be birthed. Intuition is well developed in people with this spirit animal too.

The fox also represents adaptability. You are likely open-minded, philosophically, and with idealistic tendencies. You possess vision, but vision connected to the realm of ideas, concepts, new belief systems and ideologies, and the subtle impressions & information received from the mental plane. You might be emotionally, sentimentally, and spiritually cut off at times, but your mind is brilliant! You are flexible with the capacity for multidimensional awareness. You can see multiple sides of a story, and you can tune into multiple modes of subtle perception. When you combine your evolved instincts, wit, and intellect you can produce groundworking creations, works of art, or business ideas. With sound judgment and amazing observation skills, you possess agility and flexibility of mind. You have strong willpower and fierce determination to succeed. You are driven, ambitious, high-flying, achievement-oriented, and totally determined. The fox equally represents discernment and curiosity- you approach life with a playful and inquisitive, open mind. Your curiosity and love of fun, color, and play allows you to connect with other like-minded souls. You seek out kindred spirits and other creative and innovative people who can add to your vision. The fox simultaneously suggests someone with great communication skills. You are able to express your ideas, feelings, talents, wisdom, and inner impressions in a way that inspires or connects. You might be an educator, teacher, speaker, coach, or entertainer of some kind. You love to inspire and educate others, and people generally see you as open-minded, wise, intelligent, and communicative. Judgment likely rules your life, but judgment doesn't have to be negative, so keep your mind and higher eyes set on connection and positive reinforcement. Your words and thoughts hold immense power…

Thinking outside of the box can lead to advancements in love, friendship, career, and monetary flow. One final thing to note, this is the only spirit animal that comes with a warning message. People with the fox spirit animal can be incredibly deceitful. You may manipulate others to get ahead or win in life, and your logical and intellectual nature makes you disconnected from the other essentials in life; *empathy, feeling, kindness, gentleness, grace, diplomacy, and compassion.* If this is your spirit animal, make sure you work with it in harmony with some others, such as any of the animals from the 'Emotionally Intelligent' chapter. Your mind is bright and sharp, but you lack emotional sensitivity, caring, and more humble/modest/feminine qualities. You can further be a trickster, taking on the role of the "cosmic joker!" This may be good in some social and light-hearted situations, but in others it can ruin or destroy other people's lives, livelihoods, and more serious aspects of life related to health and well-being, security, and survival. In other words, be careful of not being a prick. Keep it real with yourself and others and stay clear of deceptive tactics; "play fair."

Anything to be mindful of?

If the Fox is your spirit animal, you need to be mindful of the following shadow traits or follies:-

- Be careful of manipulation and deceptive tendencies. People with this spirit animal are the most likely to deceive, cheat, and BS others!
- Try to lose the cunning and callousness… develop greater empathy and sensitivity instead
- Be mindful of relying too much on logic, reason, and rationality
- Stay more connected to your heart-space, emotional intelligence, and sensitive self-awareness

Also, become conscious of your own manipulative and overly competitive ways; are your methods rooted in cooperation, harmony, fairness, and equality, i.e. will it lead to unity consciousness, a result that will benefit the greater whole? Or does it just serve your own interests and ego desires/needs?!

Monkey

The monkey symbolizes creativity, innovation, and color! This is a highly expressive and innovative spirit animal to have, one of the most, in fact. The monkey brings the energy of vitality, energy, life force, and originality. If this is your spirit or power protection animal, you are very clever, intelligent, and intuitive. You're full of wit, and your communication style is unique. This means you don't follow the crowd, but prefer to draw on your own unique skills, gifts, and abilities to establish your own communication shine. You're innovative, original, inventive, bright-minded, both logical and intuitive, and very passionate. People with this animal spirit tend to be musicians, speakers, entertainers, artists, poets, or motivational coaches; or excel in the acting or performance industry. You could be a creative directory or visionary, a photographer or graphic designer, or a writer or author. You have pretty advanced speaking skills, and your courage and boldness allows you to shine. Playful, curious, inquisitive, open-minded, and philosophical, you likely have many friends and social contacts. Kindred spirits and community bonds are extremely important to you. You dislike solitude and prefer to find mental and psychological stimulation through the fun and creative, or educational and intellectual, activities you share with others. There is such a high and powerful life force, spirit, creative and artistic energy, and zest and passion for life that you can achieve great success. In Chinese astrology, the Monkey is associated with fame, accomplishment, and status- rising through the ranks through talent acquisition and professional self-development, to reach new levels within and around.

Laughter, mischievous nature, optimism and positive- love of fun, the monkey is a reminder to let out your more daring and bold side. Be courageous and colorful, i.e. actively seek out connections and pathways that will service your creative spirit. The message is: embrace light-heatedness and have more fun. This zestful spirit animal enhances joy, innocence, and the inner child. Connecting to your inner child whilst allowing for imaginative & artistic self-expression provides doorways to self-awareness and growth. Self-evolution is available when you let your inner spirit soar, show off your talents and innate gifts, and be courageous in any desire you may have for seeking the spotlight. Seeking the spotlight doesn't have to be seen as something egotistical, if your intentions are pure. Standing strong in your light and your truth can actually be very helpful for others, so long as your intentions are to motivate, inspire, heal, teach, or educate; or raise the collective vibration and energy of a space. Joyous and high spirited living is integral to the monkey spirit. Sometimes, this animal can represent the trickster, a mischievous and deceitful kind of energy, so this is something you need to be mindful of. But it's in a playful and fun-loving way, it's not malicious or rooted in ill-intent. You can make the most of this influence by turning towards comedy, channeling your inner comedian, or using "trickery" to stimulate fun and games.

Compassion and empathy are integrated, while mastering mindful and empathic communication is often key to your victories. You thrive off of companionship, you are very companionable, in fact, however it's important to develop both mindful (mindfulness) and empathic (sensitivity, compassion) communication if you wish to get anywhere in life. Problem-solving and observation skills, intellect and wit, logic and intuition, and sensitivity to the needs of others creates prosperity. In Hinduism, Hanuman is the monkey god, and he is represented as strong, self-controlled, loyal, fearless, and with a strong sense of service and devotion. He is a fierce protector of those he loves and cares for. You can apply the symbolism here. Japanese culture is responsible for the well-known saying, "hear no evil, see no evil, speak no evil," which is linked to the monkey spirit. This signifies you can learn how to live with purity and integrity, choosing all things good and righteous over darkness and chaos. This ancient wisdom can also show you how important mindful speech, thought, perception, and action are. Living with honor, integrity, and commitment to a higher truth & power are key to the monkey's symbolism, as is honesty. In Mayan culture, the monkey was seen as a prophet and linked with the creative life force of the Sun, in addition to the fire element. In many Buddhist stories, the monkey is depicted as a symbol for bravery, intelligence, and comfort and protection. You can draw from all of these themes to find a deeper resonance with the monkey spirit.

Anything to be mindful of?

If the Monkey is your spirit animal, you need to be mindful of the following shadow traits or follies:-

- Practical jokes and trickery *without* harm or dark intentions... Be careful of causing havoc and mayhem!
- Being so light-hearted, joyous, and creative/artistic that you lose touch with reality

- Absent-mindedness, recklessness, and impulsiveness; remember to tend to the practical things and honor your commitments
- A lack of responsibility, focus, and groundedness

I am the monkey, mischievous yet innovative,
You never know what you'll get with me- I have so many gifts!
From bright, communicative, expressive, and highly charismatic
to colorful, intellectual, witty, and creative…

I know how to play and have fun, yet I also possess ambition,
Goals usually align to some artistic or creative vision.
If you want to receive my medicine, remember to embrace your wild essence,
as I am a symbol for physical vitality, freedom, and independence…

Chapter 5: Down-to-Earth & Grounding Spirit Animals

We are the down-to-earth and modest animals who bring a strong sense of security.
We represent nurturing, caring, compassion, and stability.
All of your practical needs can be found in us- we're resourceful and intelligent,
We know how to plan, organize, manage, and create order with intent.

Reliable, responsible, deliberate, and masters of manifestation;
Our powers come from Mother Earth and physical worldly sensations.
See, we're deeply in tune with our roots, yet we have a unique spiritual vibration,
A love of divine order and potent intuition, which stems from grounding & self-preservation.

Bear

The Bear represents ancient wisdom, grounding, reflection, rest and introspection. This is the power animal to work with for self-healing, introspection, and soul-searching. The bear brings ancient wisdom and self-knowledge rooted in primordial and primal powers and instincts. It is a deeply grounding spirit animal that connects you with the earth. Instincts and psychic powers are heightened while there is an immense sense of self-protection and self-preservation. Also, protection of loved ones. Bears have a powerful motherly instinct, so if you resonate with the bear you are very nurturing, caring, affectionate, providing, and supportive. You likely take on the role of mother or caregiver, and have amazing instincts in a parental role. Feminine qualities including intuition, imagination, astral knowledge and power, and a connection to the realm of dreams & the subconscious mind are heightened. Rest and meditation are very important and can further be learned and developed. You may frequently enjoy dreaming to receive wisdom and insight from the subconscious realm, and your Higher Self, and like to journal, introspect, meditate and engage in conscious self-reflection. If this is your power animal or protection animal to work with, you should integrate these things as part of a daily or weekly self-care and self-therapy routine and regime. Bear medicine encourages self-development and soul-growth, which can include shadow work. This is looking within at your own darkness, your shadow traits and follies, and seeking to release, heal, and overcome. Through doing this, you are then able to integrate them, so you don't fall into extremes. We must transmute our darker and less desirable characteristics- linked to the shadow self- to then rise into our light. The bear teaches you the power of solitude, rest, and introspection.

Earthly and feminine wisdom linked to the earth, a feminine principle, and ancient knowledge of our connection to the planet, the stars up above, and the cosmos sparks with the bear's medicine. Deeply instinctual, and protective of loved ones, including their home and physical foundations, the bear represents courage and fierce strength. They are not to be messed with! This sense of semi-aggression is purely defensive, rooted in self-preservation and a nurturing instinct, as suggested above. You can learn true maternal and paternal instincts through the bear spirit. Artistic, imaginative, and creative gifts also flow in abundance when in a space of rest. Relaxing, taking time out to recharge your energies and simply "be," rejuvenates you; further expanding creative life force. If you're someone with a powerful imagination and artistic visions, the bear can help you both access and ground these. Contemplating life's deeper meanings and the mysterious, ethereal, and spiritual powers & energies of the universe allows you to develop innate empathic, imaginative, and psychic gifts- and magnetic powers. Destiny can be discovered. Divine revelations, insights, and self-realization into your purpose and soul plan arise through the infinite spaces. Your life path and legacy may shine through in full force, or come out in glimpses… Considerable inspiration and higher dimensional guidance is available to you.

Getting clear on your needs, desires, and passions are symbolic of this power animal. If you're feeling directionless, stagnant, suppressed, misaligned, or swimming against the currents within- or the external tides, the bear will help to connect and align you with the greatest version of yourself; your best & ultimate self. Your life path may be shown to you in dreams, meditation, and other transcendental states if you only ask. You should know that you are protected and held in a warming and comforting embrace with the bear spirit. There's a unique combination of boldness and masculine strength merged and harmonized with gentle grace and compassion. This also helps to balance yin and yang energies within. Furthermore, personal power and authority kick in once you find your center (self-alignment). The bear asks you to lose distractions and put your energy and awareness into only what serves your soul growth and highest alignment; like family, kindred spirit connections, your children, passions, creative projects, visions and life path/purpose, soul plan, and self-care. Channeling healing powers to become your own healer is a further message and meaning of this animal, and the bear is often associated with shamanic healing powers. And, you may be called to step up into a role of wayshower, teacher, or healer one day. Bears symbolize spiritual and metaphysical teachers, and master healers.

Anything to be mindful of?

If the Bear is your spirit animal, you need to be mindful of the following shadow traits or follies:-

- Not taking action and stepping into self-leadership; getting lost in idleness, laziness, and lethargy
- Try not to get lost in isolation and solitude… only enter these places for rest, healing, self-care, rejuvenation, and dream or shadow work (also spiritual healing)
- Not controlling protective and maternal/paternal instincts, thus shifting towards aggression, violence, or self-destructive tendencies
- A lack of motivation, drive, will power to succeed, and ambition; a disconnect from your purpose, path, & passions

Stag

The stag spirit animal is a call to self-leadership. This is the power animal to look towards when you need to reclaim self-autonomy and sovereignty. The stag symbolizes self-control, taking back power, and stepping into personal authority. Confident, fearless, and courageous, the stag has strongly developed instincts & self-esteem. Your intuition is at an all time high, and you rely on instincts and gut feelings connected to your connection with the universe to navigate life. People with this spirit animal tend to become famous, successful, financially abundant, or accomplished. You can draw on your inner strength and intuitive & psychic powers to create real success in your life. Empathy, compassion, sensitivity, nurturing instincts, and generosity are just as available to you as self-leadership and strength. This is another "yin-yang" animal (like the Bear). The stag provides a sense of grounding, allowing you to expand boldness and self-autonomy and courage… But it also is a down-to-earth animal, living and surviving through Mother Earth and her benevolence. So you can tune into this benevolent, loving, and nurturing energy to enhance similar qualities in yourself. Abundance and prosperity are available to you when you get honest and real with yourself. Stay authentic- develop authenticity. You must live fearlessly while staying connected to inner empathy to create the life you want. Achievement, success, and abundance are available to you with an open and active heart chakra. The stag represents powerful heart vibrations; the heart emits vibrations that can't be seen by the physical eyes, but ripple out into one's aura and the etheric field surrounding. If your heart chakra is weak, you will likely have blocks to love, friendship, prosperity, wealth, good fortune, well-being, and health.

Direct communication, masculine attributes like healthy competition, assertiveness, and boldness, and authority and self-empowerment linked to the Sun- solar energy- are available to you. Empathy and compassion combined with these masculine 'yang' traits allow you to connect to others in a healthy way, also enhancing communication. Communication is very important to those with the stag spirit. If this is you, you might find others listening intently to your every word. A moment of eye contact can spark interest and attention. People know and sense you command personal power and are in control of yourself. Your energy and body language speaks for itself; life force is strong and evolved too, which signifies you have a lot of energy and vitality. Your energy levels are high, meaning you can thrive and continue to grow and expand on the psychological, emotional, spiritual, and physical planes. All of these aspects of self are highlighted. The stag is a symbol for balance and harmony- balancing all various bodies and aspects of self. Physically, vitality and instincts are powerful; emotionally, you possess empathy, gentleness, and emotional intelligence; spiritually you are insightful and wise, with key skills in subtle perception and evolved self-awareness… psychological, you have quality intellectual and logical powers that allow you to thrive mentally. The clear message is: it's time to take charge and step into self-mastery, so you can share your skills and wisdom and lead others. This is an excellent power animal for teachers, motivational speakers and coaches, and educators or wayshowers. It's also the perfect animal for those in a management or business position.

The stag is a symbol of love, power, devotion, inspiration, and alignment with your destiny. You should feel free to speak your truth and express yourself without fear or apprehension. Liberation of emotions- letting feelings flow, and having an open heart and throat chakra are key here. The stag spirit helps you to discern, connect to your intuition & higher mind, and see that all is interconnected. You don't want to live in fear, anxiety, or loss and separation, so why would others? High self-esteem and self-love accompanied people with the stag spirit animal. Walk gracefully and confidently that you are protected, and that you are free to be your authentic, brilliant, and shining self. Keep your intentions pure and rooted in integrity and truth too. Any manipulation, BS, or deception on your behalf will often be sensed by others- this is an extremely noble animal. Also, modesty, purity, manifestation powers, and mental and spiritual gifts & abilities are strong. All star signs can call on the stag for protection, because it offers such a grounded and powerful, protective, wisdom and energy. A white stag symbolizes purity, innocence, faith, and vulnerability.

If the Stag is your spirit animal, you need to be mindful of the following shadow traits or follies:-

- Being so head-strong and assertive that you come across as aggressive or intimidating
- Ambition, determination, and willpower to succeed that you lose touch of sensitive, empathic, and gentle-compassionate qualities
- Losing yourself in work, service, or career (at the expense of family & friendship bonds)
- Becoming disconnected from emotional, spiritual, and sexual needs

The stag is similar to the **Elk**, so you can apply the meanings and symbolism of the Elk here.

Squirrel

The squirrel symbolizes the power of resources. If this is your spirit animal, you are very abundant, resourceful, and positive. Squirrel's are optimistic and remain generally happy despite life's challenges. The message is that you can get through any testing and difficult time, as long as you remain positive minded and keep your sights set on success. This is a high achievement and accomplishment power animal. The squirrel may be small, but this doesn't take away from their power. Self-sufficiency and self-reliance can be learned through the squirrel, as can personal authority and confidence. The squirrel teaches the importance of hard work, determination, perseverance, and having aspirations, no matter how big or small. Everything related to the earth element can be experienced, increased, and integrated. Renewal, rebirth, transformation, hard work, duty, and accountability are further symbolisms, as are responsibilities, practicalities, and discernment. All of these characteristics are well integrated in those with the squirrel spirit. Mastering your own energies should take precedence above anything else, like trying to control or seek power over others. Find your own power within. The squirrel equally symbolizes change and adaptability. Listen to the messages from both the sky and the earth, because there are timeless teachings and deep insights to be found in earth and sky. By combining gratitude with foresight, you can find pearls of wisdom- and significant abundance.

Financial flow, prosperity and abundance, and seeing beyond and through physical illusions are all part of the squirrel's medicine. The material realm is here to serve our highest self and spiritual body. It is not here to feed ego, greed, negativity, hatred, fear, illusion, or separation. Through reflecting on where abundance is needed, and how you can best make use of your resources, you are able to rise above the limitations and pettiness of the material-physical realm. This spirit animal represents breaking free of cycles- cycles that may be toxic, self-sabotaging, destructive, or limiting. You should be using your observation and perceptive skills to determine how you can draw energy from the earth in a positive and empowering way, as the squirrel does. It can help to ground you. It helps to make you feel comfortable and secure, safe, and cherished. The squirrel spirit is a guide for when you're feeling out of touch with your body and Mother Earth. Excellent planning and organizational skills come with the squirrel. If this is your power animal, you're a master of long-term planning, thinking ahead for your future, and reserving your resources, finances, and energy levels for cycles of success. There's a strong sense of preparation and being diligent, also being very mindful, conservative, and sensible with regards to your security and safety. Squirrel spirit can help you if you tend to be reckless or impulsive with money and have a hard time saving. Not only is renewal of physical energies present, but renewal of spiritual life force, which in turn sparks healthy choices related to the physical and material realm. The squirrel spirit can help to ground more impulsive, uncommitted, and impractical adventure seeking types! Divine simplicity is a further message of the squirrel. This humble little creature doesn't need much, yet truly appreciates all they do have; this is a message of joy and contentment in your home and physical environments.

Positivity, looking towards the sky, symbolizing remaining optimistic, and adding some laughter and humor into your life and character are additional meanings. You should embrace multiple perspectives and open-mindedness, becoming more conscious of how your belief systems and judgments affect close relationships. The squirrel is often underestimated in this realm- they're open-minded and with a philosophical nature, and this means you can expand your horizons through gifts of discernment, intelligence, and acceptance (non-judgmental perception). Don't get stuck in a routine or rut either, embrace change and adaptability. And, let important internal shifts to occur without resistance. The squirrel represents overcoming adversities and learning through challenges. Also, going within- rest, introspection, and taking time for reflection. Self-discovery is important and this manifests through detaching from the physical realm. Set clear goals whilst aligning with a bigger picture vision, aspirations and dreams included. A further message is to be more responsive and less reactive. Instead of living in fear, ignorance, chaos, and hatred or negativity, seek to embody more light, joy, positivity, and love. Responding requires conscious thought and mindfulness, while reaction is often unconscious and impulsive. The latter creates anger, tension, hostility, and unnecessary separation. As a symbol of agility and quick movement, you can apply this meaning to any area of your life- emotionally, psychologically, physically and spiritually. Playfulness and lightness of spirit can be learned too. Draw on your wisdom, talents, skills, inner strength, creativity and innovation, love of fun, and adaptability for the victories you deserve.

Anything to be mindful of?

If the Squirrel is your spirit animal, you need to be mindful of the following shadow traits or follies:-

- Rigid thinking, an inflexible mindset, and getting stuck in pessimism or worry and doubt
- Taking life too seriously- not lightning up and having fun!
- Too much importance and emphasis placed on the material things in life… possible spiritual disconnection
- Be careful of taking on too much and overcommitting, having multiple projects or tasks on the go. Return to simplicity where you can truly appreciate all you do have, therefore attract more in the future

Mouse

The mouse reminds us of the small details in life, and they are often overlooked as a spirit animal due to their size and current treatment by humans. Mice are extraordinary little creatures, scurrying around to make sure they have all the essentials to survive; food, security, shelter… They are hard workers, and as a spirit animal the mouse represents perseverance, determination, hard-work, and persistent effort. The mouse is humble, down-to-earth, and modest with unique perception and observation skills. They're very intelligent, despite their size. The symbolism is to tend to daily chores, errands, and responsibilities in the real world. This is an extremely practical and dutiful spirit animal to have. It is symbolic of the star sign Virgo, if you know anything about astrology… Therefore the mouse represents perfectionism, being very concerned with domestic and practical matters, and not overlooking a single detail. They are small-minded but in a way that allows them to "get stuff done." Hard-working, surprisingly ambitious, modest, reserved and genuine, the mouse is connected to the earth, and therefore brings many positive qualities. You can embody greater grace, compassion, and feminine energy through this power animal. Nurturing, caring, kindness, generosity, sincerity, and humility are available for integration. Being somewhat shy and reserved has its benefits; a hidden power of the mouse spirit is that you often navigate life undetected, blending into the crowd, which allows you to take care of your own business. You don't seek the limelight and you're certainly not attention-seeking. These two qualities open doorways for collaborations, connections, and prosperity later in life. The mouse teaches the art of patience.

You're likely very subtle and intentional in your words and ways. Through being modest and shy as opposed to attention-seeking or overly bold or dominant, you possess the power of invisibility. Being overlooked isn't all bad! People underestimate you, which means you can strive towards your own successes, abundance, accomplishments, and personal aspirations and goals without bother. Sometimes, silence and humility are the greatest powers. The mouse's message is that it's the quiet ones in life who don't always need to be seen or outshine others that win the long game, or at least create lasting happiness and peace. Communication tends to be direct and gentle in those with this spirit animal. You are intelligent, observant, perceptive, analytical, instinctive, and an excellent planner, organizer, and problem-solver. You're bold and courageous in a subtle way. You certainly don't lack inner strength or determination to win in life… The key is to work behind the scenes and get stuff done without the drama or fuss. Stay committed, hard-working, and optimistic on your journey. If this is one of your personal animals, you are a real family person, likely making an excellent parent. You love creating safe, comforting, and harmonious spaces, so that your loved ones feel protected at ease. You know how to support them emotionally, spiritually, and psychologically, and provide financial and practical support too. Stay clear of impulsiveness as best as possible, as patience is your secret superpower.

Also, *think small, but dream big*. You shouldn't get too lost in fantasy or non-realistic visions with the mouse spirit animal. Certainly seek inspiration- inspiration flows effortlessly through the mouse spirit, however always remember that it's the small details that count and add up to the greater whole. You can call on other spirit animals where vision is required. Finally, the mouse symbolism and meaning asks you to appreciate yourself, further trusting in yourself. You have great instincts and intuitive powers, so trust in the subtle guidance and impression you receive from the universe. The answers are within, you have your own source of wisdom and light inside you; source energy flows through all things, including you! Practice gratitude daily, and work on cleansing your physical system to be as pure and clear-sighted as possible. Honor your physical vessel to create the best prosperity for yourself and your family.

Anything to be mindful of?

If the Mouse is your spirit animal, you need to be mindful of the following shadow traits or follies:-

- Losing touch of reality through becoming disconnected from your body; stay grounded!
- Letting others suppress you, oppress you, or bully or dominate you
- Wanting to conform to be like everyone else or blend into the crow… be yourself, stay authentic, and do things your way

- Steering away from proven routes and pathways to success. Remember that tradition serves a purpose

Bat

The bat is a symbol of rebirth and new beginnings. Transitions, transformation, and fresh starts are in store when the bat spirit crosses your journey. The bat can help you process and understand grief, pain, and trauma. It is an animal that calls for self-reflection and introspection, self-honesty, and being totally vulnerable and transparent with your emotions and feelings. This spirit animal is linked to the kundalini, the serpent-like energy that travels up your spine and equates with life force, psychic gifts, imaginative abilities, sexual energy, spiritual powers, longevity, and instincts & intuition. The purpose of awakening and being on a spiritual path- or aware of your own spiritual body- is to unblock your chakras and awaken kundalini energy. As the bat symbolizes rebirth, activating and working with kundalini energy can help you to heal on multiple levels, and access the unique traits and symbolism of the bat. These are claircognizance, clairaudience, clairsentience, psychic gifts, inner alchemy, and spiritual and intuitive perception. Insight, vision, telepathic powers, and highly evolved instincts come under the symbolism of the beat. Representing rebirth and alchemical transformation, you can discover hidden truths, talents, and aspects of your soul. Meditation, sound therapy, holistic healing, and spiritual activities are all part of the bat's medicine. You're able to get deep and explore your psyche, inner desires, and core motivations and passions; everything connected to the astral and subconscious realms are available. Hidden desires, strengths, weaknesses, gifts, talents, and personality and soul traits can all be discovered through 'going within.' A lot of answers and truths are found within our own bodies, within our cells and our DNA.

Wisdom flows through you, your body is essentially a channel. Bat energy assists in grounding you, connecting you to your body and the world around. Referring back to understanding grief; hidden sadness and pain related to past trauma are linked to this highly perceptive animal. Through darkness you find light, and with light comes self-awareness and wisdom. In fact, this is an incredibly powerful spirit animal for discovering yourself and your shadow self, or shadow personality traits & attributes. Darkness is linked to the shadow self. It's also linked to the subconscious realm, and feminine powers. You can therefore develop magnetic and astral, spiritual, and imaginative powers through the bat spirit. Also, nurturing, caring, empathy, compassion, sensitivity, parental instincts, extrasensory gifts of perception and illusion breaking; breaking illusory cycles, seeing through the veil of illusion, and finding ultimate truth. True love within is accessible as well. Going through and into the darkness allows you to come out into the light, which usually always results in self-love and the realization that true love has always been within. The bat can further be called on to help with dreams, such as diving deep into the subconscious realm to ask for insight, wisdom, and higher or spiritual guidance. All in all, a lot of wisdom from various angles- dimensions, aspects, and planes- are readily available for connection. Take note of the bat symbolism in relation to darkness and the subconscious, astral, feminine, spiritual, and multidimensional dream realms.

Past lives and memories of ancient times can be accessed. Fresh starts and new chapters within and around are sparked. You are most likely very intelligent, intuitive, and insightful- you have very fine-tuned senses which enable you to receive subtle information, emotions, and other psychic vibrations from your external environment. Rebirth comes through shedding layers of yourself that are outgrown, and no longer serve a purpose. New ideas and fresh perspectives flow when you do this… The ego transforms and old thought patterns & belief systems are filled with light. Purity and innocence are symbolic of the bat. It's about clearing space for the new to emerge, new relationships, romance, partnerships, creativity, better serving philosophies, talents and self-expression. Beginnings come in many forms, but the key is to clear the old, heal your shadow self, enter the darkness to find the light, and activate and awaken kundalini for holistic healing and wholeness. Increased visions and foresight are also symbolic of the bat spirit animal. You should work on your third eye chakra and the associated gifts. Your Higher Self comes alive, flashes of inspiration become apparent, and vision, prophetic sight, clairvoyance/clairaudience/claircognizance as mentioned all expand. Supremely sensitive, self-aware, and deeply soulful, connect to the bat spirit for immense power and inner depth. Finally, bats possess echolocation due to poor (physical) vision in darkness. This means they have amazing senses and can "see" through psychic gifts, but they have unique hearing abilities. You may sense things clairaudiently, also being open to spiritual transitions, past life exploration, and channeling or mediumship.

Anything to be mindful of?

If the Bat is your spirit animal, you need to be mindful of the following shadow traits or follies:-

- Rigid thinking, holding onto outdated beliefs, and a lack of flexibility or adaptability (including getting stuck in routines)
- Fear of darkness or the shadow realms, which is where significant growth and insight are available
- Repressed emotions, and inability to let go of past wounds, pain, and trauma
- Unwillingness to "dive deep' with yourself, and fears and ignorances of the world preventing you from accessing psychic, spiritual, and extrasensory gifts

Chapter 6: 'Higher Self' Spirit Animals

Eagle

The eagle is a symbol of your Higher Self. Vision, connection to the Great Spirit, courage, illumination, inner strength, and aligning with your life purpose are all connected to the eagle. The eagle enhances insight, wisdom, intuition, and prophecy. You are able to see the big picture, tune into higher consciousness, and receive divine revelations. If this is your spirit animal, you're an expert of visionary and idealistic qualities, meaning you can look past and beyond the trivial, petty, and mundane aspects of the material world. Getting stuck or trapped in the 3D materialistic realm doesn't interest you- you are more interested in how you can connect to your higher mind for extraordinary creations. As a message of prophetic wisdom and higher power, the eagle helps you shift, evolve, and transcend. Toxic cycles and behaviors can be overcome and transcended. The eagle spirit is concerned with truth, spirituality, philosophy, and higher truths; the ability to see beyond the veil of illusion, and uncover hidden meanings and symbolism. The eagle is a messenger of spirit and the divine. Creative and artistic visions can come to you, while genius ideas linked to the imagination and the subconscious realm are amplified. If you need to get to the root of the truth of something, see through BS, deception, or manipulation, and gain some clear sight, call on the eagle spirit. It guides, heals, protects, activates your third eye, and stimulates spiritual perception. The eagle is the ultimate "Higher Self" spirit animal to have by your side; it is a fierce protector too. There's a holistic, broader, and spiritually-aligned reality waiting to be discovered… All you have to do is rise above and past the petty triviality of the material world, and align with a higher power. Find your center too.

Clairvoyance, clairsentience, claircognizance and clairaudience are all linked to this power animal. Intuition, psychic abilities, and telepathy are available as well. You may be gifted in precognition and precognitive, prophetic, and shamanic dreaming. Eagle medicine allows you to connect to the spiritual, astral, and subconscious realms for multi-dimensional insight and wisdom. Subtle perception is enhanced. With such a strong connection to a higher power and the soul & spirit planes, compassion and empathy, non-judgement and universal love flow and expand. You should stand strong in your truth, and walk with grace, integrity and dignity. *The message is clear*: live with heart, soul, integrity, and compassion. Magic and divine synchronicities are connected to the eagle's medicine. Divinity, grace, personal power, courage, and prophetic wisdom flow effortlessly when in tune with your Higher Self, and to the shamanic and subtle realms. Evolved empathy is common in people with this spirit animal. You're bold and fearless, yet sensitive and self-aware. You know how to take charge, lead, inspire, and step into self-assertive action, yet can equally be humble, down-to-earth, compassionate, and gentle. The eagle represents a beautiful harmony and synergy of yin and yang within. Personal authority and elf-sovereignty expand when you work with the eagle. Through transcendental meditation and therapy/healing activities you may receive glimpses and flashes of inspiration, higher guidance, and insight. The eagle is a call to your soul plan and purpose, your life path, destiny, and soul mission. Secrets of the universe including manifestation and universal laws are accessible and amplified, while healing power and knowledge are equally available.

You can work directly with the Creator, in co-creation with and to the universe and its subtle, ethereal, and mystical powers. Many people with this spirit animal are inspirational teachers or speakers, spiritual leaders, healers, and artists or musicians. Working directly with Spirit is a gateway to hidden truths, secret information, and extraordinary creative & imaginative abilities. You may equally seek the help of an elder, teacher or mentor to help you acquire wisdom and intuitive guidance. You may then become an elder, master teacher, or mentor once you've attained self-mastery! Self-mastery is core to the eagle's wisdom. Other spirit animals, spirit guides and spiritual teachers can be connected to with the eagle's assistance, as this animal connects you with the spiritual and soul planes. Furthermore, there is a determined, hard-working, and persevering aspect to this power animal; big dreams and aspirations are usually associated with the eagle. Have faith, trust in a higher power, energize your vision cyclically (daily, weekly, etc.) and feel safe and comforted in the knowledge that you are protected. Majesty and power accompany foresight and premonition or precognition, as long as you're willing to lose the distractions. The eagle represents rising above the illusions and fears or ignorances of the 3D realm, also focusing, and cutting cords, that keep you stuck in limiting or self-sabotaging cycles.

Anything to be mindful of?

If the Eagle is your spirit animal, you need to be mindful of the following shadow traits or follies:-

- Getting so stuck on the big picture that you fail to see the smaller details
- Losing touch with your physical body and the material realm due to always needing to be spiritual, or remain connected to spiritual & philosophical ideals (ungroundedness)
- Believing yourself to be superior and treating or perceiving others as inferior!
- Mysticism, fantasy, or spiritual ideals that lead to illusion and disconnection from others; isolation or extreme independence

If the eagle has visited you in your dreams, you're being directed towards connecting with your Higher Self and ability to communicate with Spirit, or the Great Spirit. You may be a divine messenger and have some "shape-shifting" aspect about your soul-print (unique soul's blueprint). Alternatively, there are creative and artistic visions that need to come through, so you should be paying attention to signs & synchronicities and further engaging in imaginative, musical, and artistic self-expression.

You're here to create beautiful works of art! Stay open to the subtle messages from the ether, while never neglecting your intuition.

Hawk

The hawk symbolizes clear sight, vision, and intuition. If this is your spirit animal, you are incredibly intuitive, perceptive, and problem-solving- you have a problem-solving nature and are a master of observation. You can clearly see the bigger picture, rising above the smaller and more trivial or petty details of the material world. The physical plane is of little use to you, it is merely a tool to ground your larger visions into the world, and of course to provide security, shelter, and survival for you to continue on your spiritual mission. People with the hawk spirit animal tend to have a greater destiny or purpose; your life is filled with passion, personal power, and creative and artistic talents. You like to partake in educational and cultural pathways for self-development, and to work towards your legacy. The hawk is highly intelligent. Both intelligence and creativity, logic and intuition, and analytical and imaginative skills flow through you. The hawk is significant in Native American culture too, a symbol for receiving and tuning in to messages from spirit. As a shamanic power animal, the hawk connects you with the divine and acts as a direct bridge to the spirit worlds. Magic, synchronicities, and deep insight into life's hidden meanings and messages, including sacred laws and universal truths, can be discovered. The Higher Self is activated and awakened through the Hawk spirit. Channeling gifts are enhanced, you may start to awaken to your own clairvoyant and clairsentient ability; this spirit animal brings incredible extrasensory gifts. Psychic powers too.

Illumination, spirituality, inner stillness, contemplation, a connection to the divine mysteries of life, universal cycles and sacred knowledge, higher truths… these are all part of the hawk's medicine. A strong connection to the ethereal and astral planes are present. You can find pearls of wisdom and knowledge through the astral realm, which connects you directly to the subconscious and imaginative realms. This means subconscious insight, wisdom, higher guidance, spiritual power, and imagery, visuals, or revelations into your purpose and soul path. Your desires, strengths, buried talents, and deepest passions and gifts linked to your soul purpose are available through the astral and subconscious realms. The hawk symbolizes being able to rise above the physical plane and world, thus connecting to the more subtle aspects of spirit and the collective consciousness energy field. Past life recall, seeing into past lives, and perhaps even receiving glimpses of your future self, in future cycles when you are more self-mastered or connected to your divine light essence, can be seen and understood. Higher and spiritual consciousness are energized. Similar to the eagle, the hawk allows you to transcend and elevate, providing for steps towards self-mastery and spiritual maturity. Instincts and impulsiveness can be used as a gateway to essential survival and security means. In other words, place more importance on your Higher Self and visionary works of art or groundbreaking creations you can birth, but always listen to your instincts. Boldness, self-responsibility, duty, and service come under the hawk's medicine. Foresight, clairvoyance, prophecy, seeing past illusions, and channeling your energies into spiritual and creative or artistic visions are also amplified.

Eliminate distractions, pay attention to subconscious and subtle messages from the universe, be open to clairaudience- hearing important frequencies and communication from the realms of spirit, and clairvoyant and clairsentient gifts- receiving information from the divine through a range of senses and fine-tuned skills. Although a 'light' power animal, the hawk spirit can help you to find comfort in the dark and shadow realms, which includes your own shadow personality. This is due to such a strong link to the astral plane. Dreams are highlighted, so you can consciously work with your dreams to find guidance and inspiration; the OWL and PANTHER spirit are excellent to work with alongside the hawk for these purposes. They compliment each other.

The symbolism of the *eagle* applies to the hawk too.

Anything to be mindful of?

If the Hawk is your spirit animal, you need to be mindful of the following shadow traits or follies:-

- Reigning over others in a way that seeks to control, dominate, or oppress
- Becoming intimidating or cold in your intentions for success and creating a legacy
- Perceptiveness, logic, and intelligence to the point of losing touch with your emotions; a lack of empathy and sensitivity…
- Sacrificing personal relationships and loving family & friendship bonds (emotional warmth, companionship) through seeking self-mastery and expertise in your skills

Raven

The raven is another powerful bird spirit connected to the Higher Self and the realm of spirit. A messenger of magic, the raven is more connected to the shamanic and shadow lands than the previous two bird power animals. The raven is often linked to the star sign Scorpio. If you know anything about astrology, you will know that Scorpio is the zodiac sign ruled by Pluto, the watery planet symbolizing rebirth, alchemical transformation, power, mysticism and intensity, and spirituality. Scorpios are deep, intense, and immensely intuitive- they are also the sign of the Shaman, someone who can travel between worlds and enter multidimensional consciousness and wisdom. They are natural shapeshifters and skilled in the realm of psychic gifts, clairvoyance, and extrasensory perception, whether they know it or not! All of these qualities can be linked to the raven. In Norse, Druid, and Celtic mythology the raven is considered an animal of great wisdom, intelligence, and both intuition and intellect. The raven is a symbol of darkness, death (metaphorical), the afterlife and rebirth. Inner alchemy arises when you make peace with your own shadow self, and this is the message of the raven. You can "get deep" and explore the depths of the subconscious, astral and spiritual realms through the raven spirit. Higher self and primal wisdom light up, and this animal helps you connect to both the primal waters of divinity- connected to your lower chakras, and the celestial & light realms.

This spirit animal further teaches that nothing in the universe is random. Everything is connected through a sacred and divine web, through sacred laws. You can be shown the true meaning of synchronicity and sacred & universal laws governing our universe, further understanding metaphysical concepts. You achieve this with the raven's help through the realm of feelings, emotions, enhanced senses, and increased self-awareness and spiritual perception. Through the darkness linked to astral forces and multidimensional wisdom and awareness, you can explore aspects of your past self, the programming and belief systems, patterns of behavior, and emotional and psychological forces that used to drive you. Inner desires and driving forces that are rooted in intensity and soul-nourishing sensations can be accessed. This is how you open new portals and doorways to new growth, through going into your past and being open to the memories that arise, the good and the bad. The raven teaches that even painful, dark, or negative emotions and experiences can be a catalyst for great change. This is true alchemy. The third eye chakra is associated with the raven spirit, and becomes awakened when you work with this bird's medicine. Gaining access to manifestation powers and innate healing, divine, and clairvoyant and spiritual gifts are common with the raven. You're able to perceive subtle energy, see behind physical and material situations and any manipulation or BS and deception attached, and gain clarity bathed in white light. Purity, innocence, faith, a connection to the Great Spirit, and angelic consciousness are linked to the raven spirit. Creative and imaginative gifts too. You're able to connect to creative life force in a way that activates powerful visions, for example through tuning into the collective consciousness. Spiritual ideals and revolutionary concepts and philosophies come through, as you are a channel; the raven spirit assists in awakening your higher energy centers. Universal archetypes and extraordinary works of art, music, poetry, writing, or visionary creations can come through.

The raven acts as a messenger of spirit, which includes secrets from the hidden and unseen realms. You may find ancestors, spirit guides, other significant power animals, and archangels or ascended masters come through- divine contact and channeling and spirit contact through the light realms. The raven is the perfect spirit animal to work with for ancestral communication, healing and transformation, accessing past life wisdom or memories, and unlocking dormant DNA that can lead to the awakening of hidden talents, skills, and soul gifts. Finally, you can discover the true meaning of perfect vision in both a metaphorical and philosophical sense and a physical one. Observational, perceptive, and problem-solving skills run deep with the raven spirit. Creative forces and powers of the universe and cosmos are available for you to tune into. Trust in your power and the subtle and intuitive impressions you receive. Divination is strong and mystical powers flow through you. If this is your spirit animal, you are mysterious, confident and attractive. You have a strong aura, a powerful personal presence, and a somewhat intimidating personality! But this is not a bullyish or overpowering energy- it's a character trait and inner power that commands attention and authority, and you likely use it to help, inspire, or connect with others. Commanding attention allows you to be open with your intuition and wisdom, sharing it with others and raising the collective vibration. Your connection to the source increases other people's light. You're simultaneously fearless and bold, and extremely self-expressive and passionate. A final meaning and symbolism is healing and letting go of the past…

Anything to be mindful of?

If the Raven is your spirit animal, you need to be mindful of the following shadow traits or follies:-

- Be mindful of using your personal power to intimidate others or hurt their feelings
- Supersensitivity and hyper-emotionalism may be common and come in sporadic (or frequent) bursts
- Be careful of extreme isolation and solitude, or timidness, shyness, and feelings of a lack of security
- In your need to detach, you may come across as selfish and inconsiderate, also neglecting important relationships & practical commitments

Crow

The crow is similar to the raven due to the connection with magic and divination. You can work directly with the creation and co-creative powers of the universe. Magic pulses through the energetic universe, but only if you're willing to tune into the frequencies and vibrations. Everything in the physical universe exists on a basis of frequency and vibration, and this is a primary teaching of the raven. Sounds and subtle energy, colors and spiritual life force are available in every moment. The crow shows you the power and reality of presence, living in the moment and being present. Sacred laws shape our human experience- everything is interconnected. Thoughts shape reality, and emotions, feelings, philosophies and beliefs give rise to the physical world; everything begins on a subtle and unseen level... There's a divine order for everything. Excitement, a sense of wonder, and joy can be yours when you connect with spirit, and with the sacred and divine energy that flows through all things. Following your highest joy is connected to the crow spirit. You may experience celestial and spiritual sensations, and the wisdom and self-knowledge that accompanies, through following a creative path. Artistic, imaginative and creative gifts are strong with this spirit animal. Also, through connecting to the spiritual and ethereal qualities and dimensional. Higher dimensional consciousness is available for you to tune into. Unity consciousness too. In fact, the crow helps you to feel expansive and blissful feelings or self-love and interconnectedness.

Trusting in yourself, spirit, and your higher self is symbolic of the crow. People with this spirit animal tend to love peace and harmony over anything else, but they also feel comfortable with the chaos, drama, and darkness or distortion of the world. They see how creation and positivity can be found in destruction and darkness. Every negative situation is an opportunity for learning and growth, self-evolution and taking steps towards self-mastery are available in every experience. The crow symbolism portrays the highs and lows of life, and that there is divine inspiration in both negative and positive events. Stay optimistic, listen to your instincts & intuition, and be open to alternate views and mindsets. The crow can assist you in being flexible and open-minded, adaptable to new ideas, schools of thoughts, philosophies, and world views. Cultural and educational activities are common in those with this spirit animal; business ventures and partnerships, creative collaborations, artistic inspiration, and new doorways to professional and personal development flow effortlessly. You will find yourself attracting a lot of these things in your life. As a link to sacred laws and the divine synchronicities of life, you may find yourself noticing natural cycles more than others, being attuned to a "oneness" frequency. For example, living by the cycles and phases of the moon, or the seasons of Mother Earth. Or even larger cycles like Equinoxes, Grand Cycle shifts (2012 Winter Solstice) and other cosmic events. Abundance, prosperity and good fortune come to you easily when you live in harmony with nature. Nature is abundant, so you should practice gratitude daily.

The crow can help you with divination, prayer, ceremony, and daily routines or self-care practices, which include counting your blessings and intention setting. Meditation, mindfulness, and a strong sense of inner serenity and peace increase and expand. Your life is filled with lightness, but in a way that allows you to stay connected to inner depth and soul. The crow represents light, color, creativity, innovation and intellect but without becoming overly superficial, or at least you should stay mindful of not falling into superficiality. Connected to the astral and subconscious realms as well, you can access past life memory wisdom and awaken ancestral codes of knowledge. You may due blessings or gifts from positive karma unclaimed, i.e. things owed to you can come swimming back into your life with the crow spirit. The crow is a messenger of hidden knowledge, secrets, and everything related to the often unseen and invisible worlds. This includes vibrations and aspects of life linked to your own psychological, emotional, spiritual and physical driving forces, and your past actions. Further, the crow helps us to recognize that all things "dark" and seemingly "insignificant" actually hold great power; many people overlook the crow, yet it is very similar to the other spirit animal birds that gain respect. Why is this? Well, this fact alone can teach you not to judge yourself and/or others. Perhaps it's your judgment for others that results in you being wrongfully judged or dismissed… karmic forces influence us all, and we're usually further unconscious of them. This also teaches us the power of working behind the scenes and not being afraid to remain invisible to some. The power of invisibility is present. If you're going to blend into the shadows, however, you must also maintain your boundaries. Self-protection is a key message.

Anything to be mindful of?

If the Crow is your spirit animal, you need to be mindful of the following shadow traits or follies:-

- Be careful of over-adaptability and a lack of boundaries; self-protection is paramount
- Don't use magical or alchemical powers for darkness, ego, or destruction (there's a possibility of dark or black magic with this animal!)
- Be mindful of manipulating, deceiving, or conning others- trickster energy may be present
- Never use prophetic or intuitive gifts for selfish motivations or egotistical desires… keep rooted in the light and pure, authentic, and loving connections

Beetle

The beetle is connected to ancient Egypt and the realm of god and goddess energies, or frequencies. You can really get in tune with your ancient, spiritual, primal, and divine essence and nature through the beetle spirit. The beetle is all about magic, the divine, divination, and your own spiritual powers. You are a sensual, creative, imaginative and majestic creature; this is the message of the beetle. You are one with the divine and the universe is one with you, benevolent and abundant energies are everywhere. Through the ethereal and spiritual realms, you can access hidden gifts, like clairvoyance, psychic abilities, telepathic powers and profound intuition. It is a feminine spirit animal as well, bringing in feminine qualities and enhancing gentleness, empathy, compassion, nurturance, kindness, and instincts & intuition, receptivity, and personal magnetism. People with this spirit animal are incredibly lucky due to such strong receptive and magnetic powers. You are likely a master manifestor, excel in empathic and mindful communication, and are sensitive to the needs of others. Your unique sensitivity combined with nurturing and compassionate qualities is what makes you succeed and thrive in life, and form more meaningful and prosperous connections. The beetle teaches that you can be alone and thrive in independence, while simultaneously being very lucky in the realm of community connections. This animal suggests you have lots of kindred spirits, soulmates, and family bonds. Regarding manifestation, you know how to tune into psychic and intuitive powers and birth through new ideas, concepts, and universal archetypes. You can birth universal and cosmic blueprints as well, new paradigms, philosophies and wisdom that this world hasn't seen yet. People with this power animal are very deep, wise, intelligent, intuitive, and in tune with the subtle and astral realms…

This is an excellent spirit animal for creative ventures, projects, and self-expression. Expansive, abundant, prosperous, and ever-lasting opportunities & blessings are available, as the beetle symbolizes infinite potential. Also, creative magic, co-creation, tuning into your Higher Self for passionate and conscious self-expression, and raising your vibrations through healing and spiritual awareness. New levels of self-development and inner balance arise. Channeling and mediumship, accessing spiritual gifts, tuning into the divine and higher consciousness, and being a conduit or messenger for spirit come with the beetle's medicine. You're able to let go of old chapters and cycles and release anything that doesn't serve you. This includes old or limiting belief systems, mindsets, emotions, behaviors, and relationships. You can see through deception and get straight to the light of truth; you're able to see through BS & manipulation, seeing past illusions. You may be able to see through the superficial aspects and dimensions of society or social situations, and instead view from the soul and a spiritual, higher vibrational, reality. Healing, release, and closure on a deep level are available with the beetle spirit. Letting go of the past makes space for the new to emerge, which includes new opportunities, collaborations and connections, and educational, professional, and creative pathways to abundance. The beetle teaches the true meaning of life chapters and cycles of growth. The beetle asks you: Does this serve your higher self? Or does it keep you stuck in self-sabotage, a past cycle or destructive timeline? The beetle further instills courage and fearlessness in you, so you can take on the world in a modest and humble yet powerful way. Many people with the beetle spirit are changemakers and groundbreakers! You possess supreme compassion and sensitivity, grace, kindness, generosity, gentleness, sincerity, and integrity. Integrity and morals are high in this spirit animal's recipients.

Physical instincts, vitality, achieving your dreams and goals, and patience linked to determination and hard work are further meaning & symbolism. You should focus on the big picture and dream big, while paying attention to the smaller details and individual steps that take you to the finish line. Spiritual illumination, self-realizations, and self-actualization are available. The beetle spirit signifies peace, harmony and a down-to-earth and chilled vibe above anything else, so you should consciously avoid the ego games of others and drama, or chaotic situations that bring you out of balance and alignment. It also teaches self-love and self-care and how important they are. Nurturing yourself is healthy, you can't give to others or share your light, joy, or generosity with the world if you're in a state of depletion, or lack and poverty consciousness. Honor and value yourself- you should see yourself as worthy and hold yourself in high esteem. Compassion, empathy, clairsentience and emotional intelligence amplify through the beetle spirit. You're very self-aware and persevering, sticking with whatever you start (relationships, plans, projects, etc.). The message is that patience, persistence, calmness, inner stillness, and determination conquer all things… Stay committed to self-renewal, transformation, purification and enlightenment.

Anything to be mindful of?

If the Beetle is your spirit animal, you need to be mindful of the following shadow traits or follies:-

- Becoming lost in the drama, gossip, or false stories of others; stay in your own lane
- Thinking you have to be everything or do everything for everyone
- Sacrificing self-care and your own abundance in the name of compassion and selfless… aim for balance and harmony of individual needs vs others' interests
- Losing your modesty & humility to conform or blend into the crowd. Be authentic! Be true to yourself.

I am the beetle, a master of magic,
I can connect you to a timeless truth, for I am a *soul magnet*.
I am deeply magnetic and can help you attract and manifest;
Instinctive, psychic, nurturing, and gentle, my feminine qualities are the best.

As a symbol of enlightenment, I can help you transcend old cycles,
Synchronizing you to your inner godly shining spiral...
Reclaim abundance, embrace renewal, and align with vibrations of the heart,
as I am the spirit animal to call on when you need a *New Beginning* or *Fresh Start*.

Chapter 7: Spiritual & Evolved Spirit Animals

We are the evolved spiritual masters of the earthly plane,
We represent higher consciousness, universal truths, & are here to show another way;
a way rooted in love, unity, and harmony- our energy is infectious,
as multidimensional beings with many talents, we bring through multiple energies and
perspectives.

The universe is colorful, magical, and musical… infinite potential is real
from dreams to clairvoyance and unconditional love to purity,
or extraordinary instincts and the power of invisibility;
Call on us if you need some assistance in evolving to new heights,
You never know what you will find, for our reality is infused in joy & light!

Cat

The cat is a symbol of independence, powerful instincts, and listening to your senses and inner voice. People with this spirit animal are independent, faithful, affectionate, and explorers. They love venturing off to explore distant lands and worlds (or different areas!). You have potent instincts and a powerful intuition- psychic gifts too. Ancient Egyptians revered cats for their ability to see things humans can't, specifically their capacity to transcend dimensions. Cats are mystical explorers of the universe, able to tune into multiple dimensions and timelines. They are known as messenger spirits to many cultures, acting as messengers between Spirit and this physical realm. Cats' senses are extraordinary; they're psychic, telepathic, instinctive, clairsentient, clairaudient, and clairvoyant. This means, if this is your power animal, you can pick up on a range of subtle, emotional, psychological, astral, physical, and spiritual forces and frequencies. You're not just bound to the physical world and dimension, in other words. Curiosity, agility, sharp mind and wit, self-autonomy, and intelligence also come under the cat spirit's powers. You're open-minded and philosophical, deeply intelligent, observant, perceptive, and wise; you enjoy exploring new places and are likely an adventurer at heart. You live with a lot of passion and affection for others in equal measure. Loyal, loving, caring, and extremely protective, the cat represents our paternal and maternal nurturing instincts. They may like to wander off, but they are equally protective and nurturing. The cat symbolizes solitude and introspection too. People with this power animal are prone to sporadic or cyclic periods of introspection and self-healing, time to themselves to rejuvenate and engage in self-care. As master groomers, the cat spirit teaches you how to take care of yourself and step into self-sovereignty. Self-reliance, developing talents and skills with little outside help- perhaps only guidance, and making your own money or acquiring resources to support yourself are symbolic of the cat. This spirit animal signifies responsibility and survival.

Powerful magnetism and instinctive self-awareness, in addition to a Higher Self connection link here. You're so intuitive that you have extrasensory gifts, and psychic powers that may wow or shock others. You will feel a drive towards spiritual illumination, self-actualization, and enlightenment. Acquiring wisdom and knowledge of the self is strong with this spirit animal, as is discovering mysteries of the universe… Also, hidden and deeper meanings to life and self, including sacred and universal laws. The cat spirit is so powerful that you can see through the veil of illusion, looking into hidden dimensions and beyond the material-physical, 3D, world. The cat teaches that there is more than meets the eye, there are lots of invisible and subtle layers to reality, and with keen sight and a higher vision perspective you too can access this. Vision, higher perspectives, spiritual sight, and a love of the unknown, you are very skilled at reading between the lines. This also makes you a BS detector- you're able to see through manipulation, false motives, and the darkness and deception of others. It also asks you to be honest with your own darkness and deception, asking you to step into truth and authenticity. The cat spirit can be direct and blunt, as is seen with this animal's actions when they want to be left alone, desire food or sleep, or don't want affection. Further, the cat spirit symbolizes courage, confidence, and supreme bravery. They are fearless with hearts and spirits of warriors. Ancient Egyptians admired and respected cats because of these qualities, in addition to their multidimensional and transcendental/enlightened nature.

This spirit animal can assist you in putting your trust in both the universe and the unknown, and in your intuition. As a spiritually evolved power animal, this lovely and balanced feline energy provides protection, strong physical vitality and foundations, and a love of luxury. They crave companionship and intimacy, yet equally need their space. They thrive in the daylight where they seek connection with others, however simultaneously love darkness and solitude. The cat therefore shows the importance of inner balance- balancing your inner yin and yang energies. Harmonious relationships should be a priority in your life, in addition to the gifts and abilities that are developed through introspection. And through feeling comfort in the darkness and shadow realms. Social connections VS independence, companionship VS solitude, and healthy attachments VS self-reliance; the cat is perfect for anyone wanting to unify and harmonize their inner dualistic needs. Furthermore, the cat brings the vibration of deep relaxation, of contentment and inner serenity. Wisdom expands from this peaceful state of acceptance and stillness. Finally, due to having impeccable vision the cat spirit signifies being able to see in the dark, developing visionary and seer-like qualities, and precognitive gifts. The cat is sometimes linked to magic and the healing arts, so be very mindful of not falling into black magic or the dark arts. Spells, witchcraft, and alchemy should be kept to the light only. *The message*: align with your Higher Self and a higher truth, transcend distractions and extremist behaviors, and connect to the mystical life force and magic of the universe, without becoming disconnected and ungrounded. Preserving your energy, grounding, self-protection, and knowing when to take action for inspiration and forward movement are other key meanings of the cat spirit. Hold yourself in high-esteem and with high self-worth, knowing you have many gifts, talents, and skills that can help others on their path.

Anything to be mindful of?

If the Cat is your spirit animal, you need to be mindful of the following shadow traits or follies:-

- Try not to become disconnected from your body and physical environments, including intimate relationships, for your love of adventure and the unknown
- Be conscious of imbalances that may arise; always seek a unification and aim for harmony
- Stay self-aware and in tune with all of your "bodies"- your emotional, psychological, spiritual, and physical bodies. People with this spirit animal tend to go too far into one area for significant periods of a time, and neglect the others!
- Stay open-minded and flexible, adaptable, and attuned to multiple perspectives (don't become rigid in mindset)

Chameleon

The chameleon represents adaptability and spiritual evolution. People with this spirit animal are incredibly adaptable, open-minded and flexible. You're able to see multiple perspectives and are extremely gifted in subtle perception, problem-solving, and using a combination of logic and intuition to make the best decisions in life. This is a highly skilled, perceptive, observant, intelligent, and analytical spirit animal. Chameleons are masters of camouflage, and this can be applied to your mind, emotions, psychological thought processes, and both spiritual and physical bodies. You're blessed with a rich imagination and amazing creative and artistic skills. You have a colorful and evolved inner world, meaning you're attuned to the spiritual and subtle realms of feelings, emotions, astral wisdom, and cosmic life force. Artistic vision and profound spiritual wisdom and insight too! Your emotional intelligence is on a whole new level. You're empathic, down-to-earth, kind, loyal, and sensitive to your surroundings (and the needs of others). You may be quite selfless and even self-sacrificing, due to your pleasing, genuine, and adaptable nature. The chameleon spirit is a symbol for purification and cleansing- taking steps to cleanse and clear your auric field and begin a path of self-mastery. Highly evolved with a connection to your soul, you are a deep person. You enjoy exploring life's deeper meanings and mysteries; you equally look for symbolism everywhere. You're the type of person to notice patterns in nature, how colors emit certain feelings and emotions, and how sounds each have specific frequencies that can be used for self-discovery, or for healing. Clairvoyance is integrated and evolved in those with this spirit animal.

Spiritual gifts are strong as well. Psychic, open to telepathic communication, and highly intuitive, you have evolved senses. Extrasensory perception is common with people with this spirit animal, and you are very likely multidimensional. Astral encounters, out of body experiences, lucid dreaming, and transcendental states are accessed easily. It's rather effortless for you to tune into your holistic, spiritual, and multidimensional body. This in turn opens you up to creative inspiration and vision, profound higher mind wisdom & insight, and the capacity for musical and imaginative magic! You're attuned to color frequencies and sound vibrations in a way other humans aren't. The way you perceive reality is unique. You're certainly original with your own set of philosophies and belief systems…The inner child is also awakened and brought to life, you're likely playful and live life full of pleasure. You believe in following your highest joy. Physical sensations, emotional cues, psychological impressions, and spiritual vibrations all make up your reality. You are in tune with your senses and pursue pleasure in your life. Being so adaptable and open-minded can help you in career, relationships, finances, business, love life, or with some creative project or health regime. The chameleon teaches that your outer world is a reflection of your inner world; all internal thoughts, feelings, impressions and reflections create physical reality. Reality is an illusion! Everything is a construct of your perceptions and inner world. Reality is subjective, and this universal truth opens you up to the world of color, sound, music, imaginative gifts, and spiritual and psychic impressions. Sensitivities are an indicator that you're in tune with your feelings and emotions too, which opens you up to your true self. This spirit animal asks you to be honest with yourself and to be authentic.

Individuality, self-expression, curiosity, innovation, and living in alignment with your truth are all symbolic of the chameleon. Sensitivity is your superpower. You're able to sense danger and toxic or harmful people and situations as well- there's a psychic and precognitive element to this power animal. Always be learning, changing, growing and evolving; seek to transcend to the highest heights, new levels. Engage in self-care, honor your sensitivities, and hone your psychic and intuitive abilities. The chameleon signifies someone with a shining and bold personality too. You are both electric and magnetic, knowing when to take the spotlight, and when to blend into the background. This allows you to conceal your emotions when needed, when you want to be more private and either secretive or self-protective. Boldness and courage are associated with the chameleon. Detaching from unhealthy emotions, toxic cycles, and people and environments that aren't good for you. The chameleon spirit asks you to get real with yourself; what serves your highest self? Finally, you are given a lesson in the duality and sometimes ambiguity of life with this power animal. Sometimes you may appear wonderfully wacky, weird in a creative, genius, and brilliantly funky or inventive way. Next, people may perceive you as crazy or strange. This is the beauty of life and the message is to embrace it all, always staying connected to your instincts and intuition. Adapt, but be self-loving and self-protective. Your personality is defined by patience, thoughtfulness and consideration, yet balancing these qualities with boldness and knowing when to take charge of your dreams and ambitions with zest. You may be an outspoken humanitarian, changemaker, visionary, or teacher of some kind. Go with it! The world needs your uniqueness, love, and light.

Anything to be mindful of?

If the Chameleon is your spirit animal, you need to be mindful of the following shadow traits or follies:-

- Be careful of manipulative tendencies or projecting on others when you feel overlooked
- You can be shy and too focused on intentionally not seeking the spotlight, yet this can suppress you and some of your greatest strengths & gifts
- Insecurities, self-doubt, and dissatisfaction can take over... Start to assert yourself more to overcome this
- Defensive, uncertain and apprehensive to make conscious change and forward movement, your lesson is to not be too idealistic, as this can create disappointments

Dog

The dog symbolizes loyalty and unconditional love. There is a reason why dogs are considered "man's best friend." There's no act of service, generosity, or selflessness too much for the dog; this spirit animal teaches these qualities and more. The dog spirit is an extraordinary message of love, service, devotion, faithfulness, loyalty, friendship, and kinship. Love and commitment are enhanced and you may be someone who has a few close friends, who you consider family, whether their blood family or not. This is a strong soulmate spirit animal. You likely have many soulbonds in this life, deep and meaningful friendships. You're affectionate and loyal to those you love, and you cherish companionship- romantic and platonic. Karmic love and the various types of soulmate bonds can be learned through the dog spirit. This spirit animal shows you the power of positive reflection and conscious mirroring, and this can apply to any soulmate, family, or friendship bond. Specifically related to karmic love bonds or soulmates with a past life connection, you can learn a lot about yourself through the relationships in your life. We often share lives with many- we have many soulmates, and we simultaneously share past life connections with others. We come into this life with soul contracts, and we usually meet kindred spirits and soul family along the way. This is what the dog spirit teaches. Actually, you can learn who your soul family is and who is part of your tribe, or who you should make part of your tribe, with this power animal's assistance.

Learning, self-evolution, personal growth, conscious communication, and positive mirroring are all part of the dog's medicine. Luck and prosperity flow to you when you're in tune with your more affectionate and positive qualities, like loyalty, kinship, sincerity, kindnesses, compassion, and generosity. The dog is very benevolent, but they're also self-protective. They're protective of those they love and they are also extremely selfless. It is not uncommon for dogs to display the most evolved and advanced form of unconditional, true, love; sacrifice. The dog spirit is here to show you the power of sacrifice and selflessness, of putting the needs of your loved ones above your own. Being selfish is not a trait emphasized with this spirit animal. Sacrifice is choosing love, and this may call you to put aside your own desires, needs, emotions, or feelings to think about what serves another best. Or what serves the whole. Collective comes first before the individual. This isn't saying lose all sense of self-love or abandon your self-care and well-being needs; it's just saying that when a moment of choice presents itself, being selfless wins. You can transcend self-entitlement, self-centeredness, and egotistical ways with the dog spirit. Further, the message is that regardless of our personal journeys, situations and relationships we may outgrow or people gravitate away from; love will always remain. Commitment and faithfulness can also be energetic, i.e. it doesn't only refer to being in someone's life physically. For example, you can choose to stay committed to love and a soulmate, romantic or friendship bond long after you've parted ways. Overcoming drama, negativity, and ill thoughts are symbolic of the dog. You can truly release all toxic and negative thoughts with the dog spirit, also transcending hatred, envy, and thoughts & feelings of separation. Unity consciousness is called for.

The dog represents our desires and how we attract luck, good fortune, blessings and new opportunities. Gratitude can be learned, the true meaning of counting and appreciating your blessings. Forgiveness is another key meaning. Through purity of thought and being birthed from sincere and authentic emotions, integrity and 'white light' increase in your life. This spirit animal is linked to the crown chakra, your highest chakra of the 7 main chakras representing cosmic consciousness and enlightenment. Spiritual illumination, faith, purity and forgiveness link here, and of course universal compassion. You can call on the dog spirit to assist you with healing, releasing painful emotions, and letting go of karmic, toxic, or negative cycles. Forgive yourself-forgive others. This is the key to your happiness and well-being, and longevity. Following your highest joy too. The dog is a symbol of hope, happiness, positivity, optimism, and good fortune. Living in alignment with your highest joy- what brings you true happiness, pleasure and connection to your heart's content- signifies your true path. The dog power animal helps you discover what is your true happiness, what your soul or creative gifts are, and how you can best express yourself for the most healthy & harmonious connections. Accessing your full and highest potential is linked to the dog spirit. Good character and a good judge of character and your own capabilities link here. If this is your spirit animal, you are not delusional or living under illusions; you follow your highest joys and seek out pleasure, but you're realistic and grounded. You likely keep your promises and know how to protect yourself and others when needed. You should be loyal to yourself, however. Try to balance self-sacrifice and being a best friend and support system for others with self-respect. Confidence, courage, and fearless devotion and passion arise from loyalty to your own needs. Strong self-esteem and self-worth are amplified with the dog's assistance. It's important to keep your spirits high. Also, be open to receiving help and not just helping others. The message is that you're naturally generous with your time, energy, resources, talents and affections. Give and receive love in equal measure, because you're a master at letting others shine in the spotlight while you sit humbley in the sidelines. You're modest and full of grace, so be open to receiving with gratitude and a light heart. Stay gracious even throughout the challenging times.

Anything to be mindful of?

If the Dog is your spirit animal, you need to be mindful of the following shadow traits or follies:-

- Be mindful of falling into extreme selflessness or sacrifice; honor your own needs too (self-care is important)
- Speak up, protect yourself, and voice your needs. Don't be afraid to stand up for yourself! Also, stay good natured but be mindful of opportunistic people...
- The dog spirit suggests conflict might be near, or you may just need to be extra conscious of the relationships in your life. Nurture close friendships
- Try not to over-do pleasure; follow your highest joy, but remember to take care of the practical, domestic, & financial aspects of life

I am the Dog, intensely loyal with unconditional love.
I am devoted to my friends and love to help and serve,
and respond lovingly and affectionately to kindness and positive words.
I truly am man's best friend;
treat me like I am family…
and I will love you to the end.

If you dream of a *white dog*, this is a symbol of purity. You are being shown that friendship and loyalty are extremely important to you right, and soon you might have to make a choice. As the dog represents unconditional love and white symbolizes purity, innocence, and faith, this choice might be a major timeline moment!

It's rare to see a white dog, and it could be that a lover, soulmate, or kindred spirit is watching over you and sending you guidance and protection. Do not turn against this soulmate. Life can be a distraction; there are multiple moments when we are presented with an opportunity to shape our destinies. The question always comes down to: *fear Vs love.*

Choosing fear and thus separation will align you with a darker timeline, one likely rooted in greed, ego, and negative karmic consequences. Choosing love, however, can open many magical portals and doorways to infinite possibilities…

Frog

The frog symbolizes purification, purification of the mind, body & spirit, and your emotions and soul. Clear out the clutter. Engage in a detox or cleanse; eat healthy and make significant lifestyle choices. These are the messages and symbolism of the frog. Internal shifts and changes in your health, well-being and daily habits will lead to long term results. Simplify your life, declutter excess and heavy emotions, belief systems, ideologies, patterns of thought and emotions, and physical clutter. Get rid of the outdated and outgrown beliefs that keep you in mental confusion or self-limiting cycles. Release material excess and examine your emotions to see if there is a person, relationship, or memory you need to let go of to move forward. Repetitive cycles that have been 'on repeat' for too long become clear with the frog spirit. Cleansing and clearing are in divine order. This can include your energy field, your aura or auric field. As human beings, we store all of our memories, emotions, thoughts, and patterns of behavior and experience in our auric fields. Our auras then interact with others, and this is how those who are intuitive or psychically-inclined- or have a pure and clean channel- can pick up on subtle energies. Purification of your mind, body, & spirit allows you to be a pure and clear channel. This then lets you act as a catalyst for your own and others' healing. The relationships and physical environments in your life may need decluttering too. A reboot or restart might be on the cards. The frog spirit animal teaches us the importance and power of transition.

Embrace changes, transitions, and transformation. This power animal is connected to the water element, the realm of emotions, instincts, imagination, subconscious forces, feelings, and internal impressions. Everything to do with the inner world- the inner you, is brought to light. Transformation comes from cleansing your emotional driving forces and psychological processes. The frog spirit asks you to "get deep" and "get real." You should take time for introspection and contemplation. Meditation, soul-searching, and finding answers within is a powerful process of self-discovery and accessing personal freedom. With these things you can learn your boundaries, such as when you've lacked the ability to say 'no' to others. Or when you have given too much of yourself, time, resources, and love or energy away. Be prepared to be authentic and honest with yourself! It's when you're honest with yourself that you can become authentic in the world, shining your light and showing your true self with complete freedom and confidence. The frog spirit asks for transparency. Linked to emotions and feelings, inner sensations help you to make sense of external events. If this is your power animal, you are likely very psychic, perceptive, intelligent, observant, and intuitive. Call on the frog spirit when you need psychological, emotional, or spiritual healing or physical cleansing. The frog can help you in times of change, connect you to inner guidance linked to physical instincts, and assist you in accessing emotional intelligence. Feminine energies are strong with the frog, especially emotional intelligence, wisdom, and empathy.

Other key themes include renewal, rebirth of the Self, holistic healing, and enhanced self-awareness. You can discover knowledge of life's deeper meanings and mysteries. You are able to remove toxic energies and patterns of behavior, and begin a personal process of transformation. Consider seeing a shaman or going on a conscious fast (detox) for emotional release. Exploring past wounds and pain are symbolic of the frog medicine, such as going deep into self-reflection to access memories related to your emotional center. The purpose is to clear and release all that no longer serves, making space for healthier relationships, friendships, and connections. Examine how you spend your time and energy and where you direct your focus in waking life. Also, renewing perspectives and refreshing your vision, like idealistic gifts and your ability to see into the future, aligned to your greater purpose and soul mission with foresight. The frog is a great spirit animal for soul vision, soul plan, and deeper purpose activities. The death-rebirth cycles of soul evolution and personal transformation can be discovered through the frog spirit animal. A further meaning is the link the frog has to ancient cultures. The frog symbolizes rebirth in Ancient Rome and Egypt, and in the latter the frog also represented fertility and resurrection. There's a link to mystery and magic with the frog spirit. Specifically, embracing our multidimensional nature and being able to shapeshift, travel the dreamspace and astral realms, and exist in and on multiple dimensions. You can connect to the unknown, ether, Spirit, and waters of divinity within and around with the frog's assistance. *The message*: never underestimate the power of cleansing your personal space, home, mind, spirit, or body.

Anything to be mindful of?

If the Frog is your spirit animal, you need to be mindful of the following shadow traits or follies:-

- Being a perfectionist and needing to order everything and everyone in your life
- 'Organizing' your emotions…. Remember to feel and listen to your intuition too!
- Getting lost in addictions, junk-food, t.v. and other toxic cycles
- Letting the darkness and heaviness of the world weigh you down; you might be on a clear path of purity, but others might not be so committed to personal growth or soul-evolution as you. Heal yourself without needing to change everyone else around you.

I am the frog, I represent purification,
Cleansing, clearing the past, and detoxification.
I can help you access emotional intelligence as well as psychic gifts-
I live in both water and on land, I am agile and swift.
Only those who treat me with loving kindness will get to observe
how I transcend limitations and restrictions of the physical world.

I symbolize spiritual illumination, meditation, and healing,
and empathy, feminine wisdom, astral insights, and soul-searching.
So look to me when you need help transcending
everything that holds you back, for my energy is truly soul cleansing.

I am the Lizard, a symbol for dreams,
I have access to abilities that are often left unseen.
I can see into the future, having premonitions and visions,
It is in dreamtime where I receive my lessons, clarity, and all wisdom.

Did you know I can break off my own tail to escape a predator,
or that my power lies in my ability to rescue myself from danger?!
Listen to my message and learn how to 'let go'
and leave all that does not serve you in the past
for new chapters for your growth…

For the places often left unexplored
are the routes where questions lead to doors.
In dreams we find our deepest yearnings-
use my medicine for your journey's most enlightening searchings.

Lizard

The lizard is a message of connecting to the dream space and multidimensional realms of consciousness. Dreams are a direct portal to vision, subconscious insights, and wisdom on the ethereal and astral planes. Astral projection and astral travel are available with the lizard spirit animal. You can journey to the depths of your soul for self-discovery and profound insights into your own and the collective psyche. Through astral travel, you can explore different dream spaces and worlds, which not only enhances the type of vivid imagery and symbolism you can see, but amplifies your intuition and psychic abilities. Lucid dreaming is also available. Lizard medicine generally relates to everything to do with consciousness exploration and dreaming. If this is your spirit animal, you have a gift for tuning into the divine, opening your mind to higher consciousness, and your Higher Self, and tuning into the spiritual realms for knowledge, guidance, and inspiration. You also have a strong connection with your subconscious mind and psyche, which means you can live your life connected to both your conscious mind and subconscious mind, drawing information, memories, and wisdom deep from within to help with a variety of situations. The lizard spirit animal represents someone who is remarkably intuitive, wise, perceptive, intelligent, and clairvoyant. Regarding visions, you have a visionary quality about you. Transcendental meditation, self-reflection, and visualization come naturally to lizard spirit people. In dreams, visionary gifts are activated as well, meaning you may receive multidimensional glimpses and potent images related to your life path or soul mission.

The lizard spirit animal asks you to live with passion, purpose, and empowerment. Forget anything that doesn't serve your higher mind, spiritual path, and unique sense of service or destiny. Because of such a powerful visionary quality, combined with a cord to the ethereal and subtle realms, you may have a gift for seeing things others miss. You are a BS detector, seeing through people's narcissism, manipulation, and cunning or deceptive ways. You may actually appear strange or crazy to a lot of people- this is how intense multidimensional vision is. Such a strong connection to the subconscious mind and realm and the astral/spiritual planes allows you to see directly into your internal motivations, desires, emotional needs, physical wants, strengths, weakness, hidden talents, and virtually everything related to the emotional, spiritual, and psychological planes… You require sufficient periods of introspection and alone time. This helps you make sense of all the information and date being presented to you. If this is your power animal, you tend to seek out hidden truths and deeper symbolism in life, even in the most mundane of situations. There's always a hidden message. Your evolved sense of visions contributes to your relationships, finances, creativity, inspiration, health, and spirituality; to romance, business partnerships, family bonds, and inspirational artistic activities. You believe in holism- that we're living in a holographic, holistic, reality, and this opens portals to self-growth and self-mastery. Further, the lizard spirit symbolizes an incredible imagination! You possess artistic, imaginative, creative, and perhaps musical gifts that are on 'genius' level. Your mind is attuned to a higher power; Source, the divine, the ethereal realms of Spirit….

So you can birth blueprints of higher truth and wisdom in addition to universal archetypal concepts to uplift humanity's vibration in some way. You're a powerful creator. You should listen to your dreams and intuitive, instinctive, and psychic guidance that comes your way. Dreams hold golden keys to your legacy and destiny. If you have a great mission or purpose, your dreams will show you virtually anything you need to discover. Self-awareness, intellect, and problem-solving skills increase. Subtle signs and synchronicities are common with the lizard spirit animal, and the lizard's medicine represents being able to see through and beyond the veil of illusion to uncover deeper truths. Soul growth is on the cards as well. Precognitive powers, foresight, and premonitive abilities are equally developed. Your intuition is incredible, you're one of the most naturally psychic and intuitive people this world has seen. If you are a water sign (Cancer, Scorpio, or Pisces) or have strong water in your birth/natal chart, such as a water Moon, Venus, or Rising placement, you might be a real-life psychic. Also, a shaman, seer, prophetic storyteller, visionary poet, or mystic or spiritual healer. This spirit animal is symbolic of people who choose a metaphysical and spiritual path, such as becoming an Astrologer, Numerologist, Tarot reader, Healer, or Shamanic energy worker.

Finally, exploring the past is very important to you. It's key to your path to greatness, finding peace within, and aligning with your Higher Self. Old relationships, painful memories, wounds, and trauma from childhood or your family upbringing- or collective trauma, are very comfortable for you. In other words, you're open to "going deep" and getting real with yourself, sitting with the pain and using it as fuel to transcend, heal, and evolve. Although gentle, sweet, and sensitive, you are just as fearless and courageous when it comes to the real challenges and hardships in life. The lizard spirit represents an individual who is on a soul mission, always working towards change and peace, unity consciousness, and a bigger vision. The lizard also symbolizes change and adaptability.

Anything to be mindful of?

If the Lizard is your spirit animal, you need to be mindful of the following shadow traits or follies:-

- Getting so lost in the larger vision that you forget the smaller details
- Neglecting friends, lovers, and family in pursuit of your soul path or purpose
- Not recognizing when people don't want to change or grow; always trying to push, inspire, or coerce others into growing and evolving with you, even though it might not be their path.
- Being stuck in the past and succumbing to bouts of loneliness, depression or melancholy, and isolation

Chapter 8: Creative & Inspirational Spirit Animals

We are the creative and inspirational spirit animals with potent life force,
We lead to your highest potential- we open new doors.
It may sound cliche, but we really do symbolize your best and highest self,
So turn to us for guidance, manifestation, and self-empowerment that leads to wealth.

From communication to creativity, and expression to boldness,
Ancient wisdom to fresh cycles, and seasonal knowledge;
We are the animals that make your soul sing-
the choices you make in the present define the reality you choose to exist in.

Buffalo

The buffalo is here to remind you of your place in the universe and of the abundance that arises through authenticity. The message is to live life with integrity, honesty, and authenticity- strong morals and values. This is where true prosperity comes from and when you do so, it activates your birthright. The buffalo is a big legacy and inheritance spirit animal. All matters relating to financial abundance, security, material wealth, and aligning with a prosperous future come under this animal's domain. The buffalo spirit symbolizes incredible self-authority, personal autonomy, self-reliance, and self-sufficiency. You are likely independent and self-autonomous, meaning you provide for yourself and those you love. You're highly self-protective and protective of friends, your partner, and lover. You believe in living the good life, a life of luxury; material wealth is equated with a stress-free life, so you don't mind earning big or increasing your financial flow. In fact, these things are also linked to self-esteem and self-confidence. The buffalo spirit suggests an individual who is very confident, self-loving, and self-respecting. You hold yourself in high esteem and expect the same from others, and business comes naturally to you. You possess advanced problem-solving, organizational, managerial, and perceptive skills; you're very bright and intuitive, but also logical and analytical. Intellectual and educational pathways are a strong feature throughout your life. You're further an amazing manifestor. If the buffalo is your power animal, you can manifest virtually anything you desire, as long as you're staying true to yourself and living with authenticity.

Boldness, bravery, and devotion define the buffalo spirit. You are fearless in standing up for your beliefs, fighting for a cause, and working towards a better world. Whatever profession, service, or project you commit yourself to, you believe in service and giving it your all. Many people with this spirit animal engage in regular or frequent charity service, humanitarian or environmental pursuits, and projects and pathways that are aligned to "Selfless service." I.e. you may be extremely headstrong and self-protecting, respecting your value, time, and resources, but you don't mind dedicating a significant part of your life to helping others. Abundance, manifestation abilities, and gathering resources are your main priorities in life, however. Once you have enough personal wealth and security, this is when you are more than happy to share it with others. Generosity, kindness, and sincerity are some of your greatest strengths. You can manifest your dreams, desires, wants, and needs with a positive mindset. Focus, concentration, and setting good intentions come naturally to you as well. Your lesson is to trust that the universe has your back; trust in the power of Spirit. Also, adopting a mindset of abundance is essential for your well-being and success. You may need to be mindful of poverty consciousness, especially in youth, and perhaps victimhood and any sort of self-limiting tendencies and beliefs. But you are generally an optimistic and upbeat person when it comes to pursuing your dreams and following through with long-term goals.

The buffalo spirit animal represents a willful and powerful individual with hidden reserves of personal power, autonomy, and authority. Always listen to your Higher Self and inner guidance.

Intuitive guidance comes naturally to you, although you might sometimes mistake it for intellect or logic. Regardless, always pay attention to the subtle signs and clues from the universe. There's a mystical and spiritual reality you can tune into for guidance and direction, and I'd advise you to do so. Just always bring it back to center, to your own truth and center within. This will help you avoid distractions and the manipulations of others, while keeping you aligned to your true path, soul gifts and talents, and divine birthright of abundance. The buffalo spirit animal suggests someone who has a personal legacy to leave behind, a destiny, and a soul mission. Never underestimate long-term planning and commitment! From the small details and minor chores to the bigger visions and larger steps, the buffalo is a high-flier and high-achiever. Essentially, you have big goals, aspirations, and plans, and people with this power animal tend to be masters of achievement and career success. You may receive many promotions and level-ups throughout life. The more you master your craft and trade, the more higher-income clients you will receive. People respond to you the best when you're playing to your strengths, and staying true to yourself. You may come across as overly ambitious and level-headed at times, maybe even over-authoritative, yet this allows you to continue on your golden path and create the change you wish to. Focus on security, stability, and the physical foundations in your life… Remain humble. Modesty and integrity are incredibly important with the buffalo spirit.

Finally inner beauty and a life of tranquility and harmony are very significant to you. You dislike chaos, pettiness, and the unnecessary dramas of the world. You choose to live in peace and are deeply romantic, sweet, attentive, considerate, caring, compassionate, and nurturing. You may be suited to starting a family of your own with both traditional and inspirational values. You're a fierce believer in love; you're loyal, devoted, harmony-seeking, genuine, and both independent and companionable. *The message*: the universe is benevolent and abundant… prosperity, love, and security are your divine birthright.

Anything to be mindful of?

If the Buffalo is your spirit animal, you need to be mindful of the following shadow traits or follies:-

- Sacrificing sensitivity and other intimate and feminine qualities for ambitions, the pursuit of wealth, abundance, etc.
- Being so set on creating a fabulous future that you forget to live in the here-and-now
- Relying on faith over logic… the power of hard work and practical actions should not go overlooked!
- Sacrificing your gentler side for other people's impressions and stereotypes of you. This may sound contradictory to the first point, but people with the buffalo spirit need to master the art of balance. Some people see you as gentle, loving, affectionate, and kind,

whereas others see you as threatening and intimidating. You need to develop discernment and adapt to different people, places, and situations.

Peacock

The peacock spirit animal is a symbol of light, color, and your ability to shine! This is one of the most self-expressive and colorful spirit animals of the animal queen-kingdom. You're being asked to shine and step into self-leadership when the peacock crosses your path. Bold, charismatic, highly confident, and courageous, the peacock represents our need for love, romance, and attention. Get in-tune with your more glamorous and spotlight-loving self. Be fiery, electric, and command the attention of those you meet. The peacock symbolizes someone with a lot of gifts, talents, and hidden strengths, so this is not about commanding attention to out-shine everyone or have admirers. Gathering admirers is symbolic of having a gift or calling that can actually help others. People with this power animal tend to be inspiring, motivated, high-achieving, and divinely-guided individuals with artistic and imaginative gifts. You may be a performer, entertainer, musician, speaker, teacher, spoken word artist, actor, or creative of any kind. You could work in big media or the film or music industry. You might just be a creative person who works from home, inspiring or educating others through your passions and gifts. As long as you're following your heart and soul, the peacock spirit tells you, you're on the right path.

The message is to be beautiful, radiate confidence and self-esteem, and show off a little. Shine, allow yourself to glow, and be inspirational if you have wisdom and knowledge to share. The peacock asks you to step into magnificence. Ok, you may come across as egotistical at times, but this is part of the peacock spirit's medicine; don't worry about judgment and false perceptions. The message is to not play small or devolve to fit other people's narrow-minded world-view, judgements, or comfort zones. Many people choose to stay within comfort zones in life, however this is not what is in store for you. Radiate inner beauty. Inner beauty is very important, so be mindful of how your personality and internal thoughts, emotions, impressions, judgements, observations, and beliefs affect your outer world. Try to stay as pure and organically glowing as possible. This is a sign to take care of your health. Honor your physical body and your emotional, psychological/mental, and spiritual well-being simultaneously. Liberated and free to shine, the peacock teaches you to not give too much attention to what others think. You need to stay modest and graceful, embody social charm and grace, and be open to learning from elders, wise teachers, and people who can shine a valuable light on your life. Yet, don't take advice from people who don't have the credentials, honor, integrity, or life experience to back up their judgements. This is a key self-realization to be aware of: some people just give their opinions while others actually have real-world expertise, knowledge and insights that can help you grow. On this note, the peacock spirit is all about using discernment, logic, higher reasoning, instincts, and intuition to determine who is right for you, who you should listen to for guidance, and what path you should take.

The peacock medicine includes liberation, personal freedom, high energy, vitality, and self-empowerment. You need to be mindful of your intentions for success whilst maintaining high self-esteem. Know your worth! Access imaginative and artistic gifts as much as possible, and further perfect them. Skill and talent mastery, self-development, and acquisition are very important. Liberate yourself from negative, cynical, and pessimistic people who want to dull your sparkle; seek out inspirational and creative or successful people instead. Be courageous, fearless even, in going after your goals and dreams and don't settle for less than what you deserve. Keep your ego in check and stay modest, of course, but don't let the weight of other people's negativity prevent you from stepping into your legacy. You likely have a destiny to create, no matter how big or small. People with this spirit animal may encounter envious and jealous people on their path, so it's essential that you develop gifts of discernment and intuition and further put up some healthy boundaries. When you align with your true self, without fear, the universe sends you friends, soulmates, work colleagues, partners, and kindred spirits who match your frequency. "Showing off" to one may be warmly received as "divine inspiration" to another… Show your true colors because, either way, you're going to get judged. Live with passion, heart, and soul, and always stay connected to a higher truth. Come out of the shadows as they no longer suit you. The Creator didn't make you for you to play small or people-please your way through life. The peacock spirit animal is respectable, diplomatic, and sincere- kind-hearted and honest too. But they don't suffer fools gladly. Finally, this animal symbolizes self-expression related to song, dance, music, art, poetry, sensuality, and imaginative and divinely-inspired co-creation. You're a channel for the divine, creative energies, and Source, therefore celebrate the luck and good fortune you have been blessed with. Joy, pleasure, luck, and celebration are the additional meanings. There is a soul song and internal spark about you only you know, and the world wants to see it.

Anything to be mindful of?

If the Peacock is your spirit animal, you need to be mindful of the following shadow traits or follies:-

- Succumbing to people-pleasing and self-sacrifice, which makes you dull your shine and step away from your soul talents and service
- Letting the false judgements, envy, greed, and negativity or cynicism of others prevent your path (shine regardless!)
- Being bold and spotlight-seeking for the sake of it… Control your ego and know when it's the right time to speak, act, and shine
- Being judgemental yourself, including believing you're the only one who can do what you do. There are other experts and professionals in your field, so be open to teamwork and cooperation… because this is where the magic (+ co-creation) happens.

I am the Peacock, a symbol of self-expression,
I represent creativity, the imagination, and sound communication.
I am deeply intelligent, intuitive, and instinctive,
and I use my talents and skills to inspire and uplift.

I like the spotlight, this is no secret; I thrive in being center of attention,
So look to me if you want to increase your confidence, self-authority, and vision.
Because color defines me, I radiate beauty and self-esteem…
I may not be for you if you want to play shy and exist in the unseen.

Giraffe

The giraffe is a symbol of being able to see the big picture. This spirit animal represents having vision, a sense of idealism, and foresight. Visionary and psychic gifts are available with the giraffe spirit. You're able to see the big picture and connect to your idealistic higher eyes. The giraffe symbolizes longevity. People with this spirit animal are high-flying, high-achieving, and have big goals and aspirations. Your dreams are important, to listen to them and honor them. Giraffes are deeply sensitive, caring, and intuitive. They're equally as wise, perceptive, and intelligent. Big picture thinking allows for success, abundance, love, prosperity, and a healthy and happy life. Prosperity, material wealth, financial success, and perfect health can all be achieved with the giraffe. The message: it's time to broaden your horizons, expand your mind, and gather new knowledge and wisdom. The giraffe spirit animal is a big push towards self-study, learning, educational, cultural pursuits, and expanding professional and career-related pathways. There's a sense of longing for a higher truth… Your inner light is turned on through truth, higher wisdom, and knowledge of the self; *know thyself* applies to the giraffe spirit. Universal truths and quantum laws fascinate you, and when you choose an educational or career path you can work diligently towards your goals. The giraffe spirit represents long-term success.

Achievement, hard-work, professional victories, promotions, abundance through your talents and gifts, big aspirations, and future planning are all further associations of this sweet yet ambitious animal. The giraffe teaches that hard-work, determination, and vision combined with a practical approach go a long way. Manifestation and precognitive abilities link here too. Develop courage and boldness, go after your dreams with passion, zest, and life force. You may be destined to become an elder, mentor, teacher, guide, or someone who is respected for their wise counsel and expertise. People with the giraffe power animal make excellent teachers, wayshowers, and mentors for others to learn from their wealth of wisdom and experience. Attaining qualifications and diplomas may be important to you, but so is developing family and intimate relationships. You can call on the giraffe to help you maintain a healthy and harmonious work-play-rest balance. Balance and inner harmony are the name of the game. As for precognitive gifts and foresight, you pick up on subtle energies from the environment and then use a combination of logic, discernment, and intuition to conclude the best next course of action. Foresight is the ability to see into the future through planning, anticipation, and powerful intuition. New and fresh perspectives and further advanced analytical, logical, and observational skills are available. Look towards your future with positivity and optimism, but don't forget where you've been and all you've learned.

This is a big 'past and future' spirit animal; the lessons of the past can be mastered and integrated, as you look towards your bright future. Never look back. Never give up. Keep working with optimism and passion towards your bright future, even when times get tricky or challenging. The giraffe spirit also represents sadness and grief. Why? Because to achieve something significant and become successful, we often have to let go of people and past situations and relationships that kept us playing small. Take the wisdom and positive memories and leave the sadness and sense of loss behind. Loss can be fuel to your inner fire. It can serve as inspiration to your Higher Self and self-alignment, however it should never keep you stuck, repressed, living in fear, or stagnant. Failures, detours, and setbacks are integral to the path of someone with the giraffe power animal. The message is to embrace change, failure, and hardship so you can reach greater self-awareness and self-mastery within, which then manifests outwards. Inspirational qualities, confidence, self-empowerment, victory, and alignment with your soul plan arise from loss, but for each sacrifice you make you create legacy. Legacy is strong. Never steer away from the big picture, and make sure you pay attention to messages, signs, and symbolism or imagery in dreams. You live primarily through your conscious mind-consciousness, but this doesn't mean you should neglect your subconscious mind and the invisible, subtle, world of spiritual life force energy.

Anything to be mindful of?

If the Giraffe is your spirit animal, you need to be mindful of the following shadow traits or follies:-

- Don't get lost in grief, sadness, and pain, or stuck in self-inflicted suffering
- Try not to let others take advantage of you and abuse your generosity; you're kind and a natural giver, thus you might naturally attract some takers in life
- Put up healthy boundaries and don't let anyone tell you who you can or can't be. Negative people, cynics, and the judgements of others might temporarily steer you off your path, so don't be susceptible to the limiting judgements or false perceptions
- Always stay authentic, as inauthenticity will lead to wrong turns and endless detours…

Rabbit

The rabbit is a symbol for fertility, creativity, and sensitivity. Psychic and sensitive abilities are available through the rabbit spirit, as are advanced empathy, self-awareness, and artistic gifts. Everything linked to fertility is inherent within this spirit animal's medicine. The rabbit teaches you how to connect the astral and subconscious realms where artistic, imaginative, creative, psychic, empathic, and intuitive gifts are rich. Passivity is favored over dominance, receptivity over forceful action, and gentleness over aggression. The rabbit connects you to the realm of emotions, including emotional wisdom and intelligence, yet this animal is not short on logic either. Logic, key analytical and perceptive skills, observation, higher mental reasoning, and analysis, the rabbit is an excellent problem-solver. If this is your spirit animal, you know how to tackle problems with the perfect combination of emotional involvement and detachment. You're both emotionally intelligent and logical- connected to your feelings and intelligent. In fact, this rabbit spirit is highly intelligent. Discerning too. Your sensitive nature is what will bring you the most abundance, financial flow, and prosperity. Good luck is a further symbol of the rabbit. Innovative, creative, skilled perceptively, multidimensional, and an excellent original and independent thinker, people with the rabbit spirit animal tend to thrive in both business and creative fields. You make an excellent organizer, planner, and manager, and can dream up inventive new ideas and concepts in a heartbeat. Your creative visions are down-to-earth and modest however, just as the rabbit chooses to make a home in the earth. You too enjoy creating physical foundations and structure that lead to increased artistic and financial endeavors. You have a bright future with the rabbit by your side.

Rabbits come alive in Spring, so make use of the energies of this season. This animal teaches you the power and significance of cycles- seasons, life cycles and chapters, and evolutionary cycles of the mind, body, and soul. You're very good at manifestation. You possess evolved manifestation powers and connect to subtle and mystical energies daily, so you are in tune with universal laws and cycles, like the law of attraction. You have a gift for manifesting resources to you, and can usually attract your heart's desires without stress and with minimal effort. You should make the most of the Spring's vibrations by starting new projects and giving birth to new conditions during the Spring months. Emotional, psychological, physical, and spiritual conditions, new mindsets, and fresh starts can be born. Your life is symbolic of planting seeds, both literally and metaphorically, so the new can grow. Tune into your own cycles & rhythms within for wisdom, enhanced instincts, intuition, and higher reasoning. Honesty, nobility, self-accountability, and integrity are all associations. The rabbit teaches you how to be perceptive, wise, and intelligent, yet also philosophical, intuitive, and open-minded. Adaptability and surrendering to change are key traits to possess. Vulnerability is another gift that can be embodied. Through such sensitivity and compassion (self-compassion and compassion for others) you're able to see things others miss, magnetize things to you, and go with the flow. Both vulnerability and adaptability serve you well in times of need or distress. Always be open to communicating your needs, feelings, beliefs, emotions, and desires, because self-expression is core to the rabbit's spiritual symbolism. Authenticity, communication, and open and mindful relating and expression are gifts to strengthen and contemplate regularly.

Also, connect to the energies of Mother Earth and Gaia, as magic is all around you! Magic occurs from within and then ripples out, and vice versa. The rabbit spirit is here to show you how to develop a close relationship with spiritual and universal energies for self-healing and working directly with the earth. Your personality is benevolent, creative, artistic, wise, mature, emotionally balanced, serene, down-to-earth, and magnetic. You are a master of manifesting your heart's desires in addition to basic security and survival needs, and need intimate and authentic connections to nourish you. You like to nurture and provide for others, but you equally need to be cherished, loved, and supported. Companionship is a key quality you look for in any partnership- romantic, business, or a friendship bond. Gentleness, grace, acceptance, surrender, flexibility, self-evolution, transformation, and self-protection are other key associations.

Anything to be mindful of?

If the Rabbit is your spirit animal, you need to be mindful of the following shadow traits or follies:-

- Social anxiety, timidness, being shy and reserved, and becoming fearful of the smallest things
- Running away from problems and disagreements or confrontation instead of facing them head on… Also, laziness and idleness are core follies
- Being overly flexible and adaptable; learn to ground and center yourself and your energy
- An overactive sex drive! Overpowering libido can lead to impulsiveness, which can result in a disconnection from your responsibilities, duties, and practicalities

I am the Rabbit, a symbol for fertility,
you can tune into my energy to enhance your creativity!
You'll often see me upbeat, full of zest, and bouncing around,
as I love the sun and air, yet under earth is where I'm found.
I feel warm and safe near natures heartbeat;
It is Mother Earth who comforts and reminds me of my unique sensitivity.
Finding joy in my senses and pleasure in my surroundings,
use my medicine for creative projects, fresh starts, and new beginnings.

Parrot

The parrot is the ultimate symbol for light, color, self-expression, and communication. All aspects of written, verbal, and spoken communication come under the parrot's realm. You are a creative, artistically gifted, and colorful individual who excels with conversing with others. You've mastered your communication skills, or should be taking steps to, and have a healthy and integrated sense of self-talk. These are the stories you tell yourself, which are almost always rooted in optimism and creative self-expression. You're intellectual, logical, and highly bright! Your mind is alive with ideas and concepts, and you know how to direct these in an assertive and conscious way. You love community connections. Community groups, organizations, clubs, professional environments, and vocational projects are your favorite pastimes. Also, you are an excellent storyteller who excels in poetry, writing, communications, the spoken word, and anything similar. You may be working towards becoming a spoken word artist, musician, poet, performer, entertainer, actor, or speaker. The way parrots mimic sound provides insight into your own potential and ability to communicate on the highest levels of expression. You are sensitive, self-aware, psychically-inclined, emotionally intelligent, deeply wise and perceptive, and both imaginative and intellectual. You thrive in many mental and psychological planes, yet are also spiritually evolved and enlightened. If the parrot is your spirit animal, you understand how song, sound, and the universal laws of vibration and frequency work. Mindful and empathic communication is essential to develop for your best life.

Take note of how you use your voice, tone, and words chosen. Speak to heal, educate, uplift, and inspire, not to destroy or create separation. There is great power in your voice. As for color and creativity, you are incredibly fun-loving, upbeat, and optimistic. You go through life with passion and vitality, and are genuinely enthusiastic about developing new friendships, connections, and business partnerships. Companionship and social bonds alike are extremely important to your self-esteem and social image or identity. Always seek harmony, love, unity, compromise, balance, fairness, equality, and cooperation. Conflict is not your strong point. The parrot spirit further teaches how to be mindful and honest in your deals, and never succumbing to manipulation or deception! Act with integrity. Emotionally, you are balanced and open with a harmonious and positive disposition. You radiate warmth, calmness, serenity, unity, and grace; you're very comfortable in your skin and don't feel anxious around others. Your social life, professional connections, and romantic and platonic bonds make your world… You don't do well in isolation or solitude, so watch out for any periods where you've been alone for too long. Only use these life chapters for introspections and developing your gifts and talents. People with the parrot spirit always end up gravitating back to pathways of community.

The parrot simultaneously symbolizes the soul's many colors. The universe reflects back the stories we tell to ourselves, therefore the frequencies you emit outwards will come back to you. You may have mastered the law of attraction- your manifestation skills are certainly on point. The parrot's medicine included finding beauty within and then reflecting- or positively mirroring- that inner beauty outward, into your social connections and environments. Further symbolism: you're a natural diplomat, counselor, and speaker, and an excellent listener. You embody a high frequency of emotional intelligence, empathy, and compassion. You're nurturing, caring, benevolent, understanding, and full of social grace and charisma. Habits can be negative or beneficial, so be mindful of the repetitive motions you go through in your life. Observe your own daily routines, habits, thought processes, behaviors, and mindsets. Are they serving your soul and Higher Self, or your ego? Finally, the parrot represents natural cycles and stages of self-evolution in life. Inspirational qualities and pathways are many.

Anything to be mindful of?

If the Parrot is your spirit animal, you need to be mindful of the following shadow traits or follies:-

- Manipulation, deception, false pride, and ego
- Judgment, being overly scrutinous, intellectual or spiritual superiority, and being self-critical or too critical of others. Also, indecision.
- Gossip, slander, low vibrational communication, and unmindful outbursts; always think before you speak (live with dignity, grace, integrity, modesty, and intention)
- Don't suppress your big and colorful spirit in the name of humility… Learn the balance between being modest and repressed or people-pleasing

THE ZODIAC SIGNS
AND
SPIRIT ANIMALS

Chapter 9: Aries

I am Aries, the Zodiac's child,
I represent desire and want, liberated and let wild.
I am the inner flame that knows what it needs,
satisfying my desires replace inner peace.
A quick witted mind and passionate nature
make me a natural born leader and expressive communicator.
I am the initiator, the warrior… the leader;
I go after what I want with a fire that's courageous.
Impulsiveness, action, and a pioneering spirit define me,
I know how to command attention and don't follow, but lead.
I am fiercely willful, confident, and ambitious;
Passionate, expressive, independent, and tenacious.
I need to learn how to be less demanding, controlling, and overpowering,
as my ruler is Mars, the planet of war, aggression, and competition.
Yet, I have powerful instincts, high energy levels, and physical vitality.
my light is a source of inspiration for others when I lead with some
compassion and empathy.
I am assertive, strong, and bold to initiate plans,
for I am the first, Aries- the Ram.

What's my shadow, do I have any lessons?
I desire to come first and win at all costs- my extreme competition is birthed from
overpowering instincts.
I can be brutish and domineering, becoming the bully and tyrant,
I need to learn how to be more caring & sensitive, also playing well with others.

Key Animals: *Your Personal Animal Guides & Spirits*

Horse

With such strong physical instincts and vitality, the horse is undoubtedly one of your personal animal guides, Aries. You are bold, passionate, fiery, and courageous, and you live your life full of enthusiasm, zest, and life force. The horse is a symbol for freedom and movement- powerful instincts and physical stamina too. So you can call on the horse spirit when you need a boost or reminder. Your power comes from your physical instincts, well, so do the horse's. You need to feel free and liberated to express yourself, travel, and follow your passions, which are largely rooted around adventure and exerting your immense energy levels. The horse can help you to move gracefully and with nobility so that you don't run over anyone (a metaphor for your overpowering spirit). There's nothing wrong with wanting to be number 1, or running full speed ahead. Just make sure you do so with integrity, a sense of gentleness, and some empathy and higher awareness, just as the horse does. In fact, the horse is the perfect spirit animal for love, business, self-care, health and spirituality matters, and both money and romance. For love and sexual synergy, i.e. 'are you compatible?'- look up what other signs have the horse spirit, because this is a powerful indicator that you have very similar love styles! The horse is here to teach you- and perfect the balance of- that there's nothing wrong with being energetic, youthful, and enthusiastic; just remain graceful, diplomatic, and sensitive to the needs of others simultaneously. Also, this majestic spirit animal can help you tame your inner wild beast, learning that sexual energy and connection is one thing, however there are many other dimensions and planes to connect with others on. You have a strong libido, yet it doesn't always need expression. Self-control and self-mastery are available with the horse spirit.

Crocodile

With such fiery and electric energy it can be hard for you to slow down and explore your emotions. The inner realm of feelings, empathy, and sensitivities are not your strong points, Aries. Yet you're equally incredibly passionate with a highly evolved sex drive. It's important that you work with the crocodile spirit, from time to time, therefore. The crocodile will assist you in making sense of your powerful emotional currents, which you do possess. This can be a tricky area for you, as you're always on the go. You like to tackle life head on and with full force, but to access the inner realm of feelings and self-reflection you need to really go deep. As a primal animal who represents potent instincts and strong reproductive desires, this animal is the perfect one for you to explore your innermost yearnings without feeling judged. Not feeling judged or restricted is important to you, even when delving into the more trickier parts of your innermost self. You must make time for conscious contemplation, introspection, and going within. The crocodile allows you to explore yourself and innermost workings and desires, without feeling like you have to change your fundamental nature. Some of your greatest blocks to self-growth are feeling like someone is trying to change you, like you can't be your independent self, and as if you have to appease or people-please others, watering down your big spirit. The crocodile helps you to understand it's ok to be self-autonomous *and* be open to change and wise counsel or expertise from others, simultaneously. Not everything has to be in ultimatum; some people see crocodiles as bloody-thirsty monsters, for example, while others see them as cute and adorable. There is a great message in this.

Bat

The bat is one of your personal animals because the bat symbolizes rebirth, and you are one of the most sexually active and expressive signs of the zodiac. As the warrior ruled by Mars, the planet of masculine sexuality, will, action, vitality, and energy, and, at a lower vibration, lust, aggression, and competition; it's essential you learn how to channel your sexual life force energy properly. Without the energy of the bat, you could begin exploding, lashing out on others emotionally, psychologically, and even physically. The bat spirit helps you to ground and center yourself. You're able to channel your powerful libido and life force into conscious and mindful communication & expression. Instead of reacting, you start to respond… with enhanced self-control. Self-awareness increases and you can embody more emotional intelligence, sensitivity, and empathy. The bat is psychic and intelligent, so this power animal is great for transcending intellectual comfort zones. This animal teaches you that it's ok to be seen as normal in the eyes of society, while simultaneously tuning into spiritual and subtle gifts. Call on the bat if you want to merge some spiritual & psychic instincts, higher seeing, and outside-the-box imagination with your intellectual gifts and methods. You thrive in the realm of the higher mind and intellect, however you lack in other areas. The bat can help you change this- it's one of your best spirit animals for spiritual self-development.

Coyote

As a symbol for divine detours and recognizing there are setbacks on the path to success, the coyote is an ideal spirit animal helper for you. Aries make excellent leaders, managers, business CEOs, and self-employed people. You like to set your own rules to live by, and this means you're destined for success and big achievements. Your'e determined, hard working, intelligent, organized, and incredibly ambitious; yet, you also have an issue with listening to authority and taking directions from others. Your lesson in life based on your shadow personality traits is to learn how to be part of a team, listen to the advice from others, and show humility when you fail. The coyote is therefore the perfect spirit animal for you, as the coyote always stays committed, even through the hard and low times. Victory isn't always yours, yet you should be modest, graceful, and practice humility when someone else wins, or when you are forced to take a loss. A spirit animal of failure and success, lows and highs, and staying completely committed and determined throughout all of it, this power animal is perfect for developing acceptance while refusing to give up. The coyote can further help you to see multiple perspectives when you have your eyes set on one assumed or projected goal. Letting go is sometimes the best way to attract what is meant for you… Also, the message of the coyote is to 'lighten up,' therefore this is a great animal to connect to for when you've been in ambition-mode, neglecting your sense of fun and play. You love to laugh, Aries, therefore turn towards the coyote when you need to be more youthful, fun, and free-spirited. Read up on this animal's shadow traits (follies) too to see what you need to transcend. *Hint*: manipulative and mischievous energy!

Fox

The fox is all about rationality and intellect, additionally this animal does *not* symbolize emotional empathy or sensitivity. So this is the perfect animal to work with for all business, educational, and financial matters. You share a close resonance with the fox because you have a secret cunning side. I am not advocating going through life stomping over others or taking and using as if humans were objects. But, it is important to be honest with our true selves. You are ruled by the God (planet) of war himself, Mars. This means you possess more of a fiery and powerful spirit than many others. It also signifies that you excel in business, giving orders, taking charge, and creating your own security, stability, and abundance. This requires level-headedness and emotional detachment- making decisions with your head and not your heart, in other words. Your own survival is just as important as anyone else's. Thus, the fox lets you tune into your more calculated and cunning side without feeling guilty. Shame, self-abuse, guilt, and self-blame serve no-one! Call on the fox when you are in a totally psychologically attuned mindset, when you need practical and logical advice and higher guidance. Discernment, rationality, analysis, and headstrong nature define the fox's medicine; just try not to mix business with pleasure or confuse the fox's healing powers with the type of energy you should embody with friends and family. The fox spirit serves non-sentimental, level-headed, and business pursuits only. Further, the fox helps you to discern the difference, knowing intuitively and through common sense and observation which relationships and situations call for more emotional sensitivity and involvement, and which require detachment and objectivity.

Eagle

The eagle connects you to your Higher Self. Geographically, Aries rules the head, so the eagle is the perfect spirit animal to align you with your Crown chakra. Your crown is where your everyday 'I' consciousness merges with the cosmic or collective consciousness energy field. The eagle assists you in transcending ego and connecting to visionary, imaginative, innovative, artistic, and intuitive gifts and powers. There is not much else that needs to be said here. You can look up the *Eagle spirit* meaning and symbolism to discover more, as everything written applies to you, your strengths, and what you should be working towards. The eagle is your Higher Self animal, without a shadow of a doubt.

Cat

The cat is your go to for all areas of sensuality, playful expression, and romance. The cat serves your desires for companionship, affection, sensual self-expression, and unleashing your wild and primal side. The cat is a symbol for sexuality, coupled with connecting to your inner priest or priestess, the ancient part of you that knows it's connected to a divine and spiritual world. Cats were respected and revered by ancient Egyptians, you see, and in the modern day world cats are equally seen as a symbol for power, freedom, independence, sensuality, and sexual sovereignty. You can call on the cat spirit to help remove blocks, tensions, and frustrations in romantic and platonic companionship bonds. You can get more playful, loving, affectionate, nurturing, and caring with the cat's help. Also, more instinctive and psychically-inclined! You sometimes need help in this area, and the cat is the perfect animal to assist you, but, more importantly, help you feel *comfortable* in these subtle and spiritual realms. You need to feel comfortable in your own sensual, divine, and spiritual nature to open up to others fully. Furthermore, this spirit animal enables you to embody greater empathy, sensitivity, emotional intelligence, and motherly/fatherly instincts. Overall, this is a wonderful companion spirit for everything related to home, family, friendships, romance, love, intimacy, and personal self-growth & development. The cat teaches you the true meaning of independence vs healthy attachment, self-autonomy vs codependency, and self-authority vs softening to accommodate those you love. You are further fearless and courageous like a cat, thus you can work with the cat spirit animal to strengthen these innate gifts.

Frog

The frog is an unseen helper and spirit guide in your life who teaches you the importance of purity. Transcending karma is deeply integral to your path, as Aries has strong karmic influences. This gives the frog spirit a unique meaning and influence in your life. As the very first zodiac sign who strives to be number 1, come out on top, win, outshine others, etc. accumulating negative and positive karma is common to people with Aries Sun or any other significant Aries placement. Purification can help you clear your karma. As a symbol for the water element, the frog can help you cleanse, clear, align, transcend, and evolve. Any situations you need to outgrow, including mindsets, behaviors, and unhelpful habits, can all be overcome. The frog spirit asks you to be honest and accountable, and also live with a gentle and sincere heart. I am not saying you're not sincere, but you are the only sign ruled by the God of war and aggression himself (Mars). You have a tendency to see everyone as competition, even the people who were sent into your life to help you. Thus, the frog spirit animal is perfect for clearing mental clutter, emotional chaos, and spiritual and physical systems that don't serve your Higher Self, or best interests. Call on the mighty yet humble frog to help you get clear on your emotions, needs, internal triggers, desires, and daily responses. This power animal allows you to transform while making the unconscious conscious. Purification, emotional intelligence, and cleansing are three key qualities to visualize in addition to work on in your meditations and spiritual practices.

Buffalo

Abundance, resourcefulness, ambition, potent will, determination, and great organizational skills are qualities shared by both you and the buffalo. This is the spirit animal to turn to when you need grounding. Self-authority flows with the buffalo spirit's help, yet you also live with more sensuality. You can develop modest and down-to-earth qualities that allow you to be both high-achieving, and graceful in your approach to ambition and self-assertion. Cycles of nature and Mother Earth and your own internal cycles can be learned through the buffalo too. The buffalo's assistance is perfect for when you want to come back into your body. If you've been on a particularly ambitious, practical, or money-driven streak, you can remember the importance of self-care and daily beauty and health rituals (without losing your fierce passion to accomplish, dream, and succeed). The buffalo enhances respect in yourself and others, and because there is a sensitive quality to this grounding spirit animal you don't run the risk of falling into the extreme of becoming power hungry and overbearing. Similar in attributes to your own astrological glyph, the Ram, the buffalo increases zest, inspiration, passion, life force, and a connection to nature and your body. 'Don't live in your head….' Return to your heart and the sacred space where child-like innocence, wonder, and awe arise. The buffalo is both serious & hard working and carefree & spontaneous, just like you. With regards to innocence, the buffalo lives in the forest, not outside of or apart from it. This is a great message for how you should play and work well with others, being part of a time without losing your own sense of self-leadership or personal authority. The buffalo understands and respects that Mother Earth is benevolent and abundant, she provides for all of her inhabitant's needs. In this respect, you shouldn't see yourself as "above" nature or the creatures (animals and humans!) you cohabit physical space with. We are all one, even if you do have your own strengths.

Giraffe

The giraffe is your spirit animal for connecting to your visionary self and long-term idealistic goals. This animal helps you see past the mundane and attune to something greater than yourself, and you certainly possess these capabilities! Your recurring problem or block is that you are so focused on creating material wealth, security, and stability, that you often forget about these "higher" planes and frequencies. The giraffe can literally see far and above, and this symbolically means that you too can develop foresight for developed intuition and cosmic insight. Look above and beyond your everyday goals or routines. Seek to enhance your psychic gifts and abilities, which lead to evolved clairvoyance, clairsentience, and claircognizance. Extend your vision out… further…. Further… Yes, that's it. There's nothing wrong with living a materialistic life, yet this should also be balanced and merged with spiritual sight, vision, and wisdom. Read up on the Giraffe's symbolism to see what else you can embody and increase.

Power Animals for Protection

Hawk

Your two main power animals for self-protection and self-preservation belong to the 'Higher Self' spirit animals. These animals connect you to your higher mind, intuition, and intellectual power. You are one of the most intellectual and independent signs, Aries. Your sign rules the head, the part of your body that links to the Crown chakra and higher ethereal realms of cosmic consciousness and spirit. Yet, you're deeply logical, rational, and connected to your physical body. This essentially means that higher forces and insights flow from the top of your head into your body, so the hawk is the perfect animal to assist you in fine-tuning and mastering your innate gifts, skills, and talents. The hawk symbolizes clear sight, vision, imagination, intuition, and the ability to read between the lines. Unlike other signs, such as the water signs, who do so in a way that is outright psychic and even telepathic, your ability to see beyond and through the veil of illusion is rooted in real-world facts. You draw from a range of experience and logical ideas to get to the root of truth, uncovering wisdom and self-knowledge in the process. You're deeply observant, intelligent, and quick-witted, and love solving problems and finding solutions with your amazing brain. So, tune into the hawk's medicine to enhance your perception. You might even find some new ideas and perspectives linked to the realm of spiritual wisdom and advanced imagination shine through.

In terms of self-development, the hawk can show you how to find power in a healthy way- a way that doesn't dominate or oppress others! There's nothing wrong with wanting to shine, achieve victory, or step into self-empowerment. Your karmic lesson in life is to do so in a way that doesn't bully or oppress others. The hawk is happy to shine brilliantly without seeking praise or admiration, they know they're the best at what they do (subtle perception, intellect, instincts, logic and higher reasoning, sharp intuition…), yet they don't do so with vanity or egotistical pride. If you wish to create a legacy of your own, you will need to learn how to *be the best* without falling into your shadow traits.

Crow

The crow is your second secret helper. When people hear 'crow,' they usually think of suspicious activity and darker motives. This is because there is considerable power in the shadow realms, and all healers, shamans, and spiritual teachers through the centuries have understood this secret fact. The crow represents magic and divination. Well, we could all do with a little magic in our lives. Your issue, dear Aries, is that you tend to be so realistic and focused on the tangible that you forget the magical universe we live in. YET, because your sign physically rules the head, which links directly to cosmic and universal consciousness, you can access these realms and dimensions rather effortlessly. All it takes is a shift and a choice, a choice to be open to the Great Spirit and the benevolent-mystical powers of the universe… Learn from the crow. Work with the crow's medicine and energy. You can work directly with the co-creative powers of the universe, such as by incorporating more color, sound, and self-therapy into your life. These three tools or pathways are perfect for seeing past the material and physical distractions and connecting to something deeper, to something timeless. All ideas, concepts, wisdom, truth, and manifestations are rooted in the abstract; in the spiritual or non-material. If you want to manifest more abundance, live your dream life, or simply experience more joy and amazement in everyday waking life, explore how sound, color, and holistic practices can help you transcend your comfort zones. The crow is the perfect spirit animal to seek guidance from, because the crow is in this world but not of it. In other words, they are able to transcend and evolve past the mundane, while still being connected to their intellectual, observant, and materially connected selves.

Animals You Should Work With for Integration

Based on the qualities you lack, you should work with the following spirit animals to integrate more balance, harmony, and unification of opposite (or dualistic) forces in your life.

All of the animals from 'Emotionally Intelligent' spirit animals (Chapter 3); the **dove**, **deer**, **dolphin**, **turtle**, and **swan** are perfect for you. I strongly advise creating your own self-development plan and spending sufficient time researching, exploring, and integrating the energetic qualities of these animals. They are attributes you lack! As an astrologer, I can tell you with full honesty and conscience that you are the *least* sensitive and gracious sign of the zodiac. I advise journaling, adding images of them to your vision board, or setting an intention to receive their guidance in dreams; or during transcendental meditation. You will find through patience and openness that the symbolism of these animals are what's missing in your life. Working with them- building a personal connection with them, even- will create improvements to all areas of your life.

The **elephant** is also another great one for you, as the elephant connects you with timeless and ancient wisdom, without feeling ungrounded. Physical instincts are incredibly important to you, they make up your entire world. Material reality is essential for you to be happy- you are an animal-ruled sign, after all (your glyph, or astrological symbol, is the *Ram*; an instinctive and high energy animal with stamina and powerful life force…). Feeling in control and connected to your body is essential. Without this real-world, physical body, and material/tangible connection, you feel lost. The elephant is all about being at one with Mother Nature and connecting to the grounding and stabilizing forces of the earth, yet the elephant also brings a gentle, feminine, and nurturing energy into the mix. This is important for you, especially if you're looking to become a mother or father. The elephant spirit represents maternal and paternal instincts, community and family values, and qualities including kindness, grace, humility, caring, and compassion. You can find comfort, solace, and inspiration in the elephant spirit animal due to how nurturing and considerate, and equally strong and security-driven, they are.

In fact, the elephant is perfect for you to connect to your more gentle and compassionate side, without falling into fantasy or selflessness; two qualities you strongly dislike. The elephant is one of the most sensitive and caring, least to mention loyal and affectionate, animals. However, as mentioned already, they are very grounded. Any spiritual insights, astral impressions, or imaginative and psychic visions you receive will be very much rooted in the material realm. See the elephant spirit animal as a bridge of sorts between your primal & instinctive self and your spiritual & higher one. There's a lot of wisdom, ancient memory, and empathic awareness to be found with this majestic animal.

Chapter 10: Taurus

I am Taurus, earthy by nature enriched in indulgence.
I find pleasure in the physical comforts of life,
receiving great satisfaction from sensual delights.
Down- to-earth and highly grounded,
material needs are placed as a daily reality.
Defined by determination, endurance, and practicality,
my mind is highly rational and I possess a strong sense of responsibility.
It is routine and reliability that make me feel at ease,
physical wants and desires bring me my peace.
Combined with my practical nature and need for security
is expression, creativity, and a deep love for beauty.
I'm artistic, creative, imaginative, and benevolent,
and I'm deeply caring and loyal with a strong sense of independence.
Compassion, nurturance, and empathy are some of my greatest strengths;
I'm romantic, intelligent, and more commitment-prone than the rest.
Art and nature allow me to express, for I am sensuality in form…
I am the divinity of the abundance of our earth, Taurus- the Bull.

What's my shadow, do I have any lessons?
Well, I can be lazy, idle, and lacking in motivation.
I love security and physical comforts so much that I can turn toward materialism,
so I need to learn to balance this with spirituality and inner Soul Visions.

Key Animals: *Your Personal Animal Guides & Spirits*

Swan

Ruled by Venus, the planet of love, female sexuality, sensuality, beauty, and romance, you are the epiphany of the swan, dear Taurus. The swan is without a doubt one of your personal spirit and power animals. You are as kind and benevolent as they come, and these qualities are amplified with the swan's medicine. The swan spirit can help you to slow down and connect to your true, authentic, and loyal self. You're affectionate, generous, outgoing, warm, bubbly, friendly, and genuine. All of your words, affections, and actions are sincere, and you're just as companionable. A sweetie at heart, you're a big romantic! Yet you're equally as practical, dutiful, and responsible. Well, in addition to representing grace, serenity, calmness, beauty, and tranquility, the swan is also a symbol for divine love. When swans mate, they mate for life, and this symbolizes your loyal and dependable nature. You can work with the swan spirit to enhance the personality traits that are already there. Your character is kid and giving, faithful and trusting, and compassionate and full of love… Venus makes you a natural lover and giver- you're certainly not a taker. For matters of love and romance, look towards the swan spirit for inspiration and direction when you need a reminder of the beauty of monogamy. Faith and devotion amplify through this power animal, and regardless of your gender you can attune to the divine feminine, gentle, spirit and sensuality the swan brings. Read up on the swan's symbolism to find out more, as you are the swan.

Dove

Similar to the swan, the dove portrays your peace-loving and serene nature. The dove is all about harmony, which is what you seek. Business bonds, friendships, family connections, and potential lovers- you look for harmony everywhere, and in everything. Conflict turns you off. You dislike confrontation, drama, and chaos at all costs. So, the dove is one of your personal spirit animals. You can call on the dove to help you calm your nerves or stress levels. The dove is excellent for instilling peace and calmness, and for further reminding you of the power of silence. We live in a chaotic and hectic world with so much noise; the dove advocates silence, and it's from silence where all sound arises. This spirit animal allows you to create your own mood, tone, and frequency, putting your own unique vibration out into the world. Instead of getting pulled into the chaos and drama- or false stories and currents- of others, you begin to set your own frequency. Thus, you create, nurture, evolve, manifest, magnetize, and attract. The dove is perfect for you, because in addition to all your positive traits you are also known for being incredibly stubborn. An inflexible and stubborn mindset is one of your worst personality traits, in fact. Therefore the dove allows you to recognize that harmony and unity should come above your peace. Why get stressed when you can work together in cooperation, synergy, and solidarity?

Turtle

Slow and a BIG lover of retreat and personal space, 'aka' self-care, the turtle is one of your power animals. The turtle spirit connects you to your already well-developed sense of emotional intelligence. You're emotionally mature, intelligent, empathic, self-aware, and balanced. You're one of the most balanced signs emotionally, Taurus, and the turtle spirit helps you master these innate gifts. In terms of self-care, you live and breathe rest, play, introspection, time for study or education, and personal space. You need your down time and you're extremely chilled, laid-back, and down-to-earth. Well, the turtle lives in both sea and on land, and this represents your own gifts and strengths. As an earth sign, you feel most comfortable when in a secure and safe environment. Security and strong foundations are a large focus and necessity for you. Yet, you're ruled by Venus, a feminine planet who symbolizes emotional depth, intimacy, and feminine forms of expression, such as romance and sensuality. The turtle therefore grounds you while energizing your natural gifts. You're able to connect to both your earthly grounded nature and spiritual, emotionally vulnerable, and sensitive watery-one. People admire your vulnerability, openness, and sensitivity, so I wouldn't overlook the natural and inner beauty the turtle can instill. This is one of your most powerful spirit animals for inner balance and harmony.

Cow

Overlooked and under-respected, the cow is your secret superpower animal in times of need. The cow is the perfect symbol of subtle power and humility. Modest, unassuming, graceful, and full of empathy and compassion, you are an incredibly sensitive and mature being, just like the cow! The cow teaches you how to forgive others. The cow as a species is used, abused, and tortured-humans generally do not treat this animal very nicely. Yet, the cow stands strong and forgives, on repeat. This spirit animal is here to show you how to forgive others, while staying sensitive, benevolent, and compassionate. Do not let the world turn you closed or disconnect you, in other words. You are a natural giver, not a taker; you're a lover, and not a fighter. This means you're more prone to being used and taken advantage of, sweet Taurus. The cow helps you to see how people create their own bad karma through their own deceptive or abusive actions. You're not responsible for anyone's actions, intentions, or energy. You're only responsible for your own. You're responsible for your reactions and responses too, and this is the cow's main teaching. Through age, maturity, and experience, you can come to see how sensitivity, empathy, compassion, forgiveness, and inner strength are the attributes that will get you through any situation in life. It's also what keeps you going, allowing you to continue to attract loving, supportive, and abundant friends and partnerships. Not everyone is meant for you, and that's ok! But the people who are meant for you will honor and cherish your beautiful qualities, as long as you continue to live with grace, integrity, and modesty… This is the message of the cow.

Fox

The fox appeals to your more intellectual and analytical side, which you have. All earth signs have a strong logical, rational, and analytical side, and this is because you draw your observations and reflections from earthly sensations. You are connected to your senses and further *believe* in the power of senses, of receiving information and subtle impressions from the physical world and environments surrounding you. The fox is intelligent, witty, and highly observant. So are you. You're not only sweetness and empathy, you're also very tuned in. People often overlook your brilliant originality and innovativeness because you're so humble, yet it's there. The fox can therefore assist you when you need to be more logical and less emotional. Business, monetary, practical, and organizational matters are all ideal for calling on the fox's assistance. Deeper analysis can be developed with the fox's help. One excellent way to work with the fox spirit is to visualize the fox relaxed, playing, or content and affectionate next to one of your *Emotionally Intelligent* spirit animals. This is a powerful method of creating a feeling of unity, warmth, and friendliness between two different spirit animals that represent different things. This creates harmony within and between them on a subtle-astral level. For example, visualize (in meditation, or silent reflection/contemplation) the fox relaxing and content nearby a dove. This will instill feelings of peace and acceptance surrounding your analytical and discerning qualities and your yielding, submissive, and peaceful ones simultaneously. Picture how they are totally at one with each other, relaxed, cool, calm, and in a state of acceptance and vulnerability to the other. There's no fear present, no harm being caused by either animal. You can do the same with any of your feminine and gentle power animals, bringing solidarity and harmony to your left brain and right brain characteristics, to your mental and emotional gifts.

Bear

One of your best animals to work with for grounding, security, and staying focused and driven is the bear. The bear symbolizes ancient wisdom, rest and contemplation, dreaming and the subconscious mind, and paternal and maternal instincts. This animal is excellent for connecting to your inner sage and wise wo/man, which is what you are known for anyway, Taurus. You're wise, intelligent, perceptive, and romantic, with a gentle and warm heart. These qualities, alongside being ruled by Venus, the 'yin' planet of female sexuality, sensuality, pleasure, inner beauty, etc., allow you to access the dream states and astral worlds of spirit rather effortlessly. Out of all the non-water signs- water typically being associated with divinity, the ethereal realms, and subconscious & astral forces- you are the only sign to be able to enter these mystical and special places. (At least, at ease… it comes more naturally to you than all other fire, earth, and air signs.) The bear can amplify these innate gifts. The bear provides the medicine of attuning to your dreamy, sensual, and down-to-earth self while not becoming disconnected from reality. It's the perfect combination for you. Further, the bear is the ideal spirit animal to call on for guidance, wisdom, and protection if you were thinking about starting a career in the Healing Arts or spirituality. Astral insights enhance and can be found through the bear's ethereal assistance. And, your nurturing, caring, affectionate, providing, and instinctive qualities become stronger and more integrated. This is certainly a special power animal for you, one that may even create miracles in your world.

Stag

Similar to the bear, the stag is perfect for you for all matters of self-leadership. Whether you're your own boss or working for someone else, the stag helps you to find your power and self-esteem within. Self-authority, intellect, intelligence, instincts, and intuition are all developed with the stag spirit. You can acquire better skills of discernment, and navigate all of life's situations with ease, grace, integrity, diplomacy, and modesty. People love the fact that you're a genuinely respectful person, Taurus. Call on the stag as your personal spirit animal for protection, guidance, and elevation in any life event or experience. *The stag is your personal power animal!* Read up on the stag symbolism and energetic qualities to find out more.

Dog

Loyal, friendly, companionable, generous, and totally selfless to those you love, you are the dog. The dog spirit is already strong within you, so it's important to work with this animal for shadow work integration and self-mastery. The dog's symbolism includes loyalty, friendship, unconditional love, trust, companionship, generosity, sincerity, and service. When you tell someone you love them or that they're your friend, you mean it. Your affections and gestures are genuine, honest, and from the heart. You're a deep person, yet you don't always like to show this outwardly or in public. People who know you, however, know how loyal, kind, caring, generous, and funny you are. You possess a unique type of depth- a deep and authentic need for genuine relationships- combined with a lightness of spirit. You have a very humorous side, but not everyone gets your jokes or your laughter. That's ok. The people who see you on a real level cherish and value you beyond belief, you have many admirers and real friends, both clear and some more secret. The dog is your faithful companion in all family, friendship, home, domestic, and community circle matters. If you're looking to call on the dog spirit in matters of work and business, this is fine. But stay mindful. Boundaries are important. Some people might use and abuse your supremely benevolent and giving nature, and showing too much sentimentality or emotional vulnerability and openness around bosses, peers, colleagues, or authority figures is not advised. Give a little- show a little of this softer side, and then hold back. The dog can assist you in listening to your inner voice to know who, why, and when you should show your most authentic, loving, and affectionate side to. This is the animal to turn to for balance in your personal and professional life.

Buffalo

Extremely similar to your own astrological glyph, the buffalo helps to bring out your inner Bull. The Bull is your zodiac's ruling glyph, and this makes you headstrong, determined, ambitious, willful, and a little stubborn! You are admired and respected for your tenacity, inner strength, and powerful sense of self-respect. People know not to play you or take you for a fool, yet you're equally sweet, generous, and gracious. You're full of grace, consideration, and compassionate and empathic qualities, in fact. So, the buffalo is the perfect spirit animal to work with on a daily or regular basis. The buffalo helps you to overcome limitations and restrictions, both physically and spiritually. As the sign of material pleasure and seeking the finer things in life, like luxury, material comforts, abundance, and strong foundations of security, Venu's influence coincides perfectly with the buffalo spirit. They compliment each other. Just like Venus, the buffalo is on a path of pleasure, seeking security, stability, and physical comforts. Yet they are also sensual, down-to-earth, intuitive, and capable of real (and deep) emotions and gentleness; sensitivity. They're sensitive and self-aware, responsive to the needs and interests of others and further other people's well-being, safety, needs for support and care, etc. Working with the buffalo spirit over time will provide you with the perfect balance of your more masculine self-authoritative and assertive side, who also strives for financial security and prosperity, and your compromisable, sweet, nurturing, and family-oriented side. The buffalo can also teach you how to protect yourself, which is essential due to you being a giver in a world of many takers…

Rabbit

In addition to all your will, determination, preservation, and practical and responsible characteristics that make you an excellent boss, manager, or planner & organizer, you're also very creative. You have many artistic and imaginative gifts, and the rabbit is the perfect animal to help bring these through for you. You and the rabbit share a similar set of qualities: a deep love of home, your roots, and security. Grounding, feeling at one with and safe in your body and the earth, and material/physical structures are very important to you and the rabbit. Further, abundance and fertility link here, and this is what you can increase with the rabbit spirit. The rabbit is excellent to call on if you're seeking inspiration or a boost of energy and vitality for creative and artistic projects, or any professional or intellectual pursuit in general. One of your flaws is succumbing to laziness and idleness. You can be lethargic, surrendering into the safe bubble and nest of home and security you've created. This may be great for self-care and nourishing yourself through pleasure and comfort, but it's not very good for putting yourself out there in the world. Nor is it good for living up to your destiny or soul mission, or embracing your passions and life force in a way that makes you strive towards your dreams, ambitions, and aspirations. The rabbit may crave physical comfort and strong foundations above all else, however they also have highly evolved life force, energy, and enthusiasm. Take inspiration from the rabbit, as there is a wonderful balance between your personal and professional life available.

Power Animals for Protection

Beetle

The beetle is one of your animals for self-protection. This can help you know, through psychic instincts and visions, who is good for you (or not). The beetle enhances your sense of self-protection and self-preservation, in addition to potent intuition. As a feminine sign, you have a natural affinity with sacred laws. The beetle allows you to tune into your higher mind and Higher Self, and the quantum spiritual energy field, which includes access to dream states, your subconscious mind, and subtle and spiritual energy. The beetle represents manifestation abilities too, therefore this power animal provides the midas touch to any project or venture you're working on. This spirit animal helps you to connect to your inner god or goddess, the divine essence that bonds you with the universe, and to an ancient and primordial energy. Instincts, psychic gifts, and clairvoyance are incredibly evolved in this animal, so you can work with the beetle for any spiritual, shamanic, healing, or self-development pursuit. Primarily, the beetle assists in helping you see the sacred essence of life and self, and this can protect you whilst instilling confidence in many situations. Further, the beetle is ideal for life chapters or moments when you feel yourself becoming lost in the crowd. If you've started to conform, lower your values, or alter your truth to fit in, the beetle spirit will realign you with your most authentic self.

Also, the **Raven** is ideal for you. The raven is another one that connects you to your Higher Self and the spiritual realms. Read up on the Raven symbolism to see how you can integrate its medicine, wisdom, and energy.

Deer

Your perfect holistic animal, the deer teaches you sensitivity and strength. The deer is compassionate, empathic, wise, intelligent, perceptive, and deeply nurturing and instinctive. Yet the deer spirit is much stronger than many originally assume. The deer teaches us how to be humble and modest, while appearing shy and reserved to the outside world. There's an aspect of illusion here, which is done solely to protect itself. This is your hidden secret power, Taurus, and therefore the deer is one of your most loyal spiritual companions on this earth journey. As a spirit animal of protection, the deer is an important wayshower and pathfinder on your journey. You can learn and integrate some key shadow traits with the deer.

Firstly, you can be vulnerable and naive, innocent to the coldness and mean spiritedness of some people. Some people are deceptive, brutal, and bullyish, and as a lover with a gentle and pure heart (just like the dear), you can overlook this. The deer helps you to transcend idiot compassion, i.e. letting others abuse you, take advantage of you, and walk all over you, and move towards a more healthy space of self-love. Self-love is the seed for healthy and mutually respectful and supportive relationships. Secondly, the deer spirit teaches both patience and the art of boundaries, both of which are significant in your search for wholeness. Without boundaries, you begin to feel used, and this can make your own inner darkness come out; stubbornness, holding a grudge for a lifetime, or a temper that can be explosive. When you truly master the art of boundaries, honoring yourself and setting clear parameters on how you should be treated, you reflect love and a healthy type of innocence out into the world. The deer symbolizes purity, beauty, and grace, as do you, Taurus, when you're at your best.

Animals You Should Work With for Integration

Based on the qualities you lack, you should work with the following spirit animals to integrate more balance, harmony, and unification of opposite (or dualistic) forces in your life.

Lion *and* Panther!

Both the lion and panther fall into the instinctive and primal spirit animals. These are the qualities you can lack. The lion teaches you self-leadership, and how to leave your comfortable bubble of self-care, self-nurturance, and rest to interact with the world. The lion represents community, brotherhood/sisterhood, and family you see, and as much as you do have a social side you're also incredibly introspective. You like your own company. You genuinely love to be alone! Yet this is not a forevermore-solution, it's only good for you for periods. You must eventually 'return to the pack,' for want of better words. The lion can teach you that it's ok to enjoy your own company and solitude, flourish in self-care and introspection, and get a little lost in laziness and pleasure-seeking from time to time, but you must then come out of it. Inner strength is developed with the lion, in addition to an increase in masculine self-authority, assertiveness, and yang qualities. Furthermore, being so compromisable and benevolent, generous, and harmony-seeking can make you lack the motivation and drive needed to succeed. Self-leadership qualities are often diminished due to either sincere innocence, i.e. not realizing the people you're trying to play nicely with are in a more cunning and ambitious mindspace; or, intentionally sacrificing your own desires for wealth, success, victory, achievement, or self-respect in the name of oneness. Harmony should never cost you your peace, Taurus. Being a leader, assertive, or willful doesn't have to equate with throwing people under the bus. Nor should these qualities be seen as synonymous with a cut-throat business attitude. The lion is here to show you how to be a bold and dominant leader, *within and in unison with* your beautiful, fair, and sensitive Venusian qualities.

As for the panther, this power animal provides a unique type of inner strength that blends well with your sensual and feminine nature. You naturally find harmony and synergy with the water signs- they're considered your most compatible matches in both love and friendship. The panther is a personal spirit animal guardian and protector to all three water signs, so you can find solace and comfort in this spirit animal. The panther gives you a sense of balance, inner serenity, and acceptance. In a patriarchal and extroverted world, not everyone understands what it's like to be sincerely, introverted, or passive and gentle. A lot of emphasis is placed on logic, competition, and other dominant-yang characteristics. The panther is a deeply feminine animal with powerful instincts and senses linking to the astral realms. There's a strong subconscious force and link, and this means you find a natural resonance with the panther and her qualities. The panther can teach the true meaning of self-care, self-love, and finding comfort in your own skin. This instinctive animal is bathed in sensuality, the panther's coat is majestic while her aura emits mysterious and sensual vibrations. While the lion provides you with the masculine strength you need, the panther strengthens your instincts that are connected to the spiritual, astral, and subtle realms. Both are useful for self-empowerment and your holistic self.

Peacock

You are one of the most modest signs of the zodiac, so-much-so that many people don't get to experience your wisdom, gifts, and talents. Well, the peacock is all about expression and showing off your talents and sparkle. When this is done in a healthy way, the message from the universe is that there's nothing wrong with seeking the spotlight. It's your birthright to shine, and unlike other signs you are actually (sincerely) humble. Whilst the fire signs have a problem with ego and self-serving tendencies, and the air signs are just as dominant and expressive; you're gentle, passive, and considerate. You are more than happy to take the back seat, dim your light a little, and let others take the lead or show off their gifts. But this is not what your Higher Self and the divine wants from you, at least not all the time. The peacock will help you to step into your true colors, live with authenticity, and speak up. In addition to showing your many beautiful colors, the peacock spirit asks you to use your voice more for sharing your truth, wisdom, and talents. Don't shy away from your most brilliant and passionate self. Work with the peacock spirit animal for full embodiment of your most expressive, passionate, and multi-talented self. Also, you can find true meaning in your deeply ingrained beliefs of teamwork, harmony, and compromise through actually stepping into the light more. Modesty and humility should only be displayed in moderation, otherwise people begin to overlook you and undervalue all the magnificence you have to offer. The peacock teaches you that your talents and wisdom are important too, perhaps even more so than the ones who have to constantly show off, shout, or seek attention and praise in excess.

Chapter 11: Gemini

I am Gemini, the Zodiac's joker;
A quick witted mind and intellect define my nature.
I am the one who loves to be social,
my character is defined by a need for other people.
Stories or conversion, my mind knows no bounds-
in both reason and rhyme is where my logic is found.
Rational and intuitive with an expressive sharp mind,
I possess the ability to adapt, every time.
I can multitask and am one to easily initiate ideas
with a mind rooted in rationality and a vision like the seer's.
I'm logical, smart, perceptive, and witty,
I communicate eloquently, passionately, and effortlessly.
Self-expression is my gift, from the realms of intellect to imagination,
and I know how to use my mind for connection and manifestation.
People know they can turn to me for sound judgment,
as I am highly intelligent, intuitive, and logical.
I can lack empathy and depth, yet my cerebral gifts make up for this,
I love to converse and share knowledge… my mind is a gift.
I am a dual sign by nature that easily swims
between the different realms of Gemini- I am the Twins.

What's my shadow, do I have any lessons?
I can be manipulative, cunning, secretive, and deceptive.
I don't mind spreading mistruth and I love to gossip,
I must learn how to be more honest, embodying greater integrity & self-knowledge.

Key Animals: *Your Personal Animal Guides & Spirits*

Crocodile

The crocodile is the perfect power animal for you, because this spirit animal is all about getting deep with your emotions, feelings, and internal sensations. The crocodile asks you to get real with your past and explore your trauma. This includes ancestral and family trauma, painful emotional, unhealed wounds, and tricky experiences you once weren't willing to look at. The crocodile exists in both water and on land, and is also very primal, so this is a much better animal for you than all the others who bring the energy of emotions and feelings (except for the dolphin). The crocodile represents your basic drive, survival and security needs, and instincts. They are cute, charming, funny, original, and unique with the personalities to match, yet they also have an aggressive and forceful side. This symbolizes your spirit. You're charming, full of wit, incredibly intelligent, affectionate, and sociable, yet as a masculine air sign you are more dominant and forceful than others. You're also a fierce striver toward home, roots, and family, and you therefore resonate with the security and self-preservation gifts of the crocodile. Thus, work with the crocodile when you need help making sense of your inner waters- the realms of feelings, emotions, instincts, and processing impressions and subtle sensations. You're able to do this without feeling shame in your own shadow self, or from another perspective; you're able to go deep with the more tricky emotions and sensations while still feeling acceptance with your less desirable traits. The crocodile has come to terms with both its charming, loving, affectionate, and family-oriented side, and its self-protective, fierce, ancestral, instinctive, and survival-centered one. So should you!

Dolphin

The dolphin is your subtle protector and energizer. The dolphin symbolizes all of your strengths and all of your weaknesses simultaneously, so this is a great one to work with for shadow integrations and healing. It's through our shadow where we find our light. The dolphin is a symbol for play, community, self-expression, wit, humor, and emotional intelligence. The dolphin is both highly cerebral, gifted mentally, and emotional intelligence. This is the perfect balance or unity you should aim for in life. You often focus so much on your mind and mental and cerebral gifts, yet this undermines the power and significance of your emotions. You can find just as much joy and satisfaction in emotional bonds and connections. The dolphin helps to awaken and energize your sacral chakra, the center of emotions, interpersonal relationships, creativity, artistic gifts, sensuality (essential life force), and sexuality. It's only when you've integrated these aspects of yourself that you can become a whole, unbalanced, and complete person. You have many strengths, but one of your major follies is emotional aloofness. You can find the realm of emotions and feelings tricky, and this is when you start to detach, break down, or fall into depression, melancholy, isolation, or loneliness. Or have mood swings. Your key to a happy and long life is to work on healing and harmonizing the qualities of your sacral chakra. The dolphin will assist you in having more fun, learning how to play and express yourself artistically and creativity, while remaining connected to a serious side of you; advanced emotional intelligence.

Coyote

The coyote represents your inner cunning, Gemini. Coyote is the spirit animal to work with when you want to develop what's already there. This spirit animal is less about helping you to develop new talents, and more about mastering what's already inside of you. The coyote's symbolism is everything connected to the higher mind; intellect, logic, rationality, discernment, intuition, potent observation, and perceptive skills. Laughter, community, and the spirit of connection are also enhanced over time. If you need assistance balancing willpower to succeed with expression and light-heartedness, the coyote can help. As a sign of duality, you tend to fall into extreme, so one moment you could be depressed and down, or simply highly methodological and attuned to an intellectual or analytical frequence; and, the next, you could be completely "up," light-hearted, full of excitement, and almost forgetting your responsibilities all together. You seem to bounce through life on a high, going from extreme to extreme, certainly earlier in life. The coyote helps you to find balance, while further finding wisdom and light in the harder times. This spirit animal teaches that life is a multidimensional experience, and there's hidden wisdom and meaning in even the lowest times. Sometimes you may need to be light, optimistic, and in a pursuit of fun and pleasure. Other times, you will be asked to be serious, practical, and focused on domestic issues or your educational and professional goals. The coyote is here to show your discernment and intuitiveness so you can know, through your rational & logical higher mind and your instincts & feelings, which path is best in each present moment. Your personal karma is entwined in duality, Gemini. Your lifelong lesson is to find unity, harmony, and synergy in dualistic forces.

Fox

The fox is another intellectual higher mind oriented animal that is close to your heart and interests. You should develop a personal relationship with the fox for the best results in life. Just like you, the fox is incredibly sharp-minded and intelligent- full of wit and killer instincts too. You should listen to your gut feelings more, and further engage in meditation, spiritual healing , and perhaps psychic development work to enhance these innate skills. As you turn towards your strengths- your 'light side,' you naturally overcome your follies, your 'dark side'- and vice versa. The fox helps you work through internal blocks to honesty, truth telling, and accountability. Do you know your shadow traits? I can tell you. You are one of the most gossip-prone and manipulative signs of the zodiac. It's not that you're a bad person (or you very well might occasionally be), it's just that you enjoy talking and sharing your ideas so much that you sometimes lose touch with reality, i.e. the truth. Or enjoy the fun associated with the drama and excitement of truth distorting. With fox as one of your personal spirit animals reflecting your core personality, you have real issues with honest communication. Another reason for this is being so cerebrally active- you have so many ideas and so much knowledge, observations, and insights running through your head, that it can all come out in a rather judgemental or pushy way. The fox, therefore, helps you to make sense of your brilliant and bright mind, accept your strengths, and heal your less desirable traits. Slow down. Think before you speak, and learn to listen more. Working with the fox will allow you to let go of your tendency to BS, deceive, and spread mistruths for good.

Monkey

The monkey provides a doorway to mindful and empathic communication. Compassionate and empathic, yet equally intelligent and witty, the monkey enables some soul-searching in a way that works for you! The water signs may resonate with emotionally intelligent and serene water animals; the earth signs may prefer to work with grounded forest animals… Well, you too need some compassionate and empathetic energy in your life, but in a way that allows you to play to your strengths. Mischievous, fun-loving, flirty, intelligent, upbeat, positive, and spirited, the monkey has nurturing and caring qualities in addition to all of these core personality traits that you share. You're logical, original, multitalented, logical, expressive, and an excellent communicator. Charity and service can be learned through the monkey spirit. If you've been feeling withdrawn or prone to a bout of isolation and loneliness, the monkey spirit animal is excellent for re-finding your sense of passion, fun, sociability, joy, and community. The monkey can help you establish social bonds and ties in your life. Additionally, the monkey is perfect for showing you how to have fun without playing tricks on others or deceiving them. 'Clean and pure fun' in other words. If you need to ground and be more practical, picture the monkey next to one of your grounding animals, the stag or the mouse. Imagine the stag spirit relaxed and content next to the monkey, both chilling and content with each other's energy. Or picture a monkey holding a mouse with gentleness and sensitivity. Use this visualization technique in your meditation or when calling on your spirit animal helpers in a more ceremonial space. It's simple, yet powerful.

Stag

The stag represents your assertive, headstrong, and practical side, and is particularly good to work with regularly in youth and early- mid adulthood. Frivolity, a lack of commitment, irresponsibility, and being impractical and too excitable are some of your worst traits. The stag symbolizes self-leadership and inner strength and stamina, in addition to aligning you with personal will, courage, ambitions, determination, and focus to fulfill your dreams. Aspirations, long-term goals, and concrete professional and personal plans are very important to the stag spirit. This is an excellent animal to work with for finding grounding, self-alignment, and integrity. Also, for honoring your duties and commitments, finding structure and order, and developing managerial and organization qualities. The stag helps you to step into self-authority and be more assertive and willful when it comes to your purpose. When older and having already worked on your shadow self, merging and balancing it with your light side, you can work with the stag to balance sensitivity, empathy, and compassion with your strong will and work ethic. The stag may be all about professional goals and ambitions, but it's also a deeply nurturing and down-to-earth animal that is very much in tune with its senses. So, sensuality and a desire to spend more time with loved ones, friends, and family can be brought into synergy with your career.

Squirrel

Also, the Squirrel is another grounding animal for you to work with. The squirrel represents gathering resources and multitasking, in addition to being a symbol for Mother Earth and your connection to her. As a cerebral and energetic air sign, you tend to be on the go. You're always moving around, upbeat and full of zest, and full of ideas and inspiration. This can make you a genius or it can make you scattered- it all depends on your mood. The squirrel helps you to be more responsible and find wisdom and guidance in the smaller things. Details are important too, so you shouldn't solely focus on the big picture. Your optimism is contagious, and everyone knows they can turn to you for joy and excitement in life. Yet, this isn't good for financial, domestic, practical, business, or grounded affairs. You need to stabilize and align your internal energies, while simultaneously *paying more attention* to what's going on in your immediate and physical environment. It's all very well to have your mind buzzing and alive with ideas, information, concepts, and new and innovative creations, however this doesn't help you take better care of the relationships or material structures in your life. The squirrel is at one with nature and has made their natural environment their home. They honor, cherish, and respect the physical and material foundations and structures they find themselves in, because they know this is the key to their success and abundance. You will find wonderful longevity, self-confidence, and increased resources when you start to take a leaf off of the squirrel's tree.

To add, the *Mouse* is another personal animal you should read up on and seek to integrate. The mouse is humble, modest, and knows how to make itself invisible to get on with the task at hand. This spirit animal is perfect for when you need to learn how to calm your inner "party animal" to get to work, without being pulled into other's playful or fun-seeking motives.

Chameleon

As a Mutable sign, the chameleon belongs to you (and Virgo, Sagittarius, and Pisces, the other mutable signs). Your powers of adaptability and camouflage lie in the mental realm of the imagination, intellectual gifts, and advanced cerebral powers of communication and persuasion. You have a real gift for seeing multiple perspectives. You're philosophical, open-minded, curious, and inquisitive… you're inventive, original, intelligent, and innovative. And, you know how to multitask when it comes to thoughts and speech, which signifies you can be attuned to many different frequencies in one conversation. Your mind is like a holographic cosmic computer, Gemini. The chameleon helps to bring out these qualities and further strengthen them. Clairvoyance, vision, higher perspectives, and evolved self-expression can all be developed with the chameleon's assistance. *Read up on the chameleon spirit to find out what else you can learn.*

Peacock

The peacock represents your alter-ego, or perhaps your real world visible ego?! The peacock displays its beautiful colors to shine and attract a mate, and this is what this animal is trying to teach you. Self-expression, color, creativity, originality, and embracing your unique inner sparkle are the keys to success, financial prosperity, and true love in this life. The peacock is both a powerful spirit animal to work with and one of your personal power animals. You may already find a resonance with the peacock, as you instinctively feel many shared attributes. With such profound and clear and concise communication techniques, the peacock shows you it's ok to express yourself openly, authentically, and without fear or apprehension. Obviously, be mindful and conscious in your speech, but don't be shy. The message is the peacock is to live up to your full potential, let your colorful wings be known, and embrace your role in the spotlight. You may develop your gifts early on or a level of expertise and mastery might not come until later in life; it doesn't matter, as the peacock teaches you that life's a journey. You must accept your emotions and feelings to shine like the star you are. You must embrace your need for deeper intimacy, companionship, and connection. Stardom and stepping into a self-leadership role where your talents are known should not be separate from family ties and close relationships. Call on the peacock when you need assistance accepting that you can be emotionally vulnerable with loved ones while receiving prestige and recognition publicly.

Rabbit

The rabbit represents your inner pull towards artistic and creative projects. The rabbit can help you enhance your fertility, both physically in terms of reproduction and creatively relating to giving birth to new projects, conditions, and artistic visions. This spirit animal assists you in overcoming social anxiety and irrational worries created by an overactive mind. As you're ruled by Mercury, you tend to be more influenced by Mercury Retrogrades and shifts in the planet of communication than others. When Mercury is direct, you are (generally speaking) happy, upbeat, optimistic, ambitious, and full of zest and life force. But when Mercury is Retrograde, which happens 3- 4 times per year, or in an inharmonious position, you suffer from mood swings, pessimistic thinking, and stress and anxiety. Well, a Retrograde period or any other low cycle where you're not feeling upbeat and enthusiastic is a chance to connect to the spiritual and subtle planes. You are incredibly extroverted, yet this takes away from your ability to introspect and attune to your imaginative mind. There are multiple frequencies, planes, vibrations, and dimensions of consciousness. A lot of creative and artistic inspiration can be found in the subtle, astral, ethereal, dream, multidimensional, and spiritual planes. So learn from the rabbit, embrace inner stillness and silence, an energetic mindset that opens you up to the fertility and natural beauty of Mother Earth (and the natural world). It's from this space where new ideas, universal archetypes, ingenious insights, and original concepts flow. Furthermore, the rabbit is ideal for when you're feeling lazy and lacking the "get-up-and-go" energy you usually have. This is because wisdom, truth, and inspiration can be found in your sensuality, when you slow down and connect to your physical body sensations. Call on the rabbit when you need to embody more depth and sensitivity to the wonders and co-creation powers of the universe.

Power Animals for Protection

Parrot

A personal favorite and an animal in the physical realm you resonate deeply with, the parrot is your personal power animal that can help you through any situation. All you have to do is think of the parrot and your mind will come alive with clarity, ideas, and the perfect choice of speech or responses. Whomever you're with, and whatever situation you find yourself in- business, home, school, with peers, around strangers, in a stressful situation, or when people turn to you for wisdom and to lead the conversation; the parrot is your loyal and faithful spirit companion. The parrot, like you, signifies communication, self-expression, light, color, and independence. An original and sharp, witty, and intellectual mind defines the parrot spirit. They are able to converse with anyone and everyone, while further mimicking speech patterns and words. This has a deeper meaning. It means you too can "mirror" people's communication style and thought processes. From direct conversation to moments of silence where body language is observed; and the art of listening to direct engagement- the 'flow' of ideas and information exchanges; you are given a chance to be a master communicator with the parrot. And this is what you love, Gemini. You take pride in your intellectual and speaking skills. Also, in how you relate to others. Many people see you as a social butterfly, not for your emotional depth (you need to work on this), but for logical, analytical, perceptive, communication, imaginative, and intellectual gifts.

Perform a visualization meditation at least once a week with the parrot as your main focus. Get into a comfortable and sacred space, with herbal incense or a smudge stick to cleanse the air of impurities (like Sage or Palo Santo), make sure your undisturbed, and perhaps dim all artificial lighting, only using candles or natural sun or moon-light shining through your windows. Then, close your eyes, take some deep breaths, and picture yourself sitting in a jungle or rainforest. You can see the tall and ancient trees surrounding you; you hear the subtle call of birds singing in the background, and perhaps a stream of water flowing, from a river or waterfall. You might be aware of a cave or beautiful mountain or hill in the background… Sit peacefully in the center of this jungle-rainforest scene, knowing you are safe and protected. Now, visualize a parrot flying down eloquently and gracefully in front of you. This parrot has many colors! Let the parrot sit in front of you for a while, speaking to you telepathically. Simply absorb the subtle healing vibrations and energy of the parrot, basking in its wisdom and guidance.

How does this make you feel? What internal sensations come up? Are you reminded of an experience where you shocked others and wow-ed yourself at your amazing communication skills? Does it bring up memories of real telepathy or supersonic information exchange-flow you and another once shared?! Reflect on the feelings, emotions, thoughts, memories, and sensations that arise… Then, ask the parrot with gratitude and love in your heart for guidance. Ask this majestic bird to stay by your side, protecting you in times of need. Take a moment in this tranquil and comforting jungle scene to connect subtly to the parrot, so you're now connected through an ethereal and timeless cord.

The parrot is a symbol for your Higher Self and higher consciousness. It is your personal power animal of protection, inspiration, and internal guidance when you need a pick-me-up or mental boost. You can enhance this visualization meditation by playing rainforest sounds, a type of meditation healing music. Many free tracks can be found on Youtube and other various sources.

Raven, Hawk or Crow

Three of the animals from the *Higher Self* category are your additional power animals. Read up on their symbolism, and use the parrot meditation exercise as a foundation to expand your self-study and self-development practice. The rave, hawk, and crow are powerful animal guides and helpers that can help you navigate life's currents, and connect to your strengths and best qualities. Adapt the visualization scene to something more suitable, for example a cave, green open pasture, the top of a tree, or even your own home or personal space. Work with these animals regularly for self-mastery and integration.

Animals You Should Work With for Integration

Based on the qualities you lack, you should work with the following spirit animals to integrate more balance, harmony, and unification of opposite (or dualistic) forces in your life.

Dog

The dog teaches you loyalty and the true meaning of companionship. You are very companionable, but you are also one of the most fickle and non-committal signs of the zodiac. You can be so upbeat and falsely positive that you become superficial, telling fibs and white lies, and further running away from friendships and relationships as soon as they begin to get deep. Superificality is one of your downfalls, and this rubs off on the relationships in your life (both business and personal). The dog symbolizes kinship, friendship, and emotional and spiritual bonds that stand the test of time. Unconditional love, loyalty, and lasting friendships can be learned through the dog spirit. In youth, you are extremely lustful, flighty, frivolous, and irresponsible- you give your time and attention to people, places, and projects, and then- quite literally- get up and leave! This is a trait shared by you and your opposite sign Sagittarius. This doesn't serve you for very long, so eventually you will have to learn how to be more practical, grounded, and responsible in matters of platonic and romantic intimacy. The dog is the perfect spirit animal for integrating the "staying-power" needed for successful relationships with longevity. Your happiness lies in the bonds you make, as you are arguably the most sociable star sign. Thus, why always run away? Why can't you show and express your emotions? And, what's wrong with being vulnerable and opening up about your feelings, desires, and innermost needs for intimacy and companionship? There's nothing wrong with these things, and this is what the dog will help you master.

In addition many Geminis tend to be cat people, therefore you can find further meaning and guidance through reading up on the cat spirit animal. While dogs are loyal without fault, cats are independent; while dogs crave frequent affection and physical contact, cats enjoy their own company… Being aware of the dog vs cat differentiations and further seeking to harmonize, balance, and integrate them is the missing piece of the puzzle to discovering your true (and complete) personality.

Deer *and* Dove

Both the deer and dove help you immensely in becoming more sensitive, peace-seeking, and calm inside. The deer represents empathy, self-awareness, spiritual and higher perspectives, nurturing, caring, sensitivity, and feminine qualities. The dove symbolizes peace, harmony, serenity, receptivity, and being more passive and submissive than dominant and forceful. As a masculine air sign, you tend to be the latter (dominant and forceful), so working with these two animals, *closely*, can be your secret weapon when people begin to underestimate you. Also, when they develop the belief that you lack emotional depth and are incapable of slowing down! Prove them wrong. Just make sure your intentions are pure, i.e. you actually want to work on yourself.

Any of the *Emotionally Intelligent* spirit animals are advised for when you need to calm yourself and develop inner peace and clarity. But, the deer and dove are advised above the swan and turtle because you feel more comfortable on land than in the water, metaphorically speaking. (Water is symbolic of emotions and depth.)

Chapter 12: Cancer

I am Cancer, ruled by the Moon,
I represent the natural cycles and rhythms of nature's mood.
Caring, compassionate, nurturing, and motherly,
I am the provider that looks after those in need.
Connected to the waters of the tides we all swim-
Lunar and her energies are grounded deep within.
Just like the darkness, the subconscious that rules the soul,
I am nature's force that allows for emotional growth.
Possessing the ability to merge with others and feel
the root, the cause, the suffering left to heal;
my emotional maturity and intuitive wisdom
shine through for others, with a protective instinct.
I am sensitive, dreamy, and deep with advanced imagination,
and I possess psychic gifts and advanced intuition.
I am both practical and otherworldly- I love both domestic and spiritual life,
and when I give my heart I shower my partner with endless love and light.
I can be self-sacrificial, shy, and super-sensitive,
yet I am also an empathic caregiver and loyal & unconditionally loving nurturer.
I have great strength, yet I need affection from those I love,
for I am the Zodiac's caregiver, Cancer- the Crab.

What's my shadow, do I have any lessons?
I can be moody, withdrawn, hyperemotional, and prone to deception.
Manipulation is my downfall, yet it comes from a place of love,
I crave intimacy so much that I tend to fall into codependency traps.

Key Animals: *Your Personal Animal Guides & Spirits*

Panther

Mysterious, sensual, psychic, and elusive, the panther is certainly one of your main spirit animals, Cancer. You are one of the most deep, sensitive, sweet, and astrally and psychically connected signs. The panther is the animal that best represents majestic spiritual powers of advanced telepathy, psychic instincts, intuition, and ethereal wisdom. The panther is connected to an ancient wisdom, power, and sensuality, all of which stem from their mysterious and feminine nature. Well, you too are like the panther, when at your best and with your strengths integrated. So the panther spirit can assist you in wonderful ways for accepting and embracing your divine feminine nature. Also, to accept and develop psychic, instinctive, and intuitive gifts. The panther is here to teach you that not everything can be seen with visible eyes- there's many frequencies, realms, and dimensions. The subtle and astral planes of existence are not available to everyone, at least not naturally and effortlessly, but, for you, they are. You are ruled by the Moon, *the* planet of instincts, the subconscious mind, and the astral realm and ether. You are essentially the panther spirit when in a state of acceptance and remembrance, but it's key to not deny or repress these innate gifts. I've met many water signs- Cancer and Pisces specifically, who seem to think there is something wrong with being sensitive, dreamy, and emotions. We have society to put some blame on for this. Yes, there are some shadowy aspects to work on; for example, succumbing to bouts of moodiness, depression, and isolation- or super/hyper-emotionalism and sensitivity. Yet your inner power, strength, and higher guidance come from these invisible and subtle realms… The panther is here to be a wayshower of the power and significance of divine sensuality, sexuality, and subtle and invisible instincts, even if you don't shine in the same way the fire or air signs do. *Read up on the panther to discover your inner authentic vibration, because you are the panther!*

Dove

The *Emotionally Intelligent* spirit animals are your faithful spirit helpers and guardians. All of these animals best represent your true glow, your inner voice, and your desires for self-expression and connection. The dove represents purity, peace, and serenity, qualities you find an extreme resonance with. As the sign of unconditional love, you display strong levels of purity in all that you do. You're a natural mother, nurturer, protector, carer, and soul-provider. Whether it's friends, family, or strangers, everyone knows you possess evolved instincts and a genuine desire to help, protect, and nurture. Due to being ruled by the 4th house of home, security, roots, physical foundations, and security, you prefer peace and harmony over conflict or chaos. In fact, a non-peaceful and combative environment disturbs you on a deeper and unexplainable level, you're totally opposite to Aries, for example, who is ruled by the planet of war and competition. Thus, the dove is your perfect animal for recognizing that it's ok to choose peace and harmony over the chaos and upbeat temperaments of an extroverted and somewhat superficial society. Your home is your protection while your inner home- making peace with your nurturing and caring qualities- allows you to embody unconditional love. This is where the rest of your strengths arise, dear Cancer.

Also, through inner peace and fully accepting that you may just be unique, in terms of being anti-conflict and preferring a peaceful life, you can heal your wounds, which largely stem around being a people-pleaser and overly self-sacrificing. You must make peace with yourself first, embracing the differences- some people are just a little more combative! We're also living in a patriarchy, currently, while your sign represents matriarchal and feminine values. This is the true path to peace in your external world and relationships.

Deer

The deer is another powerful guardian animal for you. The deer represents gentleness, purity, sensuality, grace, honesty, integrity, and truth, and this is what you strive for. Your shadow traits or follies include manipulation. In your desire for connection and intimacy you become quite manipulative and deceptive, when at your lowest, yet your strengths include sincerity, service, and unconditional love. You are one of the most compassionate, caring, and empathic zodiac signs, therefore working with the deer helps you to overcome your less desirable traits whilst working towards your 'light' ones (the ones to embody). Devotional and affectionate, the deer is often overlooked, mistreated, and used for selfish gain. But why, when the deer has such a pure and loving spirit? This is something to reflect on. The deer, like you, is a nurturer and powerful support system and provider, however their power is subtle, and thus it's often misperceived as weakness. In a world of takers and users, kindness can be seen as weakness to those less evolved and misguided souls. Fortunately, the deer is here by your side to teach you how to develop inner strength so you can stand strong in your truth and in your caring and empathic nature. You should not change for any illusion or any being's false motives; this is the message the deer carries. Humility, integrity, and compassion can be strengthened while innocence, purity, and emotional intelligence taken to new levels. These qualities allow your self-esteem and confidence to shine, which is important as such a sensitive and impressionable soul. Find support in others who share this spirit animal, such as fellow water signs and the earth signs Virgo and Taurus. You find a natural synergy here, and gentle people who are equally loyal, kind-hearted, and giving/generous assist in showing you that it's ok to be yourself. You don't have to suppress your inner beauty and love for anyone- there are many people who share your values.

Swan

The swan is a symbol of purity, unconditional love, and soulmate bonds, topics and themes that are integral to your life. The swan is similar to the dove, so the message for the dove applies here. Additionally, you seek deeper and more meaningful bonds than most others. You dislike superficiality and are stimulated by depth, soul, sharing, intimacy, open-hearted bonding, and sentimentality. So is the swan! Swans mate for life, therefore they are the ultimate symbol of monogamous, life-long, and committed love. Turn toward the swan if you need help healing from painful sexual memories or trauma, and from wounds of the past. Issues in sensual, emotional, physical, and sexual self-expression can be overcome with the swan spirit, as this beautiful and serene animal teaches you how to open your heart and trust again. It's the perfect spirit helper for platonic, romantic, family, and sexual love, heartbreak, and loss. Fears surrounding intimacy, love, and rejection that come with being so sensitive and deep can be eased through the swan's gentle and compassionate, unassuming, nature. And, you can overcome idealistic types of fairy tale love belief systems, which keep you trapped and stuck in lifelong cycles of loneliness; or chasing after the wrong partner.

Turtle

Selfless, instinctive, self-aware, telepathic, psychically gifted, spiritually in tune, and astrally connected, the turtle is one of your personal animals. The turtle helps you align with your strengths in a grounded way, while simultaneously seeing that it's ok to go slow and take your time. Others may want to charge full steam ahead, giving into impulse, impatience, and unresolved core wounds along the way, but this is not your way. You don't mind going slow and taking your time, taking periods for introspection and soul-searching, or even missing out on the excitement. You understand that life is a journey and that there's lots of wisdom, joy, and inspiration to be found in silence and personal retreat. The turtle is perfect for these things. Also, this spirit animal opens doorways to soul-evolution and personal transformation through intentionally disconnecting from the drama and stories of others. You are able to go within to access soul gifts and talents, further directing and channeling your energy on more meaningful pursuits. Be sure to look up the turtle's shadow attributes- what you need to overcome and transcend (*Anything to be mindful of?*), to get the full picture.

Dolphin

Although the dolphin is emotional and sensitive, this supersonic creature equally symbolizes your love of play and community. You're not all sentimentality and introspection, you're also incredibly creative, passionate, and artistic. You have many imaginative and artistic gifts, and are wise, perceptive, and intelligent too. The dolphin represents all of these things- a fine blend and balance of intellect and logic, including other qualities associated with the higher mind and intelligence, and emotional intelligence, instincts, and psychic powers. The dolphin is deeply spiritually evolved and self-aware, so you can work with the dolphin spirit to help balance your inner feminine and masculine attributes. This is the *best* animal to work with for inner yin and yang balance, harmony, and unification! Play, community, artistic expression, teamwork, and pure liberated fun can be balanced with taking on the role of nurturer and provider.

Elephant

The elephant is your perfect healing and grounding spirit animal. The elephant brings the energy of ancient wisdom, memory, grounding, and being in tune with your instincts and the world around. The elephant senses vibrations through the ground, representing a strong connection and bond with Mother Earth. You can awaken ancient and primordial powers with the elephant's assistance. Family and karmic wounds, healing from ancestral trauma, and letting go of the past are part of the elephant's powers. As the sign of the natural empath and, to many, 'witch,' you possess natural shamanic and spiritual powers. It's essential to disconnect from the mundane 3D world and tribulations every once in a while, to connect to something greater than you. Also, to access intuitive, psychic, and extrasensory gifts. Not only will the elephant aid you in healing and raising your inner vibration, but this powerful majestic animal also assists anyone wanting to step into a teaching or healing role. If you are destined to be a spiritual teacher, healer, or wayshower for others, this animal is ideal. The elephant signifies nobility, integrity, truth, honor, compassion, clearing past wounds and pain through self-development work, and sage-like wisdom. As you can be quite dreamy and lacking in boundaries with a 'go with the flow' nature, call on the elephant for grounding, direction, and stabilizing internal spiritual and emotional energies.

Crow *and* Raven

Magic, divination, spiritual powers of illumination and expression, and divine energy are all attainable with the crow's assistance. You're already known for being deep and connected to the subconscious, astral, and non-physical dimensions, so working with the crow over time will provide opportunities for self-mastery. Everything begins on an unseen and invisible level, and this is where all extrasensory abilities, artistic gifts, and dormant abilities come from. One must go into the darkness to come out into the light. Unlike the panther, who is also concerned with astral and feminine powers linked to darkness and the shadow/spiritual realms, the crow allows you to attune to your higher mind through these invisible cords of consciousness. All aspects of imagination, manifestation, divination, subtle perception, intellect, and Higher Self realization come into play, and can further be integrated and embodied for holistic living. You're more emotional and spiritual than you are intellectual or physical. You do possess potent instincts, yet these are primarily drawn from your advanced emotional empathy, intelligence, and vulnerability. Therefore, it's important you work with some of the bird animals, which can connect you to the air element and to the intellectual & logical realms of ether and the imagination. In essence, we are complex, holistic, and intertwining multidimensional beings with many different bodies and subtle energy systems. Using your advanced emotions and spiritual gifts to access higher mental reasoning might work for you, but do consider attuning to a different frequency for the boost and level up needed. Finally, the crow can protect you from the manipulations of others, strengthening your boundaries through increased mental powers, and shielding you from darker energy or harmful projections, of which you require protection for.

Another bird from the *Higher Self* category, the ***raven*** asks you to look within while attuning to your Higher Self. The raven is your secret super-spirit animal! Read up on the raven to discover how it can shine its wisdom and light on you.

Personal exercise:

Refer to the visualization meditation given to Gemini on pages 141- 2. Perform this with the raven (instead of the parrot). Apply the raven's key symbolism and medicine to your meditation. Do it as little or often as feels best to integrate and body the healing powers and qualities of this majestic bird.

Lizard

A personal favorite (my Moon is in Cancer!), the lizard is your dream spirit helper. Everything related to dreams, visions, psychic impressions, higher perspectives, deeper truths, the meaning of life, exploring the quantum and astral realms, lucid dreams, shamanic and spiritual powers birthed from frequent dream exploration, and multidimensionality come under the lizard's realm. The lizard is a shapeshifter who can travel dimensions, including the dream worlds, at will. Your planetary ruler is the Moon, symbolizing instincts, the imagination, a powerful link to the subconscious realm, spiritual and psychic powers, and evolved knowledge of sacred and universal laws. You live everyday life connected to your instincts, which stem from higher self-awareness and the invisible ethereal cords of a divine and holographic reality. (You do this even if you're unaware of it!) The lizard enhances all dream, psychic, and visionary abilities. On the one hand, the lizard helps to strengthen and perfect the gifts that are already innate within you. It is an excellent spirit animal to work with from childhood to early-mid adulthood, and beyond if you choose to become a healer, shaman, dream therapist, or similar. On the other hand, the lizard can be called upon when you need to tone down your spiritual and otherworldly divine attributes. The lizard's follies include getting lost in the bigger-picture vision and thus forgetting, or neglecting, the smaller details. Also, distancing yourself from intimate and family bonds in pursuit of a greater soul path, plan, or mission. The lizard may connect you to multidimensional worlds and lucid states, but it can also help to ground you when you get lost there. Establishing a deeper bond with the spiritual and astral/ethereal realms is synergistic with feeling grounded, safe, and secure in your physical body. Your body's a channel for higher consciousness, insightful thought forms, and wisdom to shine through; the lizard allows you to realize that you are in this world but not of it. This means staying grounded and protected within your divine earthly body.

Dog

Loyal, caring, devotional, unconditionally loving, affectionate, and full of sensitivity and deep and honest emotions, the dog is one of your personal protectors in times of needs. The dog teaches you discernment, wisdom, and patience when establishing friendships. In youth, you can be very trusting- some Cancerians don't learn the lesson of gullibility and naivety until later in life. This means you go through life with a sense of naive trust, vulnerability, and gullibility. You lack boundaries and discernment. You're open-hearted, open-minded, and extremely loyal and nurturing. And, you're understanding, giving, generous, and in genuine want and need of love and connection. Put all of this together, and you may already see how detrimental this can be. The world is not all rainbows and sunshine, unfortunately. There are some cold, mean-spirited, and abusive people in this life. The dog helps you to develop both intuition and discernment while protecting yourself with healthy boundaries. This is not asking you to become cold, detached, reserved, and totally cut off from society, quite the opposite. It's asking you to be mindful and selective in who you show and give your love to. The dog truly is man's best friend, so as the *Great Nurturer* and *Caregiver* of the zodiac it's no wonder this is one of your personal spirit animals. Listen to the subtle yet powerful wisdom of the dog. The dog is friendly and open with everyone, also radiating and reflecting joy and positivity to all they mean. Yet they dog equally knows how to guard itself, protecting loved ones, family, and friends from potential threat and danger.

Rabbit

Your personal fertility power animal, the rabbit is ideal for when you want to expand, enhance, and ground creative and artistic gifts. Without rewriting the information already presented, find the rabbit spirit animal symbolism and incorporate it into any self-care or self-development plan you have. Remember that fertility is not just limited to reproductive fertility or creativity; it also refers to the act of giving birth to new conditions, whether they be emotional, psychological, physical, or spiritual.

Power Animals for Protection

Cow

The cow is here to ground you and center your energies when you become a little spacey. Going with the flow, being overly giving and self-sacrificing, and possessing a very dreamy and spiritual nature can often leave you open to the harsh judgements and hateful, or harmful, projections of others. Not everyone has your back, not everyone has your best interests at heart, and some people truly are vindictive, vengeful, and abusive (emotionally, psychologically, or physically… or spiritually in terms of psychic attack). The cow usually pops up on your path when you have given away too much, either too much time, love, emotion, support, protection, energy, money, understanding, compassion, etc. I know it's hard to believe, as it took me nearly 30 years to understand the true meaning of this, but there is such a thing as 'idiot compassion.' Idiot compassion is when you take empathy and compassion too far, and begin to lose self-love and self-care in the name of having unconditional compassion for your abuser or oppressor. It's something very few signs possess, namely only Cancer and Pisces. The cow is a beautiful, noble, dignified, loyal, and loving animal with equal measures of compassion, empathy, and instinctual self-awareness. Yet the cow is one of the main animals tortured and killed globally. There is a message in the cow spirit to be found here.

Turn toward the cow when you need help establishing boundaries and grounding, centering, and aligning your energies. A personal example… There's been many times in life where I've been way too self-sacrificing and giving into a period of solitude, mild depression, and melancholy, sacrificing my joy and basic human needs & desires for other more arrogant, dominant, and abusive characters. The pattern seems to be that I go for a walk and I randomly see a cow! I am then jolted out of my deep sleep (spiritually/energetically speaking) and start to have intense realizations. Something occurs on a subconscious level that tells me I have been giving away my power, and sacrificing my joy, light, love, self-care, and other essential human needs for those I still want to love unconditionally. You can love unconditionally Cancer, but you don't have to sacrifice your boundaries, bank account, or pathways to self-care in the name of idiot compassion. The cow, for example, chooses to stay happy and calm even when they know, on some instinctive level, that there are some darker intentions and motives around them. This meaning should not be taken literally, as, unlike the cow, you have the power to protect yourself from physical danger. However, the cow simultaneously teaches us the true meaning of life, death, cycles of rebirth, and our eternal nature. Find joy and comfort in the present moment. Practice divine simplicity, which is finding peace and contentment in each moment, in the now, so you can live a long and abundant life. Joy, peace, and a commitment to personal well-being- with strong boundaries for self-protection, self-alignment, and prosperous living, are your keys to immortality.

Beetle

The beetle is another little beautiful animal with an immense spirit and life force. As an emotional and somewhat moody water sign who is prone to mood swings and chapters of isolation and reflection, self-care is more important for you than most. The beetle is a master of self-care. The beetle opens portals to connecting to your inner god or goddess, allowing you to heal and find inspiration in self-care, dance, your sensuality, meditation, introspection, art, poetry, music, and daily acts of self-service. The beetle may appear small but they possess mighty spirits! Just like the beetle, you are often overlooked and undervalued. You may feel under-appreciated for your cooking, care, and constant helpfulness; you likely feel unseen for your gifts and talents, due to other people expressing themselves more dominantly, boldly, and aggressively or directly. You could very well feel shy and timid or even fearful to be your authentic true self, because the world (current societal viewpoint) says passivity and gentleness aren't strengths- you should be more forceful, blunt, or competitive. We live in a dualistic world. Passive, receptive, magnetic, feminine, and nurturing 'yin' qualities are just as significant as masculine 'yang' ones.

So, the beetle is here when you need to find your power and inspiration. It further protects you when your weak boundaries pull you into the gossip, drama, manipulations, or false motives of others. If you want to develop a better balance between self-love and being the wonderful loving support system for others, which you naturally are, call on the beetle. Selflessness can be balanced with healthy selfishness, i.e. taking care of your own needs.

Animals You Should Work With for Integration

Based on the qualities you lack, you should work with the following spirit animals to integrate more balance, harmony, and unification of opposite (or dualistic) forces in your life.

Horse

Representing physical vitality, libido, and sexual life force, the horse symbolizes the dual part of your instinctive nature. You are incredibly instinctive and intuitive, but in a spiritual way. It's no secret that you seek emotional bonding and deeper, soulful, connections. The horse also represents instincts, but instinctual responses and self-awareness that are linked to your body and sexuality. You're romantic, deep, sweet, sensitive, and often taken on the role of caretaker. Yet this leaves you feeling disconnected from your more primal needs and sensations, which you do have! Primality is the key message and medicine with the horse. In addition, physical exercise, movement, and energy levels increased by the horse can help you transcend your comfort zones. As the home-body who thrives in safe, comforting, and warm home and domestic environments, adventure and excitement are not your strong points. You choose the creature comforts of home, close friends, and family any day, and you lack the get-up-and-go "high flying" energy others with this spirit animal have, such as Aries and Sagittarius. The horse is perfect for amplifying excitement, zest, and inspiration in a fiery and yang way. Vitality is increased.

To add, diet and lifestyle choices can be improved, because when you have more vitality and enthusiasm to connect with others, explore the world, and transcend your comfort zone, you want to make better well-being choices. All manifestations of health and well-being can be sparked, while health ailments, disorders, and internal imbalances can be overcome.

Coyote, Fox, or Monkey

All of these animals are perfect for when you wish to access your logical, analytical, and intellectual mind. These three animals assist you in developing level-headedness, problem-solving, and intellect and analysis over emotions and instincts. You can't always rely on emotions, psychic impressions, and instincts, Cancer. You have a mental or intellectual/psychological body too. The coyote, fox, and monkey each have unique qualities that will push you to new heights of self-evolution within and around. Consider how you can integrate them for better balance. Working with these power animals are great for accessing less wise past versions of yourself, previous 'you's' that were bewildered as to why certain friendships or relationships ended. Relationship breakdown can be due to a number of reasons, and although there is absolutely nothing wrong with being intuitive, sensitive, and emotional, many people don't resonate with this form of relating or connecting. Call on these three animals for complete self-mastery and integration of polar opposites within. Your relationships, communication style, and confidence levels can improve considerably with regular effort and attention to the neglected parts you've been rejecting.

Chapter 13: Leo

I am Leo, the heart of the Zodiac,
I am strong, fierce, and protective over those that I love.
I am the fire and passion supporting life for creation,
with magnanimity of spirit, benevolence, and good nature.
With a highly expressive essence that can bring joy to others through my light,
I possess supreme confidence, and believe I am always right!
I take pride in my heart, my knowledge, and my intellect-
and the Sun shines through me as I wish to be the best.
Creation and destruction both define my inner nature,
my spirit and inner fire both empower and over-power.
I command the attention of those around,
demanding acknowledgement for the beauty I've found.
My presence and sense of purpose are here for all to see;
I choose action and excitement over inner joy and peace.
Kind, caring, and standing up for those I love,
I am protective and supportive with an ability to lead with heart...
Passionate, confident, and divinely charming,
I am the Zodiac's center, Leo- the Lion.

What's my shadow, do I have any lessons?
I can be demanding, egotistical, bullyish, and overpowering.
I am a drama queen/king who wants to seek the spotlight,
therefore I must learn how to tone it down and give others a chance to shine.

Key Animals: *Your Personal Animal Guides & Spirits*

Horse

An active and instinctive primal animal with lots of vitality, the horse represents your upbeat and optimistic spirit. You crave movement, travel, fun, excitement, and companionship, just like the horse. The horse is one of your best animals to call on when you are physically moving around, going on regular trips or travel breaks, for business and/or pleasure. This animal reminds you of the power of physical instincts and enthusiasm, genuinely being excited for life, your projects, and the connections you keep. Secondly, the horse represents libido, and finding synergy between romantic longings- gentle and sensitive approaches to sex and intimacy, and more impulsive, primal, and electric ones. You have a very strong sex drive Leo. But you're one of the few signs who can embody such dualities in equal measure; romance & female sexuality and pure passion & masculine sexuality. The horse shares these traits. Nurturing, instinctive, loyal, caring, sensual, passionate, fiery, wild, and untamed, there's the perfect blend of feminine and masculine attributes to draw from, which makes you feel comfortable and at peace with your needs. Fantasies can be expressed in a balanced, healthy, and grounded way. Also, sexual wounds and trauma or simply painful sexual memories of a past love or breakup can be overcome with the horse's help. The horse is your go-to for all matters of intimacy, sexual expression and union, and intentions for finding harmony within. For example, if you need to tone down your primal urges and overpowering libido, you would turn to the horse to develop greater sensitivity, caring, and companionable qualities (platonic intimacy and emotional bonding). Simultaneously, if you need to spark libido you could also look toward the horse. Additionally the horse spirit animal helps you come to terms with your personal power and self-authority, which is highly significant for you. Remember to read up on the shadow aspects to overcome associated with the horse.

Crocodile

The crocodile is less valued as a spirit animal, yet it provides some profound insight and medicine. The crocodile assists you in transforming primal and survival focused instincts into higher pathways to connection and intimacy. The crocodile spirit is a bit of an enigma. Some people look at the animal and see an aggressive and dangerous beast who should be feared, without exception. Other people observe a cute and normal animal who is like all other "potentially" dangerous animals, a being who only appears threatening due to its basic needs for security, food, shelter, survival, etc. This is essentially you, dear Leo. Thus, the crocodile is the ultimate symbol for your light and darker attributes, or your positive and negative sides. On the one hand, you can be dominant, aggressive, overpowering, forceful, and somewhat abusive. More passive and self-sacrificing water and earth signs tend to see you as narcissistic or bullyish, at times. There is some truth in this. (Apply yin and yang here for deeper understanding.) On the other hand, you are incredibly courageous, responsible, practical, providing, protective, and caring. You tune into self-authority and other forceful dominant & bold qualities so you can support and take care of yourself and your family. You're a benevolent nurturer who is fiercely protective, but those not in your close circle see you as something different. So, the crocodile is here to show you how to make peace with your polar light and dark attributes, and strive for a healthy balance and harmony. Once you accept your shadow personality traits you begin your journey toward the light, which inevitably leads to wholeness. Work with the crocodile for deeper understanding and integration in these areas, and- remember, although you have some less desirable traits to overcome and transcend there's nothing wrong with having power.

Deer *and* Swan

The deer and swan are two animals that reflect your inner soul and psyche, but they are often overlooked or unseen. As a fire sign, you are dominant, bold, assertive, expressive, willful, and intellectually gifted with many masculine attributes. You like to take the lead, and you're more forceful and active than passive or receptive. However, you are noble and gracious with a pure heart. You're one of the most generous, benevolent, and loyal signs of the zodiac, and these qualities make you possess *soul*. You're much deeper that you may have others think, so your two secret spirit animal helpers are the deer and swan. The deer symbolizes your strong sense of nobility. You have a soft and romantic side, which is usually hidden behind a hard and bold eternal demeanor. Around people you trust, you are warm-hearted, sensitive and protective, nurturing, and supremely kind. You should work with the deer more frequently to tap into your divine feminine attributes and essence, and further let this side of you be seen to the world. In love, business, friendships, romantic or sexual bonds, and family, connect to the spirit of the deer for all expressions and manifestations of inner 'yin' enhancement. Embodying more grace and gentleness will, in turn, allow you to shine in your bold and courageous way with increased confidence, self-esteem, and social charm, because you will have developed greater emotional intelligence. Emotions serve as a binding force in your life, even though you like to think of yourself as primarily intelligent and intellectual.

The swan is a symbol of peace, purity, loyalty, nurturance, compassion, grace, and romantic partnerships. As an energetic and upbeat fire sign who is known for having a flirtatious and somewhat unfaithful nature, at least in youth, the swan is ideal for when you want to settle down and commit. The swan is here to show you the true meaning of romance and faithful companionship- an ideal true love or soulmate bond, with loyalty and longevity as key themes. When swans mate they mate for life! They are the perfect symbol of monogamous true love. So, in addition to peace, social grace and charm, serenity, empathy, and emotional intelligence all being enhanced, the swan also brings the lessons of transcending any player-ish ways- the non-serious fun and frivolities of youth. You have many suitors and admirers, Leo, but work with the swan when you want to dive deep into the realm of emotions and feelings, so you can then match this with a soulmate on your new evolved & mature wavelength.

Coyote

The coyote is the perfect 'divine masculine' or 'masculine energy' spirit animal for you, as the coyote represents the power of laughter. You are naturally an extremely upbeat, positive, and electric person who loves fun, play, connection, companionship, and excitement. The coyote helps to bring these qualities out of you and strengthen them. This spirit animal doesn't always have the smoothest journey- there are many trials and tribulations to experience, and many levels to master. But the coyote's medicine is all about remaining optimistic, even through the hardships and challenging times. Further, the coyote is a powerful animal for self-development work. The coyote teaches you that there is wisdom and divine inspiration to be found in every experience; detours are a natural part of life. Not everything goes your way, and sometimes you must release control in order to receive what is truly meant for you. Your main shadow traits (less desirable attributes) include being controlling, overpowering, and domineering to the point of becoming tyrannical or intolerable. You have a big ego, and you seek control in many ways. Learning to surrender, let go, and release control is integral to the coyote's medicine and healing powers. If you really want to master yourself and attract harmonious, loving, and mutually respectful relationships, work with the coyote spirit. Also, remember that other people know how to 'do their thing' and might have valuable insights, expertise, or experience to share. You aren't always right and you don't always know best… maturity and wisdom come through failures, setbacks, life experience, and being open to the input of others. You can learn greater adaptability.

Monkey

The monkey is your creative and artistic power animal to turn to for all types of personal and professional projects. Creativity, innovation, imagination, passionate self-expression, originality, and artistic gifts; the monkey encompasses it all. The monkey is mischievous and supremely playful, just like you, yet they also know how to channel and direct their energy into innovative solutions. Energetically, the monkey symbolizes evolved and fine-tuned creativity and self-expression. Ingenious ideas can come about with the monkey spirit. Life force, zest, inspiration, energy, enthusiasm, and ambition are all amplified. Luck, good health and fortune, and prosperity achieved through your gifts and talents are also enhanced. In Chinese astrology, the monkey is associated with fame, prestige, and success- 'go big or go home!' So you can learn a key message here. You are the sign of dreaming big, Leo. You believe in success, ambitions, goals, plans, and achievement, therefore the monkey is ideal to work with for all professional and creative ventures. In addition, the monkey will assist you in overcoming your shadow traits; playing practical jokes on others- at their expense, impracticality, irresponsibility, and ungroundedness in the name of fun and play. In your pursuit of pleasure and freedom you might become too light-hearted, so the monkey helps you to honor your commitments and responsibilities/practicalities while tuning in to artistic and imaginative gifts. You can elevate *whilst* grounding simultaneously.

Stag *and* Squirrel

Many people assume Leo is all fire, drama, and excitement, however you have a deeply grounded side. This is why both the stag and squirrel are close spirit animals to call on. You're practical, responsible, and very hard-working. You're ambitious, dependable, and protective over those you love, meaning you work devotedly towards creating material wealth and abundance that can be a support system for others. The stag symbolizes self-leadership, self-autonomy, courage, personal confidence, and trust in your intuition. Feminine yin and masculine yang energies and qualities can be embodied with the stag spirit, so this is a powerful one for you. You can take control, step into noble leadership, and embody greater dignity and self-esteem, while equally embodying evolved sensitivity, empathy, and nurturing instincts. The stag represents both paternal and maternal characteristics. Through grounding and connecting to nurturing and compassionate feminine qualities, you are able to align with qualities of the Higher Self, like inner strength, assertion, and self-leadership. (And vice versa.) Boldness and courage are expanded and amplified through a strong connection to Mother Earth, the physical foundations that support you, and practical recognition. And, you feel more connected to your body and the earth, providing for security and self-protection, the more you connect to your dominant and assertive side. The stag is a well balanced and holistic yin-yang spirit animal that works well with your unique energy signature.

The squirrel symbolizes your ability to gain resources and create a strong foundation and home. You're a natural parent with strong paternal and maternal instincts. You believe in practicalities, responsibilities, and physical structures, and you work very hard to protect, provide, support, love, and nurture. The squirrel is an animal who feels at home in the natural world. This spirit animal can teach you how to create strong and long-term stability and security through divine simplicity. *It's in the little things.* Appreciate all you have, count your blessings, and stay present to see what gifts and windows are around you. Through a deeper bond with Mother Earth, you begin to see the world with fresh eyes, picking up on things you may have missed when in a state of scarcity, lack, or close-mindedness.

Hawk

One of your primary Higher Self animals that connects you to the intellectual, imaginative, and spiritual realms, the hawk represents higher vision and sight. Deep insight, wisdom, and intuitive powers are available with the hawk spirit. Intelligence, seeing the bigger picture, idealism, vision, higher perspectives, imagination, intellec, logic, problem-solving, subtle perception, and powerful instincts birthed from the higher mind are all available with the hawk spirit. The hawk is your gateway to shadow self integration, i.e. exploring your darker attributes and seeking to overcome them by seeking to embody your positive strengths. The hawk helps you to transcend your need to dominate, control, and oppress others. Being cold and calculated can also be eased, merged with emotional intelligence, warmth, and steps taken towards greater sensitivity. Self-awareness linked to your Higher Self increases physical instincts and sensations, which amplify feminine qualities. Aim for self-mastery, but without neglecting close and intimate bonds. The hawk can be used in visualization exercises and when calling on the guidance from your ancestors or spiritual helpers, as the hawk compliments all of your other animals while assisting you in attuning to multiple realms, planes, and dimensions.

Cat

Feline energy is strong in you, Leo! You're one of the few signs to have both the cat and dog as their personal power animals, two animals that are usually presented as an "either-or" in society. *Are you a cat or dog person?!* The cat symbolizes your fierce independence. You're self-sovereign, adventurous, sensual, affectionate, and highly instinctive. You're very intuitive with a deep love of exploration- you crave attention and affection, but equally love to pamper yourself and exist in your own company. This is the essence of the cat. The cat teaches you how to balance your powerful sense of independence & self-autonomy with companionship & healthy attachment. You may fall into extremes at frequent or sporadic chapters of your life. Yet the cat spirit animal asks you to strive for harmony. Otherwise, you risk the habit of pushing people away from you, losing loyal companions, friends, loverss, and family members. You can't demand extreme love and attention in one moment and then be cold and distant with a snobbish attitude the next… Life doesn't work like this. Yes, I know we all love cats regardless of their follies, yet the best cat personalities are the ones who have balanced their need for affection and intimacy with a healthy sense of freedom and independence. Look toward the cat if you want to stop blowing hot and cold, and further find deeper intimacy, union, and harmony in your relationships. In addition, the cat can assist you in connecting to psychic and spiritual powers. Cats are deeply respected by many ancient cultures; the ancient Egyptians saw them as guardians to the after life, and today they are known for their psychic and extrasensory gifts. Work with the cat spirit for spiritual prowess, evolved sensuality, and balance & harmony in all areas of your life. This spirit animal is here to show you self-mastery.

Dog

The dog is completely different to the cat, as the dog needs loyalty, perpetual companionship, friendship, and close bonds. Despite you believing yourself to be Miss or Mr Independent, you can be very needy. You too need lots and lots of affection, attention, and physical touch. You desire intimacy, companionship, and love in large quantities, and you're known for being a drama queen or king when you don't get what you desire. You can pull a temper tantrum or resort to straight out theatrics, vicious but awe-inspiring displays of ego to get the love you crave. Well, the dog similarly barks or whimpers for hours on end when they're not getting the attention from their faithful human friends. The dog is the more codependent yet immensely loyal and protective side of you. While the cat is fiercely independent, the dog represents unconditional love and lifelong commitment. The dog spirit can therefore be connected with, for evolution and embodiment of your softer side, the more gentle and submissive elements to your character. The dog lacks false pride and ego- it is humble, down-to-earth, and modest, qualities you need to increase for the best possible relationships and partnerships. So, the dog can help you ease false pride and develop more trust, faith, and purity in intimate and professional partnerships.

Peacock

This peacock is one of the spirit animals that best compliments your masculine nature. This is because the peacock is all about expression, boldness, and confidence to shine. This spirit animal loves showing off its many beautiful colors, just like you. But it does so with grace, elegance, and class- charm combined with a touch of sophistication. This is the message of the peacock. If you're going to show off your charm and talents, which you should, do it in a way that will be perceived as classy, graceful, or charming, not in any boastful or egocentric way. The peacock is excellent for overcoming your shadow traits; egotistical, bossy, and attention-seeking tendencies. Read up on the peacock spirit animal symbolism to see what else there is to embody, and further what shadow traits you need to overcome.

Giraffe

The giraffe is perfect for when you want to detach from the mundane and tune into your visionary self, seeing the bigger picture. You can be very practical, Leo. You take pride in your ability to provide for your family- you're hard working, responsible, moreover take on a lot of duties. The giraffe represents achievements, accomplishments, and working toward a legacy. This animal is perfect to call on when you need to discover truth, live a path of truth, or attain higher wisdom about a partnership, relationship, or situation. Due to its physical height, the giraffe asks you to look past pettiness in addition to the tribalities of the 3D world. If it doesn't serve your soul mission, life purpose, or Higher Self, don't entertain it! This power animal doesn't have time for things beneath their evolved level of awareness, although they remain graceful and humble. Humility, modesty, and grace are three of the giraffe's greatest qualities, in fact, so work with this spirit animal when you need to balance these noble attributes with self-discipline, inner strength, self-authority, and sheer determination coupled with personal power to succeed.

Power Animals for Protection

Lion

Astrologically, you are a Lion, therefore there is no greater power animal for you than the mighty and majestic lion. Possessing immense inner strength, nobility, self-leadership qualities, and a fiercely protective side, the Lion is here to guide you in every moment of now. The Lion is your saving grace, as this spirit animal is both a strong provider and protector, knowing when to stand its ground and roar to exert power coupled with dominance, and a nurturing gentle giant. Lions love their family, they believe in community, kin, and caring for loved ones. Yet when they need to eat, organize shelter and security, and protect, they're confidence is for all to see. This is essentially your personality wrapped up. You can call on the lion in any life event, hardship, or moment or victory. At home or at work, for domestic issues or career, or in love, friendship, or romance; the lion is your forever faithful friend. This animal is here to teach you the power of loyalty. You can be independent, strong-willed, and moreover a fighter who takes pride in their boldness and strength, while still being a softie and sweetheart to family and lovers. Life doesn't have to be black or white. This was the message the lions and lionesses were trying to teach Scar in *The Lion King*, if you remember. He failed the lesson, letting his pride and ego- combined with his need for revenge- get the better of him, thus he took himself out. It was his follies, aka the lion spirit's shadow traits that led to his destruction. Watch the Lion King trilogy when you need a reminder of your greatness, also learning about the depths of your shadow. Rainforest and jungle sounds (nature healing meditation music) are ideal for when you want to stimulate your inner majestic soul essence, while simultaneously making peace with your less desirable traits.

Eagle

To put it simply, the eagle is your second main power animal. All of the symbolism for the eagle applies to your core personality and strengths, so read up on this spirit animal in detail and familiarize yourself with its qualities.

Animals You Should Work With for Integration

Based on the qualities you lack, you should work with the following spirit animals to integrate more balance, harmony, and unification of opposite (or dualistic) forces in your life.

Turtle

The turtle can help with soul-searching, connecting to the emotional and dreamy feminine waters for answers. Going within, listening to your inner voice, and disconnecting from the outside world are available. As an extroverted sign, you're not one to usually retreat, succumb to long periods of introspection or isolation, or back down from a debate or argument. The turtle is all about retreat, withdrawing into a cocoon of comfort, security, and inner world sensations. It's not as bad as it sounds! Wisdom, learning, personal growth, self-mastery, music or talent acquisition, study, and imaginative and subconscious wisdom can be discovered here. There's a lot of noise in the external world, yet most answers to the meaningful questions- the ones that relate to your life's purpose and greater mission, are within. They can only be found in the silence, contemplation, and sufficient cycles of soul-searching. As a fire sign, this emotional water spirit animal is perfect for yin and yang balance, and further finding wholeness within.

Frog

The frog symbolizes purification and detaching from drama and an overly zealous personality. You're known for being upbeat, positive, and full of life force and excitement, yet this leads to your shadow traits- superficiality, shallowness, and anger. As a fire sign, you can become very temperamental and aggressive, being prone to dramatic displays of ego and out-of-control theatrics. The frog can help you to seek greater clarity and purify your life. The frog assists in purifying your mind, body, and spirit, and your emotions allowing you to embody emotional balance and maturity. Emotional intelligence is the key attribute missing in your life, as it's often hidden way below the surface, below all of the drama, fire, and excitement. When you start to live from a cleaner and purer vibration- a mental, emotional, and physical frequency aligned to integrity, authentic and deeper connections, and spiritual values and morals, you can transform from the 'drama king/queen' stereotype into positive self-expression. Art, music, imagination, play, children, creativity, passion projects, purpose, and soul plan are key themes that run throughout your life. But when you're engaged in drama and ego, you can't align to the higher expressions of "theatrics." Call on the frog when you need some positive alchemy in your life. Ego is not inherently bad- it's only when we use ego for selfish or destructive means that it becomes negative and unhealthy. A positive ego is empowered, productive, conscious, and focused on creation as opposed to destruction, which includes chaos and drama. Thus, attune, transform, align, center, and purify. Cleanse your emotions, mindsets, and belief systems, which in turn positively change your behaviors, speech, and actions. The frog allows you to gain clarity and spiritual & subtle insight and perception so you can live with amplified truth, integrity, and focused wisdom.

You can simultaneously work with the *dove* alongside the frog, and other peace inducing serene animals. The dove is another significant power animal for protection to call on regularly to balance and calm your fire spirit. Greater sensitivity is called for with these spirit animals.

Chapter 14: Virgo

I am Virgo, the Zodiac's Virgin,
I represent purity and perfection in idealistic manifestation.
Practical, grounded, and down-to-earth,
I received my pleasures from the physical world.
Rational, reasonable, and responsible define my nature,
as I believe there is a place for everything- all things can be structured.
Combined with need for an ordered existence,
I am highly creative and love to be of service.
My desire to help others and be supportive to those in need
is one of the things in life that truly brings me peace.
I am sincere, generous, and incredibly helpful,
Practical wisdom is my strength while being of service shows my true nature.
I'm orderly, methodological, hard working, and highly efficient,
yet I also possess emotional intelligence and potent instincts.
Kind and self-aware with an ability to put others' needs before my own,
I am the Zodiac's dutiful Virgo- an earth sign who loves security, routine, & home.

What's my shadow, do I have any lessons?
I am a taskmaster who is cynical and too focused on perfection.
I can be bossy, smug, and critical, further believing I'm always right,
I am too concerned with smaller details, lacking higher vision and spiritual sight.

Key Animals: *Your Personal Animal Guides & Spirits*

Wasp

The wasp teaches you to learn through the hardships and growing pains. As the 'worker bee' of society, you are one of the most hard working, ambitious, and persevering around. You possess impeccable powers of commitment, tenacity, endurance, determination, and discipline, and are seen as dependable and responsible to everyone who knows you. The wasp is your secret little super-spirit animal. Other people might fear the sting, yet you know that a knock-back is the ultimate path to success. You take pride in your work, just like the wasp, yet aren't full of ego. Wasps are extremely humble and modest, even when they're overlooked, underappreciated or feared. Like you, they work daily towards an end result. Their goal is centered around Mother Earth's equilibrium, contributing to the one interconnected living organism or ecosystem known as 'Gaia.' Wasps are mighty and powerful, although small, and this shows your true nature; you are a perfectionist who focuses on the smaller details. You know that details, order, and organization are where it's at- these are the keys to long-term victory and success. You're deeply achievement and accomplishment focused, and you like to live a materially comfortable and abundant life. This means that giving up isn't an option for you, nor is failure, at least not long-term failure. Look towards the wasp spirit when you need a reminder of your core values, how tenacious and hard working you are, and how you can go the distance. Also, call on the wasp spirit when you need help appreciating yourself and all you do. Just because others don't see your efforts, it doesn't mean the divine turns a blind eye. The divine sees everything… You will be rewarded if you stay persistent and keep your intentions pure and true.

Swan

The swan is one of your best spirit animals to work with for peace and love. Romantic, platonic, and family connections all receive the benefit of the swan's medicine in your life. The swan brings the notion of the 'ideal type of fairy tale love.' For others, this may be a problem, but for you it's very helpful; you're already very grounded and always will be. You don't have a problem with being realistic or seeing through logical eyes, so this idealized fairytale vision of love adds to your sense of wonder and romance. It's very good for you. The swan can help you to heal a broken heart, old wounds, and past trauma surrounding sex or intimacy. Swans are monogamous and mate for life, signifying the depths of your loyalty and devotion. You are devotional yet grounded in love- utterly giving, generous, and caring, yet equally practical. These are a great set of attributes, which the swan only strengthens. You can lack empathy and sensitivity at times, and not because you lack these qualities, but because you overthink. You're a big *overthinker*, analyzing feelings and emotions out of existence, and thus become insensitive and emotionally unaware. Deeper romance, intimacy, sensitivity, nurturing, and feminine qualities are good for you. They're already within you, however the swan helps to pull them out of you more. Work with the swan when you need assistance accessing your softer, sweeter, more feminine side, and also for peace. The swan also represents peace and purity, two qualities you instinctively know you love and cherish. You're not one for drama, and the swan is as anti-drama as they come. So connect with the graceful and serene swan when you need to calm your mind, find more tranquility in your inner and outer worlds, and finally embody positive purity. The opposite of a positive expression of purification is striving for unrealistic and unattainable perfection.

Turtle

The turtle symbolizes retreat, going within to find answers, and feeling comfort in solitude. Thankfully, this isn't a problem for your sweet Virgo. You're known for being somewhat introverted, as well as loving reading, writing, studying, engaging in learning and professional goals, and doing your own thing. You're always mastering a new skill or trade or perfecting an old one. You believe in your service, work, and craft, and it shows. The turtle is perfect for when you want to connect to your introspective and solitude loving side for any activity that requires peace and quiet. When you need to detach from the chaos and drama of the world, heal from a job or relationship ending, or move on from a tricky life cycle, the turtle is your faithful friend. The turtle lives both in the sea, symbolic of emotions, and on land, representing your grounded and down-to-earth nature. The turtle can help you get more in touch with your emotions, your inner waters (feelings) without feeling like you're swimming too far afield. You need to stay connected to your body and senses to make sense of things. You like to think both logical and intuitively, rationally and creatively, and linearly and philosophically. The turtle spirit helps you to access the realm of feelings and subtle sensations without becoming disconnected from your center, which is your sense of security, your personal safety blanket of comfort and self-worth. Furthermore, this spirit animal is excellent for awakening artistic and innovative gifts. You can become more original, artistic, and inventive with the turtle spirit, while aligning with your imagination body and vibrant creative life force. The turtle can further help you to overcome depressive or anxious cycles, mood swings, and feelings of melancholy.

Cow

The cow is a sacred animal in many cultures who is here to show you the sacredness of life. The cow essentially represents sacredness, healthy diet and lifestyle choices, and the universal laws of karma or karmic exchange. We enter into karmic exchanges with many people, animals, and entities in this life. Some karmic exchanges we are conscious of, others we aren't. We're all bound by the laws of karma, yet, as an earth sign, you have a deeper connection with Gaia and her energies- even if you're unaware of it. Many Virgos are instinctively aware of their sacred womb (women/females) or their intrinsic connection with Mother Earth generally (both genders). In addition to sacredness and karma, the cow represents fertility. You can learn a lot about yourself, natural cycles, and time cycles through working with the cow spirit. The cow is here to show you the true art of patience and forgiveness. As a deeply helpful and generous feminine sign, you tend to be taken advantage of. You may attract users and takers, or simply be undervalued as well as underappreciated. This is a similar story to the cow. Find solace, comfort, and protection in the cow. Observe how they've mastered the art of 'divine simplicity'- they don't appear to have much, yet they always look content and at peace. Cows in their natural habitat brings a beautiful message of serenity, in addition to finding contentment in simple joys, physical and material comforts, and your own sensuality. Your body is a temple, a divine and sacred vessel. This is the cow's medicine.

Fox

The fox symbolizes your cognitive and mental abilities, your intellectual and somewhat cunning side. You may be an empathic feminine sign (earth), but you have a masculine ruling planet. Mercury, the planet of communication, signifies intellect, higher reasoning, problem-solving, and key perceptive and observation skills. You are incredibly intelligent, Virgo, so much so that many people underestimate you. You can appear silent and reserved, least to mention *modest*. Yet inside your brain is working overtime to create success, gain wisdom, and master your craft or skill. The fox is a silent and swift, yet extremely cunning, witty, and intelligent animal. Everything linked to the mind including logic, higher reasoning, analysis, problem-solving, and finding creative solutions comes under the fox's medicine. They're intuitive creatures too. The fox is therefore the animal to work with and turn towards when you need help with business, intellectual, or monetary matters- anything that requires a sharp mind, in other words. Working with the fox over time will also help you understand the true meaning of discernment in addition to fair play. The fox's shadow is manipulation, deception, and cunning- intentionally 'playing dirty' to get ahead of the game. This is not advised and specifically takes away from your stellar reputation. You're modest, fracious, and extremely kind. People see you as fair, helpful, and sincere, so falling into the shadow traits of both the fox and your ruling planet, Mercury, is a no-go zone. Due to ruling the mind and logical/intellectual realms, there's always a risk of you losing your genuine and warm, compromisable, and fair approach and nature. You may sometimes become cold, emotionally detached, and insensitive- not because you are these things, but because you've shifted focus away from your helpfulness and powerful sense of service towards reasoning and analysis. Stay mindful of this and remember to seek to embody the fox's strengths only.

Mouse

The mouse is a powerful spirit animal for you and one of your best, despite its small size. You are the one zodiac sign that can find considerable strength, wisdom, and prosperity in the details. You're a perfectionist who loves to focus on the smaller details, the practical and mundane things many people overlook. Yet it's the individual pieces that create the whole puzzle. Without paying attention to the apparently insignificant details, you wouldn't be able to see or appreciate the holistic vision. The mouse is modest, determined, hard working, humble, and very private, just like you. It preserves and is incredibly resourceful. It finds its own security, shelter, and food, further finding comfort in family and community. The mouse may not be as courageous as a lion or big as a bear, but it has immense spirit, discipline, and inner strength. As one of your personal spirit animals, the mouse is here to teach you the true meaning of: patience, virtue, hard work, perseverance, self-discipline, devotion, humility, and modesty. These are some of your greatest attributes, all of which can be fine-tuned with the mouse's assistance. Two further messages of the mouse are not letting others bully or suppress you, and finding peace and joy in routine. There's nothing wrong with repeating the tried and tested way if it produces results. This wisdom and medicine is deeply harmonious to your 'Virgin-Maiden' nature, which requires a sense of order, structure, and routine for your best functioning.

Bear

You love to rest and retreat, finding peace and solace in your home, house, and hearth. The bear is the ultimate spirit animal of introspection, retreat, and rest. Taking time for personal contemplation is very important for your nervous system, Virgo. You are prone to stress, worry, and anxieties- you tend to overthink, further stress about things that others see as irrational or even non-existent. You're in your mind a lot, and your ruling planet is Mercury… Nethertheless, this is not healthy and additionally leaves you with a weak nervous system, also affecting other essential systems (your immune system, for example). Your physical, psychological, emotional, and spiritual well-being depends on how well you can relax and unwind. The bear is the perfect animal to help you with this, as the bear simultaneously symbolizes powerful protective instincts. This animal is a significant provider of loved ones with strong nurturing and caring instincts. The bear loves to relax and unwind, yet is also deeply empathic, protective, compassionate, providing, and understanding. You find a wonderful balance and internal synergy of your need to destress combined with your desires to help, protect, and serve. Further, the bear is particularly good to work with during the Autumn and Winter seasons. It can help you come to terms with your own dual nature, assisting you in seeing that you don't always need to be busy. Everything is cyclic. Sometimes you need to chill out, stop busying yourself, and slow down to connect to the source of your inner power, regather your strength and resources, etc. When you take time to disconnect from all of your duties, you refind your passion, sparking purpose for the times you're meant to be motivated. In addition, the bear can open doorways to spiritual growth and healing gifts, if you feel called towards a healing path.

Hawk *and* Crow

These two 'Higher Self' spirit animals are excellent to call on when you need to adopt some bigger picture thinking perspectives. It's no secret that you take pride in your ability to notice, and attend to, the small details. Domesticity, practical affairs, daily errands, chores, business acumen, and having respect for the mundane are where you thrive, however, you must also see with vision. You can use the guided visualization meditation technique presented for *Gemini* with these two spirit birds.

Chameleon

You are a Mutable earth sign, meaning you have a natural resonance with the chameleon spirit. The chameleon represents adaptability, which, in your case, relates to how able you are as a multitasker. As an earth sign, your adaptability is rooted in your hard working, determined, and ambitious nature; the capacity to *get things done*. You can multitask, think of intelligent solutions, and tap into advanced problem-solving powers. You make an excellent organizer, planner, and manager too, so turn to the chameleon spirit animal when you need some extra motivation. Not only does the chameleon bring out your innate strengths, but it also helps you to see through and beyond illusions, coupled with tuning into intuitive, instinctive, and psychic gifts. Extrasensory perception is available with this spirit animal. The chameleon is further perfect for assisting you in overcoming blocks and limitations, specifically self-created restrictions or perceived notions of stagnation. Your mind is a powerful tool! No-one and nothing can hold you back unless you let them. Many of the material or physical restrictions you experience are due to your own making, or a result of self-sabotaging belief systems, mindsets, and behaviors. Working with the chameleon will help you to develop greater self-awareness, intuitive powers of communication, perception, and persuasion, and divine revelations as well as insights. All sorts of blocks on multiple planes and layers can be overcome and transmuted with the chameleon spirit.

Frog

The frog is a special spirit animal guide and helper for you Virgo. Your glyph is the Maiden or Virgin, which symbolizes purity, service, and helpfulness. You're immensely concerned with purity in your life, from cleanliness to creating order, and attaining perfection to making sure every detail is checked and completed. Perfectionism rules your world. And, you're extremely kind, generous, helpful, and concerned with service. The frog represents purity, cleansing, and detoxification. You should work with the frog for all health, beauty, and organization routines. Holistic health can get a boost, while healing your mind, body, and spirit benefit strongly. The frog can help bring order to financial, practical, domestic, work, and daily routine chores and tasks. It can assist in smoothing over any health ailments, in addition to bringing inspiration and courage to the task of taking charge of your spiritual well-being, psychological or emotional health, and material world. Furthermore, the frog spirit assists you in becoming a true self-leader, boss, and excellent manager or organizer without falling into supreme perfectionism. This spirit animal teaches you the difference between purity and perfectionism. You can strive for purity without becoming critical, cynical, or creating unrealistic and unattainable goals! Call on the frog when you need help maintaining or creating order, cleanliness, and a sense of cleansing and alignment in your life. Also, this is a great spirit animal to work with for shadow work and shadow healing integration.

Buffalo

The buffalo represents abundance, an ideal animal for all of your ambitious goals, dreams, and aspirations. The buffalo is your personal sense of self-authority and will. Deeply head-strong and willful, this powerful animal is sometimes seen as sweet, nurturing, and sensitive, and at other times seen as intimidating. It all depends on other people's perspectives, which you have little control over. But, the buffalo can teach you how to *gain control*, achieving self-mastery of your thoughts, emotions, and beliefs, which do affect others and your interactions. This spirit animal is here to show you inner strength, self-control, fine-tune and near-perfected self-discipline, and mindful communication. Communication is a big theme for you when it comes to the buffalo spirit… Fortunately, you are naturally a good communicator- you possess empathy and grace, intelligence, wit, and diplomacy. You're modest and down-to-earth, yet just as self-respecting and strong-willed. So you have many good communication skills that others respond well to. Yet, you do over-think and tend to over worry, therefore the buffalo can help you to find more peace and serenity in your day-to-day dealings. Stress, worry, and anxiety can all be let go of. You can find more comfort in your sensuality, your sensual body, and your senses, instincts and intuition included. Call on the buffalo when you need to increase your monetary flow and abundance.

Power Animals for Protection

Squirrel

The squirrel is a symbol for your resourceful nature. Although small, the squirrel is incredibly resourceful, ambitious, and hard-working; a real provider and protector. They are self-autonomous and self-sufficient, just like you. The squirrel helps to ground you, stabilize you, and help you feel connected to your true nature. Your best qualities come to light with the squirrel spirit animal. You are like the squirrel in many ways; you're a feminine earth sign, feeling a close resonance and affinity with Mother Earth… You focus a lot on the smaller details, and are a perfectionist, which contributes to the bigger picture and holistic vision…. You're self-autonomous, independent, companionable, devoted to a cause, focused, practical, discerning, reasonable, and persevering. Quite simply, your spirit can be seen as synergistic with the squirrel's. You may feel overlooked and undervalued throughout life or for significant periods, yet the squirrel is here to help you find your own worth and value. This means you can focus on the task at hand, gathering resources, and establishing a strong foundation, without falling into the need for external praise and validation. The squirrel is a powerful assistant in helping you realize the true meaning of service; when you're helpful purely for the sake of being helpful and kind, without hidden motive, manipulation, or insincerity, you attract more blessings into your life.

Dog

Loyal, unconditionally loving, and a symbol of purity and hope, the dog is your faithful spirit guide and companion. Like the dog, you are extremely generous, sincere, and genuine in your affections. You're one of the least superficial zodiac signs, moreover when you choose someone as a friend or lover, you tend to be in it for life. Commitment in addition to forming and keeping long-term bonds are some of your greatest strengths. The dog further teaches you the art of discernment, something you already possess- being ruled by analytical and communicative Mercury, yet a skill you need help bringing out. Discernment combined with both logic and powerful instincts allow you to sense who is good for you. Also, what people's intentions are- are their motivations true, rooted in honesty and integrity? Or is there some deception and manipulation occurring deeper below the surface?! The dog spirit helps you perfect your logical, analytical, observational, perceptive, subtle, and intuitive skills and abilities. For you personally, the dog is also excellent for dealing with heartbreak. Generally, the dog is a symbol of loyalty, friendship, and unconditional love, but for you the dog represents something deeper. It helps you to heal from wounds of the past, further reestablish trust in yourself and your choices. If you've made bad decisions in love and romance in the past, the dog will help you mature, yet without losing your sense of trust, joy, and innocence. Dogs are incredibly innocent, least to mention discerning and connected to their gut feelings. These two seemingly opposite traits can be balanced and harmonized…

You can call on the dog in any life events or experience to protect and guide you. The dog heals you on a deep and cellular level, reminding you of the power of purity, faith, and both unconditional love and self-love when navigating relationships. Personal and business relationships get a boost with the dog's assistance. Finally, you may sometimes need help standing your ground and sticking up for yourself. The dog is one of the best animals to work with for these purposes because it provides you with self-assertion and courage, coupled with sensitivity, compassion, and caring.

Animals You Should Work With for Integration

Based on the qualities you lack, you should work with the following spirit animals to integrate more balance, harmony, and unification of opposite (or dualistic) forces in your life.

Lizard

One of the primary power animals for your opposite sign, Pisces, the lizard is ideal for accessing a developed sense of vision, holistic sight, and spiritual perspective. These are areas you can lack, in all honesty. You are so focused on the smaller details, in addition to being a practical perfectionist, that you lose your sense of holistic and spiritual sight. You may excel in the domestic, business, financial, and practical fields, however there are other essential aspects of life wanting your attention (and expression). The lizard symbolizes dreams, spirituality, ancient and astral wisdom, intuition, psychic and extrasensory gifts, and clairvoyance. In astrology, it is taught that our opposite sign is the sign we can learn the most from, in terms of finding balance, harmony, and integration within. What Pisces lacks, you have; what you lack, Pisces has. So, being aware of Pisces' spirit animals is a great healing tool for seeking to embody the characteristics and qualities you may be missing. Spirituality is often the missing link for you. It's in dreams where we find life's deeper meanings. Insight into a relationship can be discovered, as can wisdom and higher guidance relating to your emotional body, psychological forces and influences, and material and physical structures in your life. Waking life is strongly connected to the dreamworlds, something other signs understand on a deep level, yet one you often only comprehend intellectually or mentally. *Feeling* is the missing ingredient when it comes to actively living, experiencing, and participating in dreaming. This isn't because you lack depth, nor is it due to being disconnected from empathy and sensitivity; it's because you over-rationalize and over-analyze. You can "think" your feelings- real world sensations and senses- out of existence, metaphorically speaking. In your pursuit of intellectual power and wisdom, you become separated from your feelings and instincts, qualities that are essential to connecting to the astral, subconscious, and spiritual planes in sleep. Work with the lizard when you want to be more in tune with the subtle, spiritual, and multidimensional planes, as there's a lot of wisdom and knowledge to be found here.

Peacock

The peacock is your second main power animal to work with for integration, and this is because the peacock helps you to *shine*! You're so modest, dear Virgo, yet you have so many hidden talents and gifts. You often stand in the shadow of the extroverted and highly expressive fire signs or the upbeat and charismatic air ones, yet, like your fellow 'feminine' water and earth signs, you are not lacking in these qualities. You choose modesty, humbleness, and passivity over anything loud or attention-seeking. You actually despise spotlight-seeking people, seeing it as a sign of weakness rather than strength. There is duality in everything, which is what the peacock teaches you. The peacock can help you realize it's ok to shine, use your voice, and get a little loud and passionate every once in a while. Overtime, you in reality come to find it necessary, firstly for the sharing and expression of your own talents, and, secondly, to help combat the things you don't like in the world. If it's in someone else's nature to fill the silence, being loud, passionate, and perhaps a little o.t.t or aggressive because no-one else is speaking, how can you expect them to stay silent? When you are too self-sacrificing or humble it makes the naturally fiery people "fill the spaces." By speaking up, being more bold and confident, and developing greater passion leading to self-expression, you naturally balance the scales. In other words, when you "give" yourself, showing yourself to the world, you "take" from the people who always steal the spotlight. This in itself balances the scales and allows for true unity and solidarity in social or community settings. Thus, the peacock is here to show you that you are doing yourself and others a disservice by always being quiet, shy, or reserved.

Also, the **parrot** is a great one for you with similar healing powers to the peacock. You're already ruled by Mercury, the planet of expression and communication, so working with the parrot will only enhance your natural gifs. The parrot assists you in shining through using your voice more, mastering communication style and approach so you can educate, inspire, and connect with others. It can instill confidence, enhanced self-leadership skills, and lightness of spirit, so you don't take yourself or others too seriously. Then, you can stop living in fear as well as excess modesty and reservation. Win-win.

Chapter 14: Libra

I am Libra, the symbol for the Scales,
I am the cosmic justice-bringer who passes judgment with grace.
I represent higher wisdom, equality, fairness, and compromise,
it's true I can be people-pleasing, yet I see with holistic eyes.
My gifts lie in communication, diplomacy, and self-expression,
as I am the one who brings justice through teamwork and synchronization.
Harmony, peace, and unity consciousness are what I breathe;
I can be an adaptable team player or choose to inspire and lead.
I am not just a symbol for fairness and harmony, I am also deeply bright.
I am intuitive, imaginative, analytical, gifted, and kind.
I'm generous, affectionate, romantic, and compassionate,
and I crave both social bonds and solitude- I am very companionable.
Balanced in all ways, one day I might be intellectual and the other gentle & sensual,
for I am both masculine and feminine; the Scales make me practical and spiritual.
I have many gifts in both the psychological and artistic fields,
I am both cerebrally gifted & analytical, sensitive, empathic, and somewhat mystical.
As an air sign with a feminine planetary ruler, Venus, representing love and sexuality,
I am the perfect balance of yin and yang- a symbol of oneness and duality.

What's my shadow, do I have any lessons?
I sometimes think I'm intellectually superior and can be condescending.
I sacrifice my own needs for others, I am overly compromising and a people-pleaser,
superficiality and indecision must be healed so I can become a true leader & teacher.

Key Animals: *Your Personal Animal Guides & Spirits*

Lion

As a masculine air sign, you have natural self-leadership abilities. Yet they need help being brought out, at times, and this is because you are ruled by the most feminine planet; Venus, the Goddess/planet of love, beauty, romance, sensuality, and female sexuality. Venus represents everything pure and selfless, so although air is a masculine element, you do have people-pleasing tendencies you need to overcome. The lion can help greatly with this. The lion is one of the most courageous and bold animals of both the physical and spiritual world. It represents self-leadership, charisma, self-esteem, self-assertion, and self-authority. The lion is both ambitious and playful, loving both duties & responsibilities as well as rest, relaxation, and play. This is therefore the perfect spirit animal to turn toward for balancing and maintaining a healthy work, rest, and play dynamic. You can learn confidence and self-authority with the lion spirit, further becoming aware of how you interact with others, your communication style, and your belief systems about teamwork and leadership. The lion helps you to perfect your sense of self-leadership in addition to how well you play as part of a team. This is important for you, as your shadow traits (follies) include being overly compromisable and people-pleasing, verging on being a pushover. You're nobody's doormat Libra, so as much as being cooperative, fair, and diplomatic is admirable, there's a fine-line between harmony and letting others walk all over you, or push you around. Work with the lion spirit when you want to heal, integrate opposing qualities, and find lasting balance between following and leading. In addition, the lion symbolizes community and family, and you are one of the most social zodiac signs! You love kindred spirit, family, and friendship bonds, further not doing too well health-wise after long bouts of isolation. The lion can assist you when you need to step back into your social circles, coupled with coming out of introspection. Take back your power, courage, and social charm and grace with the lion's assistance.

Deer

You are essentially the deer spirit. You're gentle, compassionate, graceful, charming, diplomatic, and sensitive. You're sweet, nurturing, empathic, attentive, and deeply considerate of others. You're also charismatic and passive simultaneously, something the deer has mastered. The deer is your spirit animal for finding and developing your strengths while overcoming negative personality traits. You can find your light and shadow in and with the deer spirit. Ruled by Venus, you are extremely diplomatic, sensual, and concerned with fairness and equality. You're not pushy or tyrannical at all, although you are self-assertive when at your best. The deer helps you to be seen as the caring, charming, and gracious being that you are. It's an excellent spirit animal to work with for business, family, and love matters, as it enhances all interpersonal relations. Mindful and empathic communication can also be learned and mastered with the deer. Emotional intelligence, clairsentience, self-awareness, feminine values, and sensitivity are further potent characteristics. As for shadow traits to overcome, the deer assists you in transcending supreme innocence. Innocence is a beautiful thing, but not when it leads to diminished or weak boundaries that can result in harm. Also, being overly passive and submissive can be overcome with the deer spirit animal. You can learn to apply your evolved sense of compassion and understanding for others to yourself too, transcending the need to always be the peace-maker or unifier and counselor. Your needs matter, Libra. Self-care is important. Read up on the deer's symbolism, and, remember, the deer is essentially your spirit when in its most healed and integrated vibration.

Swan

Like the deer, the swan represents your gentle and peace-loving nature. A symbol for purity, the swan brings the medicine of purification, cleansing, and serenity- finding peace within yourself and in all outer environments and situations you find yourself in. The swan is graceful and dignified with advanced levels of modesty, integrity, and sensuality. It is not an aggressive or combative animal at all, however it is protective of loved ones. Further, swans mate for life, being the perfect symbol of monogamy as well as true love. All matters of soulmates both platonic and romantic can be healed with the swan. Deep wisdom, understanding, and self-awareness can be found, in addition to genuinely discovering your truth when it comes to matters of the heart. Truth to one is different to another's truth, yet the swan best represents your values in love (and family and business partnerships). You are loyal, committal, and faithful, least to mention very romantic, nurturing, caring, and compromisable. When you give your heart, you mean it. You are not usually one to cheat or be unfaithful, although you can be very flirtatious, which is due to your upbeat and charismatic personality. Yet, you are loyal and your love can stand the tests of time, just like the swan. The swan is a wonderful spirit animal to help you through heartache, heartbreak, or loss, such as the death of a loved one; or the ending of a significant emotional or psychological bond. If you're dealing with any fantasy beliefs around love and partnership the swan can help you get real and grounded, without losing your sense of hope, innocence, and devotion. The swan therefore teaches you grounded yet real (true) love. Inner beauty, sensuality, and psychic and intuitive gifts can also be perfected, fine-tuned, and mastered.

Fox

As a symbol for your intellectual and discerning side, the fox represents all of your mental, psychological, and cerebral gifts. When you need to detach emotionally and be a bit more cold and business-like, the fox is the perfect spirit animal to work with. Keen insight, perceptive and observational skills, intellect, wit, intelligence, and higher reasoning are part of the fox's medicine. This deeply intelligent and intuitive animal is here to show you how to perfect your mental gifts. As an air sign, you are already very wise, logical, and analytical, yet there is no harm taking these abilities to the next level. Logic and higher reasoning can be balanced with intuition; problem-solving can be harmonized with imaginative skills… The fox does not suggest you need to stop being emotionally intelligent or empathic. It solely implies being intuitive combined with having discernment and common sense to know when each is needed. For example, you would be supremely detached and cunning in a family dinner around friends and family. Just as you would be totally trusting, nurturing, and emotionally involved and deep in a work setting where you know your boss is looking to you for intellect and logic; or where there is competition that you need to have your wits about you around. This is a key lesson with the fox. Instincts can also be applied in a grounded and mature way, so you can retain some sensitivity and spiritual awareness without becoming too lost in fantasy, people-pleasing, or sentimentality.

Cow

The cow is one of your personal spirit animals because it is linked to Venus and earthy sensuality; the abundance of the earth. Like the cow, you are modest and humble with a down-to-earth and gentle nature. You're compassionate and sensitive, extremely self-aware too, yet you can go undervalued and even be taken advantage of. There are users & takers and givers & helpers in this world, and, unfortunately, you're someone who tends to be taken advantage of due to your kind and generous nature. People see you as a free ride or support system, or someone who doesn't seem to mind being used from time to time. This is not the case, therefore not addressing this issue leads to resentment over time. In a moment of weakness when it all gets too much, you could explode on one of your closest supporters, for something very trivial and insignificant. Working with the cow spirit animal will help you to address issues of low self-worth, feeling used and taken advantage of, and being underappreciated. Indecision and being a people-pleaser are two of your worst qualities, Libra. The cow symbolism on a deeper level represents karmic cycles. You enter into karmic exchanges continuously, whether you're conscious of it or not. Karma can last as long as a few minutes to decades, it all depends on how quickly and able you are to learn the lesson. *Intention* is everything. The cow is a sentient and compassionate creature despite being murdered, tortured, and used en masse by our species. The cow spirit therefore teaches you how to find forgiveness, strength, and self-love amongst all the chaos and drama, least to mention injustice, in the world. When you make peace with your fate you can find comfort and contentment. Call on the cow when you need help practicing forgiveness, coupled with regarding your strength, boundaries, and self-protection to stop the negative chain of bad karma.

Hawk *and* Raven

Your two *Higher Self* spirit animals, the Hawk and Raven energies blend perfectly with your own. As a cerebral and highly gifted air sign, you have a lot of psychological and mental abilities. You're in tune with your Higher Self, meaning you like to see and perceive from higher perspectives, new philosophies and spiritual ideals included. Read up on these spirit birds for understanding and self-evolution. Use the visualization exercise given to Gemini (*pages 141- 2*) to advance your spiritual self-development practices.

Cat

People overlook you because you can be very reserved and quiet, however you have a strong self-autonomous and independent side. This part of you is often hidden behind a very friendly and warm personality- you have a lot of friends and close companions. The truth is, you're extremely self-reliant and provide and care for yourself, in addition to those you love. You also have potent instincts and psychic gifts, just like the cat. The cat is your secret spirit animal, meaning you can get ahead of the game by embodying the characteristics of the cat without giving away all your secrets. The cat maintains an air of mystery, you see. Your true nature is defined by blending into the crowd or background while possessing powerful ambitions. In other words, you're hard working, determined, and intelligent, but to others you may appear like you're not going anywhere; or like you're content with the mundane, your daily affairs. There's a hidden world you don't share with just anyone. You have powerful emotions, beliefs, and inner sensations, so calling on the cat will help fine-tune your emotions, feelings, and belief systems even more. And, this spirit animal is perfect for developing psychic impressions, intuitive powers, and instincts. You may be introverted while loving introspective activities, yet you're also colorful, charismatic, and adventurous! The cat is perfect for balancing your affectionate, sensitive, and companionable side with your freedom-loving, adventurous, and extroverted one. In fact, the cat is the ultimate introvert-extrovert power animal, a character trait unique to yourself as well. Work with the cat when you want to connect to the spiritual and extrasensory gifts innate within, as well as finding balance between companionship and self-autonomy. This mysterious yet highly self-aware animal will assist you in remembering the mysteries and depth of the universe…

Chameleon

You are one of the most adaptable and open-minded star signs Libra. You're gifted in the realm of multidimensional perception, i.e. being able to see multiple sides of a story, and many different viewpoints. You have a natural psychic and clairvoyant streak, even if it is masked behind logic, intellect, or intelligence. You feel things on a deep level and are further very much in tune with spiritual, instinctive, and imaginative energies and forces. All of this makes the chameleon one of your personal spirit animals. Positively, the chameleon allows you to be flexible, coupled with continuing to stay compromisable, fair, just, open-minded, and attuned to multidimensional awareness. Secondly, the chameleon spirit helps you to transcend over-flexibility, which manifests as sacrificing your own well-being, needs, and self-love in the name of teamwork or harmony. Like the chameleon, you have mastered the art of being a social butterfly, changing colors, mood, and vibe to match the energy required of a group, unity, or collective. But, like the chameleon, you have essential needs too, such as requirements for food, shelter, security, rest, sleep, and so forth. The chameleon is therefore perfect for aligning with your Higher Self and Lower Self simultaneously. This allows you to stay flexible, philosophical, and spiritually insightful without forgetting your physical or emotional needs. Further, this spirit animal increases confidence, self-esteem, and courage to pursue your passions and purpose.

Giraffe

The giraffe portrays your abilities of foresight, higher reasoning, problem-solving, and intelligence. Giraffes are deeply sentient and self-aware creatures. Their long necks and height symbolizes vision, big picture thinking, and idealistic tendencies. You're a strong defender of social truths, justice, and equality, and the giraffe helps you attain your goals with style and charm. They're elegant and graceful creatures, yet they're physically strong with stamina and perseverance too. All of these qualities enable mental, emotional, physical, and spiritual strength and tenacity. The giraffe is the best spirit animal to work with when you're fighting for a cause, studying for an exam or qualification, or working towards some long-term goal. Dreams, aspirations, and ambitions are part of the giraffe's medicine. Intellectual and professional gifts get a boost with this animal, as do spiritual, artistic, and imaginative ones. The giraffe's neck reaches out into the astral and etheric planes, which signifies how you too can extend your mind out to reach different planes of wisdom, self-knowledge, and power. Bravery and devotion are available to you with the giraffe. You can also work with the giraffe when you want to detach from your sensitive, empathic, and intimate nature to rise above and think philosophically or intellectually. You have two core "personality types," Libra, one associated with being ruled by Venus, and the other linked to being a masculine air sign. Like the chameleon, you can be different things to different people, so each of your spirit animals help to bring out a unique dimension of your character.

Peacock

The peacock loves to shine, so this animal can be seen as your alter-ego, of sorts. Yes, you're introverted, introspective, compromising, and gentle. You're sensitive and romantic with a very soft and adaptable side, which can make you slightly shy and passive. But you're also charismatic, innovative, creative, bold, and brilliant, just like the peacock. The peacock is the spirit animal for you for all matters of self-expression. Your extroverted and chatty side comes out with the peacock, while you find your self-esteem and confidence to shine your light, talents, and gifts to attract abundance and opportunities. As one of the signs best representing the entertainment industries, such as the Arts, film, media, acting, speaking, and so forth, you have unique abilities that are often left unseen. Age, experience, and maturity combined with years of practice are what brings you out of your bubble. Read up on the peacock's symbolism and energetic qualities to discover what you need to work on and strengthen.

Rabbit

The rabbit is your second main animal for creativity and self-expression. The rabbit symbolizes a grounded creativity. While the peacock fine-tunes cerebral, imaginative, and upbeat gifts, the rabbit helps you access creative and artistic talents rooted in the emotional, physical, and spiritual planes. The rabbit represents fertility, sensuality, and the abundance of the earth, of Mother Earth, therefore considerable prosperity as well as self-worth can be found. You can learn about nature's cycles with this spirit animal, coupled with understanding- and experiencing first-hand- the true meaning of karmic exchanges and cycles. Overall, the rabbit spirit is excellent to work with and call on for all matters of artistic, creative, educational, intellectual, professional, and imaginative gifts. Projects deeply benefit from the rabbit's intuition, instincts, and empathic sensitivity and self-awareness.

Power Animals for Protection

Parrot

You are essentially the parrot, Libra. You're communicative, cerebral, intelligent, wise, perceptive, and highly bright. You're both analytical and intuitive, logical and creative, and intellectual and imaginative. As the Scales, you're in tune with your left and right brain hemispheres in equal measure, providing for balance, harmony, and unification. You have potent masculine and feminine or yang and yin gifts. Your mind reflects this. The parrot represents communication, color, and creativity- innovation and originality included. Like the parrot, you can use your charm and wit to connect with just about anyone. Also working with the parrot over time will strengthen your powers of persuasion, as well as listening and communication skills. One of the most well-known skills of the parrot is the art of mimicking or copying human and other forms of speech. There is a deeper spiritual meaning in this, least to mention incredible level ups, self-evolution, and self-mastery!

Dove

Like the swan, the dove is a symbol for peace, protection, romance, and enhanced beauty. The dove is your faithful companion to call on when you need to increase sensuality and romance in your life. Empathy, the ability to surrender and go with the flow, divine inspiration, receptivity, gentleness, self-awareness, and compassion are all available with the dove spirit. You can find the true meaning of tranquility and serenity. Dove energy helps you find faith and trust in yourself and the universe when you feel all else is lost, or when you need some hope and optimism. The dove is perfect for you, because you use a lot of mental energy, being very analytical and intellectual, yet also need peace, harmony, and cooperation. Just like the dove, you despise conflict and can therefore call on the dove as your personal spirit guide and protector in any waking life situation. The dove may seem like a simple animal, peace is so underrated in this chaotic and extroverted, patriarchal world, yet the power and presence that comes from choosing peace is an amazing catalyst to many other things. Through choosing peace in every moment, you create a timeline of love, unity, connection, depth, intimacy, understanding, and harmony. Through choosing war or conflict or being too focused on competition, something that is pushed in the Western world, you create, either consciously or unconsciously, a future of chaos, destruction, separation, fear, perpetually projected insecurities and illusions, negativity, and endless drama. In work, love, domestic and family life, and any social or introspective engagement, the dove is perfect for restoring peace so you can find your center, self-alignment, and inner glow.

Animals You Should Work With for Integration

Based on the qualities you lack, you should work with the following spirit animals to integrate more balance, harmony, and unification of opposite (or dualistic) forces in your life.

Crocodile

The crocodile is excellent to work with for integrating your primal self. Although you're extremely emotionally intelligent, you have a tricky time accepting the raw, primal, and darker feelings and emotions. I would never advocate lust as a base vibration to live by, but some shadow traits need to be accepted and integrated in order to not fall into extremes. For example, lust, temporary feelings of jealousy and possessiveness that may come up, and other intense emotions related to sex, intimacy, and companionship. The human experience is filled with a range of emotions and sensations. Denial and rejection lead to such emotions and frequencies being stored in your subconscious mind, which build up and up until they eventually come out in an explosive and destructive manner. Acceptance leads to the *flow* of such darker sensations, allowing them to pass through. By accepting instead of succumbing to self-denial or dismissal, you raise the energy higher so it becomes deeper wisdom and understanding. The crocodile brings the energy of acceptance of your sexuality and primal emotions! They are fierce creatures who are often feared, yet they are just as cute, loving, affectionate, and nurturing. We only see their darker attributes because there is a small chance of them attacking or harming us. As a spirit animal, this is a symbol for how the shadow self can take over, moreover destroy us. The possibility of death with the crocodile spirit links to the metaphor of death and destruction. As a Libra ruled by Venus, you are a lover with a gentle feminine spirit. This signifies you prefer female sexuality as opposed to masculine sexuality; beauty, romance, caring and sensitivity in the bedroom, etc. Work with the crocodile when you need to integrate your masculine attributes in both your sexual needs and style and in the way you assert yourself in relationships.

Monkey

The monkey helps you embrace your cheeky and innovative side, which you have. Actually, this guidance may sound strange to some of you, as you are the most balanced sign. You are one of the three duality star signs, alongside Gemini (the Twins) and Pisces (the Fish). As the Scales, you have a huge array of seemingly opposite qualities to draw from, therefore you may be completely different things to multiple people. I've chosen to focus on your peace-loving and gentle side, as your planetary ruler is Venus, the Goddess of love, romance, pleasure, wealth, luxury, beauty, and sensuality. But, as an air sign, you are also very masculine, also seeking psychological and intellectual connection and stimulation as you now know. The monkey represents your analytical, curious, colorful, inquisitive, philosophical, and playful mind. It's the spirit animal best portraying you at your most bubbly, extroverted, and communicated, living unapologetically and without fear or self-doubt. The monkey can be mischievous, further love playing practical jokes on people, however this animal is deeply social. They symbolize community, creativity, self-expression, play, romance, fertility, originality, and intellectual and logical thinking. If you have found yourself being too emotional, withdrawn, moody, sensitive, or solitude-loving; or if you've currently been in a chapter of isolation and loneliness or soul-searching, working on yourself (self-development, lone wolf energy…) start to work with the monkey spirit. This is an excellent spirit animal to not only call on for all social and community engagements, but to also balance with your 'Emotionally Intelligent' power animals. Finally, if you're someone who is naturally mischievous and perhaps a bit cold and un-empathic as a result, the monkey will assist you in overcoming this toxic personality trait.

Chapter 15: Scorpio

I am Scorpio, the sign with the sting,
I am the one whose magnetism can draw you right in.
I possess an ability to penetrate deep into your soul,
my eyes attract, my glance can heal, and my wisdom helps you grow.
I am highly grounded yet can also access the unseen,
my intuitive and analytical nature allows me to perceive
subtle energy and your hidden vibration;
I am the one who can provide transformation and spiritual transformation.
My energy uplifts, inspires, and empowers,
I am intuitive beyond belief and embody an instinctive sensual power.
Independent, mysterious, and highly attractive,
I am the one others may create as their fantasy.
Highly sexual with great ability to transform-
lust and desire are alchemised into a reality free and pure.
The darkness & the shadow self have been integrated deep within,
aspects of self others may try to repress, I feel free to exist in…
I'm not just psychic and spiritual, I am also highly ambitious and resourceful,
I'm intelligent, observant, perceptive, head-strong, and willful.
My nature is defined by alchemy, rebirth, and evolution,
for I am the Zodiac's penetrative power, Scorpio- the Scorpion.

What's my shadow, do I have any lessons?
I can be manipulative, vindictive, revenge-driven, and super-sensitive.
I need to control my inner waters, as I once ruled by Mars, the God of war.
A moment of weakness can destroy, create chaos, and close important doors.

Key Animals: *Your Personal Animal Guides & Spirits*

Panther

As one of the most intense, deep, and mysterious signs, the panther is surely one of your closest spirit animals. The panther teaches you that it's ok to be your true self, connect to the astral planes, subconscious realm, and spiritual gifts. Not only does the panther teach acceptance, but this beautiful feminine creature helps to strengthen your innate gifts and qualities. You are one of the most mysterious, emotional, and introspective star signs, Scorpio. You love to spend time alone to find yourself, connect to the inner world of light and spirit, and seek deep and profound wisdom. Lucid dreaming, astral projection and travel, shamanic essence alignment, shadow work, self-discovery, soul-evolution, and introspective activities are all areas you see as essential to the human journey. You are a natural at these and immerse yourself in the shamanic, subtle, and inner realms more than most people. The panther symbolizes potent instincts, heightened intuition, and a deep and ancestral connection to these subtle and astral planes. Multidimensionality can be learned and amplified with the panther, as can psychic gifts. As someone who can see through BS, uncovering hidden manipulations, deceptions, and secrets, the panther is perfect to work with for self-healing and spiritual enhancement. For example, you can fine-tune instinctive, psychic, clairvoyant, perceptive, and dream gifts with the panther spirit. Also, call on the panther when you need help with your sexuality. Ruled by Pluto with the ancient ruler Mars makes you the most sexual sign. Pluto is about rebirth, alchemy, and personal transformation- raising energies higher, while Mars is the planet of masculine sexuality, primal impulses, physical vitality, and energy. These attributes can be strengthened and controlled with the crocodile, as we explore next, but the panther helps you soothe these with some sensitivity, grace, gentleness, sensitivity, and sensuality. At the highest vibration, the panther represents divine sensuality as well as feminine sexuality.

Crocodile

The crocodile is a unique animal not everyone understands. Symbolizing a connection to both primality- fierce instincts, physical vitality, and protective qualities, and the realms of emotions and empathy, the crocodile is a great spirit animal to work with. On the one hand, the croc teaches you how to make peace with your combative side. You were once ruled by Mars, after all! There's an innate need to dominate, control, and come out on top; you have immense drive, willpower, and self-assertion, moreover a potent sense of competition. So this assertive verging on the aggressive side can be balanced and harmonized with the crocodile spirit. The secondary meaning is the link this power animal has to the water realm, which is symbolic of feelings, emotions, and sensitivities. In fact, the crocodile is the perfect blend of your ancient and current planetary rulers, Mars and Pluto. While Mars represents competition, lust, masculine sexuality, dominance, force, power, energy, and action, Pluto symbolizes emotional intelligence, depth, spiritual illumination and transformation, soul growth/alchemy, and psychic and instinctive gifts linked to being a sensitive, self-aware, and caring-compassionate individual. If you ever feel conflicted or like your steering too far into one extreme, call on the crocodile. Working with the crocodile can lead to considerable balance, harmony, and integration of polar opposites. It's also an excellent spirit animal to work with for shadow integration work, so read up on the full crocodile symbolism to see what strengths you need to embody, and what you need to overcome.

Horse

Like the horse, you are supremely sexual, Scorpio. You are actually one of the most sexual zodiac signs, and this is because Mars represents masculine sexuality and dominance, while Pluto represents rebirth, alchemy, and spiritual illumination, which involves coming to terms- fully- with your sexuality, physical needs, and desires. As the planet of transformation and spiritual growth, the kundalini and your shadow self are main focuses for you throughout life. Sexual energy begins in the Root, the energy center of physical vitality, instincts, libido, life force, and desires for security, survival, and procreation; and then makes its way up to the Crown, the energy center of spiritual enlightenment, higher consciousness, and extrasensory perception and gifts. All water signs are spiritually evolved. Therefore rebirth and alchemical transformation (Pluto's symbolism) can be equated with awakening your kundalini. The horse symbolizes physical instincts, freedom, movement, travel, energy, vitality, and sexuality. You should work with the horse spirit when you need to come out of your funk- being so deep and sensitive means you may often get lost into emotional heaviness, or even low moods, minor depression, and pessimistic thinking. You can get too comfortable in your solitude, which may lead to self-development on many levels, but also leads to you feeling disconnected from friends, your family, and society. The horse assists you in refinding your creative and primal spark, which can lead to both increased sex drive, a driving force that allows you to reconnect with others, and energy and movement in general. The horse inspires you to connect with like-minded individuals, also seeking out kindred spirit and community bonds. Further, the horse motivates you to travel for work, education, love, new cultural opportunities, and to energize your love of adventure. Working with the horse spirit animal can benefit you on multiple planes…

Turtle

Contradictory to the horse described above, the turtle feeds your need to retreat and self-nurture. As quite a sexually-active and charismatic sign, you go through many periods of being upbeat and energetic, also perhaps pulled into other people's drama from time-to-time. You're inherently social, despite being so introverted and solitude-loving. So, the turtle can help you when you require slowing down, connecting to your soul essence, and getting in tune with your divinity, sensuality, and so forth. The turtle is perfect for connecting to your sensual body, as well as finding and accessing creative and artistic gifts. Linked to the realm of water and emotions, the turtle will fine-tune emotional intelligence, empathy, sensitivity, subconscious wisdom, your connection to the ethereal and astral realms, imaginative abilities, and deep spiritual understanding. Everything connected to the spiritual and astral planes, moreover the subtle dimensions of consciousness where artistic inspiration, creative vision, and powerful intuitive abilities are present, are available for development with the turtle spirit animal. Psychic, instinctive, and intuitive gifts can be perfected. Advanced imagination coupled with potent portals to creativity that leads to higher consciousness can be accessed. If you've been feeling disoriented, pulled into the drama or BS of the 3D world, or have lost your center, the turtle will help you align, recenter, and find solace, comfort, and peace in both your body and your physical environments. The turtle is one of the best spirit animals to work with for all activities that require peace, quiet, introspection, alone time, and enhanced self-awareness and inner stillness for self-mastery. It can also protect you when interacting with others in social environments, because it shields you from negativity while reminding you of the importance of inner calm and serenity, regardless of what's going on around you!

Swan

The swan is another peace and serenity power animal, but the swan adds the extra theme of love and romance. Swans are monogamous, they mate for life. As a Fixed sign, you are extremely pro-commitment. You're loyal, intense in love, honest, romantic, kind, gentle, and very much into being in love. You can be possessive and prone to jealousy- the shadow aspects of being a fixed sign, however you are one of the least likely star signs to be unfaithful. The swan is here when you need to bring out these beautiful qualities, and also strengthen your desires for love, romance, and intimacy. In youth, it can be hard to settle down (although many Scorpios do), but once you reach a certain level of maturity and spiritual wisdom, a lifelong commitment is certainly on the cards. Swans symbolize love, devotion, grace, commitment, purity, beauty, sensuality, sensitivity, and romance. They are graceful, sophisticated, and elegant, just like you when you're at your best. You should call on the swan when you want to overcome lust, temptation, or promiscuous ways. Also, when you feel you want to heal from wounds and pains of the past, instead of giving into your shadow side (resentment, a need for revenge… There's such a thing as the 'Scorpio Sting!'). The swan assists you in healing from heartache, heartbreak, and emotional and sexual wounds. It's tricky for a Scorpio who's been sincerely betrayed to love again, yet this is the key to moving on and finding new love, love that serves your soul. Soulmate bonds, platonic and romantic, can be established and found with the swan's guidance. Work closely with the swan, becoming familiar with all of its symbolism.

Cow

The cow represents your down-to-earth and modest nature, Scorpio. Traditionally, water and earth signs are said to be compatible, there's a natural synergy and harmony that cannot go overlooked. As a highly grounding spirit animal, the cow is the one to turn to when you need to connect to your modest, down-to-earth, and caring nature. Generosity, selflessness, empathy, sincerity, kindness, compassion, and patience can all be learned and integrated with the cow. As a sign of immense sexual power and energy, there's a karmic element to your character. On a higher level, the cow symbolizes karmic cycles, karmic repercussions, and karmic exchange. Thus, the cow can teach you to channel and direct your energy wisely. Conscious communication, sexuality, and expression can be learned, while toxic or shadow behaviors and traits can be released. Consciousness expands through daily acts of kindness, charity, and generosity, moreover living with integrity, humility, and self-awareness. When you expand your consciousness through such things, you naturally want to think, act, be, do, and behave better. This is how you transcend karma. The cow assists you in connecting to your divine essence, your innermost joy and soul spark, without succumbing to selfish or narcissistic tendencies. This is important for you, as you hold a lot of power (whether you're conscious of it or not). All of your feminine qualities are reflected in the cow spirit, so call on the cow when you wish to embody more grace, gentleness, and sensitivity, further finding pathways to ultimate wish fulfillment, as well as prosperity and abundance.

Fox

The fox symbolizes your cunning and intelligent side. You're deeply intelligent, yet you often hide behind a shy, mysterious, or apparently indifferent exterior. You project an aura of mystery, it's like you're dancing away to the beat of your own drum on your own universal tune, that no-one else can hear! This has both its setbacks and advantages. Firstly, people sometimes mistake your silence for a lack of talent, misperceiving you to not have any sustenance. This couldn't be further from the truth… You are in actuality one of the most deep and intense, emotionally vulnerable and open, and soulful signs; your intensity and soul are matched by no other, other than spiritually advanced 'Old Soul' Pisces. You like to blend into the crowd until you speak and act with intention- you only speak when you have something important to say, and you only step out into the light when you want to shine for something worthwhile. You're one of the least attention-seeking and dramatic signs. Secondly, this inherent mystery and shyness allows you to go unnoticed. You possess the power of invisibility, melting into the distance and protecting yourself through the power of your mind. You literally put up an energetic shield that keeps you free from BS, negativity, and other people's dramas and manipulations. Positively, these traits enable you to conserve your energy, focus on your talents, and observe things to a very high level. Like the fox, you are incredibly observant, further possessing fine-tuned skills of perception, analysis, problem-solving, intellect, higher reasoning, cognition, and of course intuition. You can call on the fox when you need to develop your intellectual, intelligent, and logical side, in addition to amplifying psychological gifts linked to both your mind and spiritual body. It's the perfect spirit animal for financial, business, work, practical, and organizational or managerial matters.

Bat

The bat is an ideal power animal to work with for overcoming excessive sexual fantasies and desires- lust, an overactive "inner animal," and overpowering libido. The bat symbolizes rebirth, awakening, and alchemical transformation; moving energy from the lower energy centers and chakras to the higher ones, so this is perfect for awakening kundalini and sexual energy that allows you to transcend and evolve. Self-mastery is certainly on the cards with the bat spirit. One thing you do naturally, which most star signs have a difficult time achieving, is using your sensual and sexual energy & power to achieve higher states of consciousness. Profound intuition, psychic gifts, precognition, incredible foresight and subtle perception- even clairvoyance and telepathy… these come effortlessly to you. The bat's symbolism includes these gifts. So, when you work on raising kundalini, sexual, and primal energy higher, you begin a process of self-evolution coupled with aligning with your Higher Self. The bat helps you to accept your shadow self, sexual needs, desires, and fantasies included, without falling deeply into your shadow. You should work with the bat when you need higher wisdom, in addition to a healthy balance of merging spiritual gifts with needs of your lower self. Further, the bat is here to teach you sensitivity and self-love when it comes to choosing your sexual and romantic partner or partners. As a symbol of deeply evolved empathy, intuition, instincts, universal compassion, unconditional love, psychic and spiritual powers, and all the four clairs (clairsentience, clairvoyance, clairaudience, and claircognizance), you can harmonize intense physical passions of the flesh with more gentle, romantic, and soulful notions towards sex and intimacy. It's not about repression or denial with the bat, but transmutation and transformation, something your sign excels at…

All 'Higher Self'

Read up on the symbolism of the Eagle, Hawk, Raven, Crow, and Beetle. These animals relate to your higher mind, and you possess all of these gifts and abilities! Ancient energy is strong in your unique energy signature, while accessing imaginative, intuitive, problem-solving, cognitive, higher reasoning, psychological, and spiritual-philosophical gifts can be mastered, fine-tuned, and fully integrated. Use the guided visualization meditation given on pages 141- 2 with any of these Higher Self spirit animals. Keep returning to your spiritual self-care practice until you feel the lessons have been learned. Repeat the process.

Cat

Like the cat, you are independent, incredibly instinctive, psychic, intuitive beyond belief, and mysterious. You find solace and comfort in the dark, and feel free to explore the shadow realm in addition to your own shadow attributes. The cat appeals to your mysterious side, also allowing you to amplify your strengths and release your shadow or toxic behaviors. The shadow personality of the cat is falling into extremes; being too independent Vs too solitude-loving, and then spiraling around and around until confusion and internal apathy takes place. The cat therefore helps you to find your center. You should call on the cat spirit when you want to be more affectionate, companionable, and open to love and intimacy, just as you can work with the cat when you feel you've been becoming overly codependent or reliant on unhealthy attachments. Instincts, potent intuition, and trust in yourself and the universe can also be developed. The cat instills a unique type of confidence that assists in overcoming shyness as well as long periods of solitude and introspection, two things common for your yin, feminine, and passive nature. Of all the water signs, you are the least submissive and self-sacrificing (you have ancient ruler Mars to thank for this!), but you are still inherently selfless, magnetic, and receptive, which can close you off from others and society, moreover your social-extroverted self. The cat doesn't have a problem roaming the streets at night! Energetically this symbolizes feeling free in the world around you, a love of adventure, swift movement, travel, self-autonomy, and transcendence of fear. The cat is the ultimate spirit animal to work with for finding perfect harmony between sociability & companionship and solitude & self-development /mastery birthed from introspection,

Buffalo

The buffalo represents your capacity for becoming your own boss, earning big money, receiving abundance, and acquiring lots of sufficient resources in life. As an inspirational and highly grounded spirit animal, the buffalo aligns you with highest potential, as well as your inner self-leader, business wo/man, or ambitious persona. Success, material accomplishments, and professional coupled with personal victory are important to you. You're one of the few signs who are both spiritual and material, you're interested in the non-physical, non-tangible, and invisible realm where soul gifts are present, just as much as you are in the material world of finances, resources, and accumulating things. You have the potential to earn a lot of money in this lifetime, achieve a significant level of prestige or accomplishment, or become a CEO, boss, business owner, or person of fame, recognition, and social status. You exhibit immense personal power and self-authority, you see. You are a natural born leader, despite being so emotional and sensitive, with immense driving force. You possess physical vitality and extraordinary senses of observation and perception, furthermore being extremely passionate, friendly, energetic, upbeat, and optimistic. Many Scorpios choose to live a life of simplicity, such as by living in an ashram or shamanic land community, engaging in selfless service, or volunteering in a monastery or something similar. Yet, many of you choose the opposite route, pursuing money, material wealth, success, and fortune. The buffalo can help you with both. Whatever your path, this power animal reminds you of the importance of integrity, modesty, grace, humility, and possessing strong values, morals, and ethics in your chosen pathway. Vision coupled with idealistic qualities can be developed, while staying grounded and down-to-earth whilst seeing the bigger picture or long-term view can also be achieved. You have a big spirit, yet an equally strong desire for victory in all you do. In fact, you have one of the widest selections of qualities to draw from when it comes to spiritual and material prosperity, and this is due to fiery Mars and watery Pluto. If you need grounding, direction, guidance as to which path or direction to choose, reassurance or confirmation, divine insight, and help either cooling down your need for money or amplifying your ability to attract abundance, the buffalo spirit can help. Everything related to your finances, security, practicalities, responsibilities, duties, domestic life, and business, service, or professional path can get a boost with the buffalo spirit.

Power Animals for Protection

Elephant

The elephant symbolizes your sense of royalty, ancient connection to the earth and sacredness of life, and personal power. Emotional intelligence, deep empathy, compassion, kindness, caring, sensitivity, the ability to perceive spiritual and subtle energy, and powerful instincts, as well as a connection to astral and subconscious wisdom, are all part of the elephant's symbolism. Elephants sense vibrations through the ground, and this is connected to your own psychic and extrasensory nature and gifts. Elephants symbolize matriarchy too, a return to maternal and community values. Well, despite being blessed with strong levels of personal autonomy, power, and authority, and being gifted in the realm of force, courage, and assertion; you are a feminine sign, with water being a feminine quality. The elephant helps to protect you in family, social, and work situations. It can assist you in finding inner serenity and peace, in addition to remembering it's ok to be still, stay in silence for a little while, observe, and respond with grace and kindness. Not everything needs a brash reaction or an intellectual and calculated business approach. Gentleness, compassion, nurturance, empathy, and loyalty define you, just as they do the elephant. So, aim to stay mindful, considerate, and cooperative, least to mention empathic and sensitive to the needs of others as well as your own. The elephant instills inner beauty and grace in any situation, while allowing you to maintain your boundaries and self-respect. Also, if you're looking to become a parent, start to work with the elephant. If you've been feeling disconnected from your body, sensuality, and home or living environment, family, etc., start working with the elephant more. Self-care is intrinsic to the elephant's medicine, as is self-expression, shadow integration, and enhancing spiritual and magentic-feminine gifts. You can find evolution and growth in your artistic, creative, and healing talents & abilities through the increase in sensitivity and intuition the elephant brings… Overall, this is an excellent "all-rounder" that can enhance your life in many magical ways.

Bear *and* Stag

It was difficult to decide between the bear and stag, so I've included them both for you. Both of these power animals are ideal for self-protection and self-mastery. Instead of repeating information already written, read up on the bear and stag spirit animals. Find ways to incorporate their wisdom and energy into waking life, also exploring how you can work with them in your dreams. As the sign of the shaman, you are likely a natural lucid dreamer, or can lucid dream with just a little intention and guidance. Astral projection and travel as well as using your dreams as a gateway to higher consciousness come naturally to you; you're aware that waking life is just half of existence, there are also worlds upon worlds available to explore during sleep. And vast wisdom, insight, and knowledge are available here. The bear specifically is excellent for amplifying dreams and your capacity to draw spiritual and higher wisdom, divine guidance, and inspiration there. As a grounding animal, the stag can also be your soul guide and channel in the dream space, directing your consciousness in a way that serves your Higher Self and psyche. Both animals can be worked with in the dreamspace for multidimensional awareness, as well astral insights, self-evolution, and healing. I would suggest exploring how to enhance your dreams naturally if you're not already aware of how to do so. Here are some starting points: Amethyst and Lapis Lazuli crystals, binaural beats for enhanced sleep or astral projection, special dream herbs (research required, check out Mugwort, Silene Capensis, and Calea Zacatechichi!), and doing a conscious fast, detox, or water cleanse for dream recall and vivid dreams.

In waking life, the bear and stag will both ground you when you feel a little spacey or overly sensitive, helping you to overcome overly mystical, spiritual, or dreamy tendencies. Your spirituality and ability to see from a psychic and mystical perspective are gifts, however there's also the possibility of getting lost in fantasy, addiction, isolation, lone wolf syndrome, or escapism; or simply enjoying your company so much, in addition to the imaginative and artistic gifts that arise there, that you forget to live in the real world too. These two spirit animals protect, ground, and stabilize you, while letting you live from your Higher Self and spiritual body simultaneously.

Animals You Should Work With for Integration

Based on the qualities you lack, you should work with the following spirit animals to integrate more balance, harmony, and unification of opposite (or dualistic) forces in your life.

Chameleon

As a fixed sign, you can be infuriatingly stubborn, Scorpio! You have so many amazing qualities, yet being a fixed sign means you can be possessive, stubborn with your beliefs and mindsets, and set in your ways. This isn't a type of rigid thinking displayed by earth signs Virgo or Capricorn, it's more of a: once you get an idea and believe it's the right thing to do, no-one can change your mind! This is great for projects and collaborations where you all share the same vision, but if you're trying to work in a group or as a part of a team and you're overly self-assured, without being open to the ideas and input of others because 'you know best,' it's not so positive. The chameleon represents adaptability and open-mindedness, so these attributes are perfect for when you need to release control. Your shadow includes being controlling, demanding, and overpowering- you desire a strong grip on lovers and collaborators alike. This has its advantages, but can lead to people being turned off by your dominant "my way or the highway" mindset. Chameleon symbolism also includes sensitivity, clairvoyance, precognition, access to the dream and subconscious realms, subtle perception, spiritual powers, and higher wisdom and self-awareness. Call on the chameleon spirit animal when you need to release the need to always be in control, or during a creative or business venture of collaboration that requires a sense of harmony, partnership, and unity. This power animal can equally introduce more flexibility into your life, in multiple areas.

Parrot

The parrot is perfect for working on your communication skills. Despite all of your strengths, you can be indirect and passive, also believing everyone can read your mind. Because you are so psychic and intuitive with highly evolved empathy, you often assume everyone else knows what you're thinking, feeling, and in need of. But this isn't the case- these powerful extrasensory and spiritual abilities belong primarily to the water signs, so unless you're dealing with someone with a lot of water in their natal chart, you unconsciously create a lot of ambiguity and confusion around you. Pluto has its own level of illusion, which influences the way you think, perceive, act, behave, and form emotional responses as well as belief systems. The parrot can help you with confidence, clear, and direct, moreover colorful communication. For someone with such potent life force and power, you can be surprisingly shy, overly modest, and reserved, quite literally blending into the background to the point of being perceived as a ghost or spirit! Parrot medicine rectifies this. Observe how parrots stand, sit, and communicate. Watch their body language while perceiving their fascinating colors. Take note of the fact that although they are small compared to us humans, they still possess remarkable self-esteem. They're charismatic, confident, charming, chatty, and full of zest and inspiration! Aspire to be like a parrot, as both emotional intelligence and mental abilities can be increased, integrated, and perfected.

Chapter 16: Sagittarius

I am Sagittarius, the the bold and fiery Archer,
I represent a need for independence, excitement, and adventure.
I don't like to be restricted, I need action and movement,
I am wise, majestic, philosophical, intelligent, and groovy.
I am a real catch- fiery and electric with many creative gifts;
Music, acting, innovation, teaching, or the Arts,
I go after what I want with passion, optimism, and creative life force.
I do lack sensitivity and depth, but this doesn't make me soulless,
I am capable of real empathy, caring, and loyalty.
It's true I like my freedom, I can be polyamorous and a free spirit in youth,
yet I am always committed to honesty and a higher timeless truth.
As the Archer, I embody a strong sense of reaching for the stars…
I am a lover of community, culture, artistic expression, and traveling wide and far.
I enjoy expanding my horizons while always being open to sharing my knowledge.
I do, however, need to learn to be less blunt and self-righteous.
Also replacing lust and other primal desires
with more tantric approaches to love and intimacy, an evolution of toxic behaviors.
But, I am bold, independent, fearless, intuitive, and imaginative,
I possess confidence, charisma, potent life force, and visionary insight.
My laugh is infectious too, I am one of the most positive and upbeat signs of all,
for I am Sagittarius, a natural born leader and idealist who rises from every fall.

What's my shadow, do I have any lessons?
I am very impatient, blunt, and arrogant, also prone to lust and impulsion.
I often let my desires and primal urges rule me, giving into the lower self;
Aggression, selfish & reckless behavior, frivolity, and a lack of commitment get in
the way of my strengths.

Key Animals: *Your Personal Animal Guides & Spirits*

Lion

As a creative visionary with impeccable courage and bravery, you are a natural born leader, just like the lion. The lion spirit is strong within you because you know how to command attention. You're bold, direct, assertive, extroverted, and inherently masculine, and you aren't afraid to use your voice or shine. In fact, you seek the spotlight, more than a lot of people, which makes you have a strong affinity with this courageous and noble beast. You are righteous and blunt, the positive side of these character traits meaning that you stand for truth, justice, and morals. You are fearless in sharing your wisdom, talents, and light, coupled with having a strong personal presence and power. Like the lion, you are very creative and tend to be a leader rather than a follower in your social, work, and friendship groups. The lion stands for personal truth, brotherhood, community, family, and having a healthy ego and pride. You are a big believer in kindred spirit, also loving companionships and many social bonds. You further enjoy conversing with people from all walks of life- you're one of the most sociable signs, in addition to not holding back; you're certainly not shy or reserved! Ruled by Jupiter, the planet of higher learning, wisdom, philosophy, spiritual ideals, and truth-seeking, the lion is the perfect animal to turn to when you need to increase your natural strengths and innate gifts. The lion spirit can help you truly break free of the status quo, allowing you to realize that conforming doesn't help you or the people you're trying to inspire and educate. People benefit from your strength and commitment to truth and higher laws, Sagittarius, so call on the lion when you need to amplify your sense of bravery, devotion, and confidence to new levels.

Monkey

The monkey represents your evolved level of wit and humor. Everyone who knows you is fully aware that you're extremely witty. You lighten up a room with your infectious optimism and love of life. You love to laugh, and further help others laugh as well as lighten up. Your laughter is the perfect medicine for a lot of things in life. The monkey's wisdom has a dual teaching. Firstly, the monkey assists you in finding comfort, pleasure, and solace in this unique gift of yours- it's a rare skill. There's nothing wrong with wanting to pull others out of a low mood, supersensitivity, or hyper-emotionalism, so the monkey spirit is here to help you embrace this ability of yours. Secondly, the monkey equally teaches you how to not abuse your power. The shadow side of the monkey is using wit and humor to play practical jokes on others, embody a trickster type of energy, or simply be mean. It no longer becomes a joke when kindness disappears. You can learn the true art of laughter, wit, and humor through the monkey without falling into negativity, mean-spiritedness, or abusing your social presence and power. The additional message of the monkey is higher mental abilities, including intelligence, innovation, inventiveness, originality, and problem-solving. You're deeply wise and philosophical, least to mention both logical and intuitive. The monkey spirit animal helps to strengthen higher mental reasoning, cognitive powers, analytical and rational thinking, intuitive gifts, and creative vision, innovation, and inspiration. It's the perfect power animal for you for all creative, intellectual, and innovative pursuits.

Elephant

The elephant symbolizes your royal blood and DNA. Now don't let this go to your head Sag, your shadow side does include being self-righteous and arrogant! Yet, you are a very royal person, due to being ruled by Jupiter. In addition to philosophy and higher learning, Jupiter represents expansion, luck, and social justice- high morals and ethics too. Some of your core qualities include dignity, nobility, and standing up for truth, wisdom, higher values, etc. The elephant is a symbol for royalty and ancient wisdom. They are compassionate, sensitive, self-aware, empathic, and loyal creatures, qualities you can learn from and work towards integrating. Elephants are further a symbol of matriarchy; the females tend to raise the young as a large family or community. As a masculine sign, you can learn a lot from this feminine animal. You can integrate the qualities you lack, such as sensitivity, empathy, depth, and potent instincts rooted in compassion, loyalty, and companionship. It's not that you're not loyal or companionable, it's just that you tend to be flighty, frivolous, and incredibly flirty. You start relationships and projects that you, quite simply, "ditch," either due to forgetfulness or restlessness or carelessness. I myself know many amazing Sagittariuses who have wandered off somewhere else cutting the connection without second thought. This is the curse and blessing of having such an active and brilliant mind, coupled with immense creative life force! The elephant is a powerful grounder and stabilizing presence in your life. Community, family, and longevity values can be learned, while you can master the art of patience, slowing down, moreover returning to your roots.

Bear

The bear is a symbol of dreamtime, rest, introspection, and the Healing Arts. Sagittarius is the sign of the Archer, the adventurous wanderer who shoots his arrow towards the stars... You're on a lifelong journey of knowledge, wisdom, and philosophical and spiritual values and ideals. But you also represent the seer, sage, and spiritual teacher. At a higher vibration, usually later in life after the trials and tribulations of youth, many Sagittariuses go on to become teachers, wayshowers, sages, or religious or spiritual leaders. Well, the bear represents the Healing Arts, i.e. stepping into positions of self-leadership combined with mastering quantum and spiritual levels of wisdom, self-evolution, and self-knowledge. Choosing a shamanic path could be part of your destiny, and even if it's not you'd be wise to work with the bear to help you embody the things you lack. Connecting to the dream worlds, introspective contemplative realms, and transcendental meditative states are essential for your well-being. Work with the bear spirit to connect to your inner sage and seer, in addition to finding hidden powers, dormant soul gifts, and paternal and maternal instincts. Bears are fierce protectors of loved ones. Take care of your psychological, emotional, spiritual, and physical health by slowing down and engaging in pure rest and relaxation. Study a healing or ancient craft or subject too with the bear's assistance.

Bat

As the spirit animal of rebirth, the bat is here to help you control and gain some form of self-mastery over your sexual urges. You are one of the most impulsive and lusty zodiac signs, so much so that your whole life is ruled by passion. You have a powerful libido, a strong sexual drive, and lots of sexual fantasies, needs, and desires. Your glyph (astrological symbol) is the

Centaur in addition to the Archer- the Centaur is half man and half animal, specifically horse. The horse represents sexual power, libido, and passion! As an instinctive and high in life force fire sign, you need to learn to control your sexual urges. *Tame the wild beast*. The bat is very self-mastered and has unique psychic as well as extrasensory gifts. Instead of focusing on physical wants and earthly sensations, it is tuned into a different world and frequency altogether. Read up on the bat symbolism to discover how you can achieve self-mastery, sexual self-sovereignty, and transcendence. Remember there are many realms and planes. Mastering your emotional and spiritual bodies can open new doors for you, ones that cannot be reached through giving into temptation and pleasure…

Crow

You can be a realist, which is due to your intellectual and intelligent nature. You certainly don't lack holistic vision or intuition, but you are more realistic, rational, and logical than anything super-spacey, spiritual, or mystical. The crow helps you tap into your divination powers, the mysteries and magic of the universe, and the supernatural. The crow can assist you in understanding the true meaning of divination, how everything is interconnected, and how reality itself is an illusion. Fantasy can serve a purpose, while living with soul in addition to some openness to mysticism- the mystical reality that is very real- creates internal shifts of mindset and conscious awareness that can benefit you in many wonderful ways. The crow also teaches the true meaning of sacredness, how all life is sacred. As a masculine fire sign, one of your innate follies (shadow traits) is selfishness, something that can often manifest as using visionary or prophetic gifts for personal gain. The crow is here to help you connect to your divinity, intuition, and extrasensory powers, without becoming egotistical, tyrannical, or self-serving. There's nothing wrong with wanting to live an extraordinary life, create abundance, find personal power and authority, etc., yet to do so for solely selfish or manipulative motivations reaps bad karma. It also prevents growth and causes stagnation and blocks in the long run. Turn towards the crow spirit when you want more divination and mysticism in your life, however *with* purity coupled with good intentions.

Eagle

The eagle is the perfect animal for when you want to disconnect from the mundane while connecting to the bigger picture. The eagle helps you to rise above the smaller details, details and trivialities that can often keep us stuck in pettiness, shame, envy, separation, and fear, and tune into the holistic picture. The eagle is all about vision, yet you are a natural visionary and idealist. So the eagle helps to bring out and perfect what is already within you. Connected to both the realms of imagination & psychic gifts and logic & reason, this bird is ideal for all creative, intellectual, professional, spiritual, and educational pathways. This is an excellent spirit animal to work closely with when you feel yourself succumbing to self-righteousness, fanaticism, or believing yourself to be superior. Superiority can be eased and healed with wisdom, self-awareness, and compassion for self and others. The eagle is your Higher Self power animal, therefore familiarize yourself with the symbolism and integrate it into daily life. Although a universal spirit animal, the eagle compliments the Owl perfectly, and they can be used in unison with each other; the Owl is the feminine aspect or the eagle's dual counterpart (with the eagle representing a predominantly masculine energy). Use both the eagle and owl together in meditation and visualization exercises to balance, harmonize, and integrate your yin and yang energies.

Beetle

The beetle is an overlooked animal that holds great power. Carrying a sage-like and ancient wisdom, you are one of the signs capable of telepathy. You may not access it in everyday life, but the gift is there. The beetle helps to pull out and fine-tune your psychic, telepathic, clairvoyant, clairsentient, instinctive, and intuitive powers. It's important to have some "deep" friends in life. These are the soul companions, lovers, and kindred spirits who remind you- regularly- of your spiritual essence. The chances are you have many friends who you keep things light with- the more superficial acquaintances, and the ones who feed your materialistic values. Yet keeping a chosen few super-spiritual friends closeby is just as significant. These are the ones who remind you of the magic and mystery of life; how phenomena like telekinesis and mind-reading are possible- you know the ones. Every Sagittarius needs a Scorpio or Pisces in their lives, for example. The beetle, like the water signs, is very deep, sensitive, empathic, evolved spiritually, and multitalented. Further, the beetle teaches you how to be humble, how there is considerable power in modesty and humility. This small but mighty spirit animal is at one with Mother Earth, Gaia, and the primordial spirit that flows through all living things. The beetle's medicine includes showing you interconnectedness, sacredness, and oneness. And, this spirit animal is amazing for rising above the drama and gossip of the world, something you unconsciously get lost in from time to time. Being superficial, aka always positive and upbeat, has its setbacks; it can make you lack depth and insight, for one. The majestic yet small beetle enables you to see through illusions, manipulations, and gossip or negativity to get to the root of truth, where we are all one, sacred, with a shared heartbeat. Practicing this knowledge and putting it into action simultaneously steers you towards becoming a teacher, or wayshower, for others.

Chameleon

As a Mutable sign, you must have the chameleon as part of your personal spirit animal ensemble. As a natural visionary and idealist with highly evolved intuition, imagination, and creative life force, the chameleon helps you to fine-tune any project you're immersed in. You have the 'midas touch,' and the chameleon spirit will help to strengthen this. All expressions of artistry, creativity, and so forth can get a boost and upgrade with the chameleon's assistance. Also, the chameleon helps you in becoming more sensitive, tuning into clairvoyant, clairsentient, empathic, nurturing, feminine, and magnetic gifts. The ability to surrender and go with the flow too. Despite being so adaptable, you are a fire sign- masculine by nature and therefore prone to controlling, dominating, and overly forceful tendencies. You can be arrogant and aggressive (your shadow), therefore the chameleon helps you to cool down, be more gentle and graceful, and generally embody a more feminine touch. This spirit animal's link to multidimensionality connects you to the subtle and spiritual worlds, in addition to the astral and subconscious planes. There are many dimensions and realms existing simultaneously; work with the chameleon for soul alignment, integration, and harmonization of polar opposites. Amplifying instinctive and clairvoyant gifts will also help you greatly when it comes to artistic, creative, and imaginative projects and self-expression! You can get the best of all worlds with the chameleon spirit, so stay open-minded and remember that sensitivity is not a weakness. It can serve as your saving grace in personal and professional situations.

Lizard

The lizard helps you see into your dreams, access visionary gifts, gain insight into the astral and subconscious planes, and fine-tune intuition. With your planetary ruler Jupiter, you are always seeking higher things. You love new cultures, community, learning, seeking pathways of higher wisdom and truth, exploring new philosophies, and connecting to spiritual ideals and ideologies. You reach for the stars and are deeply intuitive. Jupiter's energy and symbolism is reflected in the lizard spirit animal, just in the dreamspace. You can be very intellectual- a realist too, yet there is much more to life and yourself than what can only be seen and understood in the material realm. The lizard allows you to transcend, rise above, and break through illusions, in addition to going directly to the Source. It's in dreams where our deepest and most important desires are found. If you've gone through a chapter of restlessness, boredom, and a lack of direction, further not being sure what your path is, call on the lizard. This is an excellent spirit animal for sparking your Higher Self in a way that expands vision; creative, musical, and artistic abilities and projects can get a boost. In addition, working with the lizard spirit over time increases your susceptibility to conscious criticism, something you need to work on to ease your less desirable traits. You can be incredibly blunt, arrogant, quick to anger, and self-righteous, always believing yourself to be right and know best. This means that even a slight bit of criticism, even if it's constructive and mindful or sincere, i.e. rooted in loving kindness, may bring out your worst side. The multidimensional, spiritual, and transcendental nature of the lizard assists you in recognizing our interconnectedness. In other words, some people have pure intentions. Some people are wise, they do have wise counsel or expert advice to give. You can develop greater trust in humanity, your spirit, and the universe through the lizard's medicine. It is advised that you do so.

Rabbit

Creativity, fertility, and abundance of the earth come into the rabbit's healing powers. Inner beauty can further lead to out of beauty, glow, and attraction- a soul shine that is only possibly through the development of non-physical qualities. For example, kindness, gentleness, grace, compassion, sensitivity, generosity, empathy, tolerance, and patience are available for embodiment with the rabbit spirit. The rabbit represents your most fertile and abundant least to mention creative and artistic nature. This is the spirit animal to work with for any and all creative ventures, so read up on the rabbit's symbolism for deeper understanding and self-discovery. Stay open-minded, taking into consideration that there are multiple energies, personalities, and strengths to embody. Just because something may not be "your way" doesn't mean it won't work for you, or lead to your greatest abundance.

Power Animals for Protection

Horse

Your astrological is the Centaur (alongside the Archer). This makes the horse one of the spirit animals you find most resonance with. You share a real affinity with the horse, because the Centaur is quite literally half man and half horse. Physical instincts, potent life force and vitality, stamina, inner strength, evolved libido, and a powerful and somewhat uncontrollable sex drive are traits shared by both you and the horse. The horse is your secret power animal of protection that can guide and shield you in any situation. In addition to sexuality, the horse represents nobility, grace, and elegance, moreover a majestic vibe. Your inner 'high class' philosopher, teacher, and wise wo/man comes alive when you embody the horse spirit, and the horse loves freedom, movement, and travel. Calling on the horse in any social situation or when you're not sure which path to take fills you with optimism, inspiration, and zest, further enabling you to tune into your higher mind- the Higher Self- for the best communication, choices, and expressions. Working with this spirit animal daily makes you feel comfortable in your sexuality and other strengths, like your infectious laughter, ability to stay positive in any situation, your wise if not somewhat self-righteous and intellectually superior persona, and blunt but direct communication style.

Shamanism and other spiritual healing modalities teach that all aspects of self must be integrated for wholeness, and this includes your light/positive attributes and your shadow/negative ones. For example, you can be wise and intuitive while seeping through a bit of arrogance and superiority. You can shine your light in a way that uplifts and inspires others, or teaches them, while coming across as a little superficial. We all have a light and a darkness. As you embody the horse spirit, you crave freedom, movement, and physical and sexual intimacy so much that you can show your shadow traits in public, quite often. Fortunately, the wisdom in this book provides you with the guidance to navigate our shadow self, integrate its lessons, and then come out fully into the light; your best self. Make the horse one of your top "go to's" for future self alignment.

Giraffe

Sweet, cute, dignified, graceful, and highly intuitive and instinctive, the giraffe is a less explored spirit animal nowadays, and I'm personally not sure why. Giraffe's are beautiful with a strong connection to ancient energy and wisdom, they're one of the few animals around today that resemble prehistoric animals who have now become extinct. Their long necks coupled with their height symbolize the ability to see into the future, so precognitive and psychic powers are available when you work with the giraffe spirit for long enough. The giraffe represents extrasensory, clairsentient, clairaudient, clairvoyance, spiritual, and telepathic powers. As a majestic sign in addition to being the sign of the spiritual teacher, guide, and mentor, you are capable of advanced spiritual gifts. Being so brilliantly minded combined with having such strong intuition, as well as being quite a soulful person, allows you to access divine abilities that's usually only possible for the water signs- the people of this world who have a direct link to the subconscious, ethereal waters of divinity, and astral and spiritual planes. The giraffe can help you reach these new heights within and around, connecting you to the Great Spirit and the powers that arise there. This power animal is perfect to work with for healing, spiritual self-development, family and domestic issues, work, career, finances, professional expansion and advancement, and cultural and learning activities and pursuits. Metaphysical wisdom can be acquired and expanded through the giraffe's medicine. Further, if you've been working towards becoming a master of expert in your profession, service, or trade, the giraffe will help you reach sage-like, elder, or teacher and wayshower level. The highest vibration of Sagittarius is taking their life experiences, wisdom, and qualifications and grounding them into a focused service. Start to work with the giraffe when you feel ready to take the leap, moving from student or beginner to advanced level.

Animals You Should Work With for Integration

Based on the qualities you lack, you should work with the following spirit animals to integrate more balance, harmony, and unification of opposite (or dualistic) forces in your life.

Dog

You've got all the tools within you to be an amazing friend, lover, and parent (if you should choose to be one). Yet one area that needs serious improvement is your lack of staying power coupled with commitment, Sag. Again, you are one of the most frivolous, reckless, and flighty zodiac signs, meaning you can get up and go without a moment's notice. You neglect relationships- platonic, business, and romantic, and start connections that you suddenly get bored of. This detrimental pattern runs somewhere into your late twenties to early thirties, and even into later years in some non-committal Sagittariuses. The dog is a symbol of ultimate loyalty, friendship, and companionship. The dog symbolizes unconditional love, standing the tests of time (in love and friendship), and choosing to stay committed over flying away without a moment's notice. Everyone has a shadow, but your shadow traits often overpower your strengths, which can ruin your reputation (quite literally) or ruin life long friendships, family bonds, or an important soulmate or love connection you've been working on. Restlessness, recklessness, carelessness, and frivolity can be healed with the dog spirit. Everything the dog stands for is what you lack, when at your worst; or when younger and immature. The dog shouldn't be seen as codependent, but as a symbol of love, loyalty, and devotion. What's wrong with long-term alliances? Call on the dog when you need help realizing that life isn't all about adventures, hot and heated love affairs and flings (that are shortly forgotten), and excitement that makes you impulsive, irresponsible, and absent-minded. I.e. living without mindfulness… By all means, chase your passions- follow your heart! Just remember the impotence of close bonds and intimate relationships. Intimacy requires growth, a level of commitment, patience, conscious communication, mindfulness, and a bit of hard work and effort.

Emotionally Intelligent Spirit Animals

All of the animals from 'Emotionally Intelligent' spirit animals are advised to read up on and work with regularly.

The **Stag** is another one you can work with to develop enhanced self-authority and responsibility. The stag is ideal for when you're at the stage of life called 'maturity.' I know, despite all of your wonderful traits, you truly are one of the most irresponsible and impractical, least to mention impulsive and immature. You really need to work on your communication abilities, as well as your capacity to form- and keep- lasting bonds, partnerships, and connections. A connection can be formed by anyone, it's not that difficult. But a connection that leads to something more than a brief moment of chemistry, conversation, or laughter requires effort, time, and energy. Whether you're thinking about love or business and your long-term visions- your dreams, goals, and aspirations; you are a natural visionary, after all… Begin a process of spiritual and emotional maturity. The stag grounds, stabilizes, and brings security. This spirit animal is here to help you develop financial self-autonomy, emotional intelligence, maturity, wisdom, and developed practical awareness. It's important that you do recognize your shadow traits, Sag. *I know*, you're the jovial and upbeat one who is alway optimistic and makes others smile…

This may be true, however you also have some less desirable attributes that are masked by this "constant positivity." You can be superficial, overly blunt, and incredibly, infuriatingly, self-righteous, so much so that you often overlook real talent, knowledge, and soul glow or spark in others. Not only does this make you miss out on significant opportunities, but it also manifests as a lack of direction, motivation, and ambition, moreover a real inability to focus and commit to a person, path, or project. Do you want to be an aimlessly wandering joker or clown of the group, forever? If not, you should certainly take your spiritual and self-development journey seriously. The stag is your faithful companion who will help you transcend the games and frivolities of youth.

Chapter 17: Capricorn

I am Capricorn, the headstrong and willful Goat, ruled by Saturn,
I am ambitious, discerning, tenacious, practical, and determined.
Intellect and logic are some of my greatest gifts,
yet I am equally down-to-earth, caring, and modest.
I am an excellent problem-solver with real skills in organization,
in creating order, structures, and impeccable foundations.
With the tough-love teacher Saturn as my primary influence,
I excel in life lessons learned through self-evolution, authority, and gained wisdom.
People know I command respect, authority, and evolved power-
I share wise counsel coupled with logic, reason, and emotional banter.
I am very serious and level-headed, yet also have dry wit and humor,
My life goal is to become an expert and teacher, transcending my inner student.
I am a boss with impeccable managerial skills, you see,
I am happy to be a teamplayer but prefer to guide and lead.
One thing I do need to improve, however, is to not be so cold and callous,
I must learn to be more emotionally vulnerable; not solely ambitious.
As an earth sign, I have a very sensitive and deep side, so this need to shine through-
only then will I be the whole package, the real and complete deal to you.
For I am sweet, caring, nurturing, sensitive, extremely generous, and compassionate.
I love to provide and support- I'm protective and magnetic!
I'm wise, hubble, down-to-earth, intellectually gifted, and giving
with a genuine and helpful nature, moreover kindness that's mesmerizing…
As the natural boss who knows how to create considerable abundance & prosperity,
I am a true friend and family wo/man who thrives in both society and community.

What's my shadow, do I have any lessons?
Yes, I can be rigid, inflexible, too conservative, close-minded, and demanding.
I can sometime abuse my power, becoming tyrannical and overbearing,
also falling into toxic traits of being emotionally detached, authoritarian, and
controlling.

Key Animals: *Your Personal Animal Guides & Spirits*

Lion

You are a natural leader with immense inner strength, tenacity, will power, courage, and determination to succeed. Ruled by Saturn, you display strong levels of personal power and authority, just like the lion. You're extremely persevering, headstrong, and ambitious, moreover relaxed and chilled when needing to be. This is essentially the personality of the lion. The lion loves to laze around, soaking up the sun and relaxing in the name of tranquility and pleasure, yet they also know how to fight for what they want; they're warriors with a strong sense of devotion, force, and courage. You may not be like assertive and simultaneously hotheaded Aries or supremely passionate yet dominant Leo, two fire signs who typically embody the strength of a lion, however you know how to command respect. You possess presence. You're ambitious, practical, and determined that your aura or demeanor alone lets others know that you are a force of power. Some of your greatest strengths include self-assertion, self-authority, and a high level of ambition coupled with potent aspirations. Satun is the task-master, further representing karmic cycles and lessons, which includes the growth to maturity and adulthood. Saturn's energy includes being a 'tough love teacher,' a strong emphasis on responsibilities, and honoring as well as respecting duty, tradition, law, order, structures, regulations, rules, and foundations that aim to restrict us for our growth and lead to ultimate self-evolution. In short, Saturn represents discipline, order, and authority on the highest of levels. The lion is known as the king of the jungle- lions are fierce, mighty, and majestic; they're high up on the food chain, further more than happy to show their power and majesty. You can work with the lion spirit when you need help developing and integrating these masculine traits. Assertion, confidence, self-esteem, charisma, social charm and grace, inner strength, and leadership skills can all be expanded with the lion's assistance.

Turtle

Despite everything shared above for the lion spirit, you are also a feminine and nurturing earth sign. You're nurturing, generous, and caring, in addition to being capable of sincere levels of empathy and compassion. You are more yin than yang, passive, receptive, magnetic, somewhat submissive- although less than the other earth signs, and very kind. Being born of earth gives you a magnetic charm and soul shine that comes naturally to you, you don't have to force it, and you sometimes aren't even aware of how attractive, charismatic, or enticing you are. The turtle is the perfect spirit animal to work with for amplifying feminine qualities within. In addition to all the above mentioned, the turtle also helps you to slow down, get in tune with your psyche- your innermost self, higher mind/Higher Self, and soul essence. From this space of inner stillness and silence, peace, contemplation, meditation, and introspection, you connect to different parts of yourself. Artistic gifts, profound imagination, evolved creativity, and even a sense of vision and idealistic perception flow to you. It's important that you connect to this side of you, Capricorn. You can be incredibly business-minded, focused on how to earn , support, and provide for yourself and loved ones. Being so materialistic and ambitious is both a curse and a blessing. The less positive side of this is that you are always working and achieving- you're always "doing" and seldom "being." The turtle can assist you when personal relationships and bonds have been suffering due to putting your working life first, in addition to accessing powerful channels of creativity coupled with artistic self-expression. Further, the turtle helps you connect to your spiritual body, enabling higher spiritual awareness, perception, and new ideas. As a grounded and practical earth sign, you tend to give less time to spiritual pursuits, yet we have four main 'bodies;' the emotional, psychological or mental, physical, *and* spiritual bodies!

Deer

The deer is a powerful animal for you, as it helps you connect to your emotional intelligence. Empathy, caring, nurturance, sensitivity, compassion, sensitivity, instincts, and higher self-awareness are all expanded with the deer spirit. The deer is actually one of your personal animal protectors and faithful guides in this life, because the deer shares a very close connection to the earth, moreover the spirit of the earth. Mother Earth, healing yourself and others with plants, herbs, natural, gemstones, essential oils, and so forth, and choosing a profession or at least hobby that honors, respects, and helps the earth are key themes to incorporate into your life. Many Capricorns become botanists, tree surgeons, farm workers, environmentalists, or permaculturists if they don't choose a 'traditional' path associated with the Capricorn personality (business, finance, management, working towards becoming a CEO or analyst, etc.). The deer has a gentle spirit, yet also teaches the art of patience, self-respect, and self-love, in addition to boundaries. This compliments your personality perfectly; you are magnetic, gracious, charming, empathic, and deeply caring, yet you're equally strong-willed, determined, and tenacious with supreme patience. Saturn combined with your earthly nature allows you to work towards something with patience, perseverance, and utmost tenacity. Once you set your mind to something or create a goal and plan of action, nothing can stop you. You may be a gentle and modest earth sign, however you possess the strength and focus of someone who is at the top of their league. You should work with the deer spirit when you want to balance and harmonize your more feminine, moreover passive and receptive, qualities with masculine inner strength, stamina, and assertion. This is your ideal 'yin and yang' animal, so choose it as your protector and guide on a regular basis for your best and most balanced life.

Bear, Stag, Squirrel, Mouse *and* Bat (All the 'Grounding' ones!)

You are one of the most grounded, practical, responsible, level-headed, methodological, dutiful, and service-oriented star signs, so it's no wonder all of the spirit animals in the 'Grounding' ensemble belong to you. Your key strengths include being driven, disciplined, reliable, strategic, patient, wise, observant, highly analytical, and persistent verging on obsessive. Once you set a plan in motion nothing can stop you; you're a force of power, an excellent motivator, and a natural leader. You're certainly not obnoxious, you're more of a silent observer who gets stuff done without hassle or needing attention. Yet you do command respect and power. You exhibit natural authority, just like these earth spirit animals, and further strive towards perfection. Read up on these spirit animals' symbolism closely and with intent. Work with them on a cyclic basis-daily, weekly, every month during a New or Full Moon… as much as you can. Once you start to realize how much of a natural affinity you share with the bear, stag, squirrel, and bat, you will come to terms with your own shadow self. Recognition and acceptance of your own shadow is the first step to healing and wholeness. It's only when we work on healing our shadow selves do we attain wholeness, and we do so through integration. These four spirit animals reflect your shine- your light essence, and your shadow; your darker or less desirable traits. And, integrating your shadow lets you live your life with joy, bliss, ease, beauty, and grace, in your light! Don't underestimate the power of these four power animals in shaping your life and influencing your destiny; they are not ones to miss.

Fox

The fox corresponds with your deeply analytical, intellectual, and level-headed side. In addition to all of your beautiful feminine-nurturing qualities, you are extremely business savvy. You're money-minded, know how to create abundance, and like to live a life of material comfort & stability, luxury, and security. You do so from choosing to think instead of feel, from putting aside your emotions and instead focusing on how your intellect can best serve you. There is a calculated and somewhat cunning side to you, just like with the fox, however with mindfulness and effort the shadow traits of the fox spirit can be released. At a lower vibration, both you and the fox are prone to minor levels of deception and manipulation to get what you want. You're so ambitious that it can make you emotionally detached, deciding to go with your head over your heart. This is fine, to a degree- some signs are much more competitive than you, such as hotheaded and (at the lowest frequency) bully-tyrant Aries. But, this doesn't mean you should lose touch with your grace, integrity, or humility. The fox represents your ability to overlook sentiments for practical, financial, and work or business matters, which is a good thing. Simultaneously, you can learn that being intellectual, full of wit and logic, and business-minded shouldn't be equated with being *ruthless*. Heart, integrity, and soul can be balanced and combined with higher analytical thinking, problem-solving, finding practical solutions, and so forth. It's essential that you make peace with this stern, strict, and somewhat cold, moreover overly authoritarian aspect of your personality and core identity, otherwise you run the risk of falling into extremes, i.e. your dark side. Remember Saturn's symbolism. This is reflected in all aspects of your life, from your beliefs and morals to your communication style and approach. Be bold and direct without becoming a bully; choose head over heart, where necessary, without falling into tyrannical tendencies; be a boss at the top of your game without becoming cold, manipulative, or controlling…. The fox has potent instincts and is capable of deep love, nurturance, and compassion too.

Hawk *and* Beetle

Both the hawk and beetle complement your personality, making them the ideal 'Higher Self' spirit animals to work with for self-development. All aspects of your higher mind come alive with these spirit animals, including higher reasoning, logic, intuition, imaginative gifts, creative vision, problem-solving, fine-tuned analytical and subtle perception, key observation skills, and the ability to combine psychic instincts with intellect. You're a bit of a contradiction, Capricorn. Some people see you as a deeply supportive, protective, and providing, least to mention sweet, caring, and supremely nurturing family wo/man. Others see you as this mighty CEO, boss, or business wo/man who takes control and charge without apology! The hawk and beatle can assist you in finding inner balance, unification, and integration. Being a feminine earth sign with a masculine planetary ruler means you're quite a balanced sign. While many others have two primary feminine influences or two primary masculine influences (element and planetary ruler), you have a mixture of both. The Higher Self power animals generally relate to your higher mind, mental abilities and gifts included (which are a masculine quality), yet the mind is closely connected to the Third Eye and Crown chakras. These are where spiritual and higher power energies flow, incorporating psychic impressions, the ability to perceive subtle energy, clairvoyance and the other clairs (clairaudience, etc.), and potent intuition. Also, an access to dream states and the subconscious wisdom and guidance that's available in the dreamworlds.

You may be surprised at this knowledge, but you are able to do a lot of the things the water signs excel in, maybe not to their high level- water represents evolution of the soul and spiritual gifts on the highest level, after all. However, earth signs have similar access to the subtle, invisible, and subconscious realms. Your issue or imbalance is that you focus so much on the 3D world of possessions, resources, and assets. Making money combined with desiring to live a comfortable life isn't a problem, but this should be balanced with abilities birthed from the spiritual plane. The beatle and hawk can help you achieve this. Why do you want to find this synchronization? Well, people who have mastered the spiritual and quantum laws of the universe will all tell you the same thing: amazing manifestation abilities increase and expand once you know the secrets to the universe. Universal and sacred laws can be studied in unison with working with these two power animals, so consider researching the Hermetic Principles as well as metaphysical concepts and practices.

Elephant, Cow *and* Coyote

Without repeating information, read up on these three spirit animals. Use the visualization meditation exercise presented on pages 141- 2; adapt it so the animals are observed in their natural environment. For example, the elephant in a jungle or on an African plane…. The cow in a farm surrounded by green pastures, and the coyote free in a forest or by a stream or river of water… Push yourself to breakthrough your logical and analytical mind to reach your intuitive mind. Don't be afraid to let your imagination run wild a bit. One secret about your personality is that you have a very wild side! You love to play just as much as you like to work and study or be ambitious. Use this meditation technique as an opportunity to expand your imagination, further becoming aware of the spiritual aspects of life. Even a small effort at switching on your Third Eye, your Higher Self, can spark shifts of transformation and positive alchemy within. Alchemy is the transmutation of energy, with energy encompassing all possible vibrations, realities, and positive and negative attributes or characteristics. Start a self-development, self-care, or spiritual practice centered around the connection to your Higher Self as well as the spiritual realms.

Dog

You are an extremely loyal, devoted, and affectionate person, just like the dog spirit animal. The dog represents purity, unconditional love, companionship, loyalty, and lifelong family and friendship bonds. You are sweet and nurturing as they come, once you let your guard down. One of your shadow traits (follies) is having a difficult time accepting your emotions. You can close yourself off emotionally, as you actually love pretty intensely. Deep emotions are a scary thing for you. This isn't saying that you aren't capable of deep intimacy, love, and romance- you are. It just takes you a while to drop your barriers. Even when in a committed relationship you can unconsciously project your insecurities onto your partner, which include fear of infidelity. You do this because you care and love so deeply, also apprehensive to fully embrace the full spectrum of emotions and inner world sensations you experience when in love. There's a mental block and barrier that prevents you from experiencing the magical, blissful, and devoted love you crave so much. Luckily, this can be overcome with effort, commitment, and self-healing. The dog can assist you with this. In both love and friendship, the dog guides you towards your most loving, playful, and affectionate, moreover trusting self. Unconditional love involves accepting yourself and others, specifically your lover in this case, as they are; shine and shadow included. We all have darker attributes just as we all have positive light ones. Your problem, Capricorn, is that you can be quite judgemental, critical and overly analytical too. Instead of choosing to connect to the emotional currents and feelings, instincts, and sensitivities of life, which incorporates empathy, compassion, tolerance, understanding, and so forth, you judge and dismiss. This is solely due to such a high level of intellectual analysis and understanding, and at a higher vibration you have integrated empathy, compassion, etc. Work with the dog spirit when you wish to develop greater trust and acceptance in yourself and others, in addition to softening up. You have a beautiful heart and spirit; your life lesson is to show it more often…

Frog

The frog is ideal for cleansing, detoxification, and spiritual illumination. As such a materially-focused sign, you love the finer things in life; good food, drinks, treats, luxuries, and creature comforts. This signifies that you often become over-indulgent, greedy, and too focused on physical pleasure- pleasures of the flesh. I know, this may seem like a contradiction; you're extremely conservative and self-disciplined, right? This is true, but you do go through multiple chapters where you give in to excessive pleasure-seeking and indulgence. The frog can keep you on track with your diet, lifestyle, and exercise goals, henceforth. Thai is the best spirit animal for you when it comes to health, well-being, exercise, self-care, daily routines, and honoring your physical body. Spirituality doesn't have to be seen as something "out there," it's very close to home. Your body is your home, as well as the earth; it's a sacred temple. The frog, therefore, assists you in paying closer attention to your sensuality, emotional and psychological health, physical well-being, and energy and vitality levels. Purification is in divine order. Purification, cleansing, and fasts or detoxes are what the frog assists with, so don't overlook the power of such a small spirit animal. The frog may be small, yet its medicine is great. It pushes you towards better self-care and health rituals and regimes, something, as a Capricorn, you take pride in- your ability to create order and plans is one of your utmost strengths. Thus, apply the same reasoning and methodology to daily lifestyle choices. See your body as a project. You set a goal, create a plan, and follow through. Simple! Remember that health is not exclusive to physical well-being, it also includes emotional, psychological, and spiritual health. Being mindful of this will help prevent succumbing to shallow or superficial tendencies...

Further, the frog is linked to both water and land, making it a perfect spirit animal for developing and embodying emotional intelligence. Sensitivity, empathy, emotional wisdom and maturity, and all other feminine qualities are linked to the element water, while patience, practical awareness, wisdom, self-knowledge, self-accountability coupled with a high level of responsibility, and so forth, are connected to the earth element. The frog is here to show you how to live in harmony, to be both sensitive & compassionate and strong-willed and dutiful. You should take the frog's energy and medicine seriously, as it can lead to healing and self-evolution on so many levels, and in so many life areas.

Peacock

The peacock symbolizes your desire to shine and take the spotlight, something that's important to integrate during this lifetime. You are incredibly modest, down-to-earth, and humble. You're respectful, sincere, and very friendly with virtually everyone you come across. Despite being a boss, your own boss, you know how to play well with others as part of a team or cooperative. These are all great attributes to possess. In saying this, your evolved level of modesty can hinder your capacity to *shine*. Fellow earth signs Taurus and Virgo share the same issue as you. Call on the peacock when you sense you've become too modest, selfless, or humble. Stepping into the spotlight doesn't have to be equated with ego. In fact, the water and earth signs run the least risk of becoming egotistical, self-centered, and bullyish or tyrannical, as they are naturally passive. You are more dominant and assertive than the others (alongside Scorpio, who also shares a masculine planet), due to Saturn's energy and influence, so this helps you step into self-assertion, self-empowerment, and personal levels of authority and confidence. The peacock is here to tell you it's ok to be bold, live fearlessly, and shine. Shine when you want to inspire others, or educate, uplift, or help them in some way; not to over-power, control, or suppress. This is a key shadow personality trait with your sign, you can become oppressive and controlling simply because you feel suppressed or controlled. It's an unconscious behavior and pattern of thinking that stems from the sheer level of control, discipline, and authority, combined with respect for structures and regulation, that Saturn places on your life. Some things are out of our control, and this is one of them for you and your psyche, the way you think and perceive, etc. You control others when you feel you've lost control. You try to suppress others when you feel suppressed. It's one of your worst character traits, yet, fortunately, the peacock can help you overcome this. Shine, be colorful, show off your creative and innovative skills, and let others see you in all your glory. Shining to inspire or educate is not the same as seeking to control overs or intimidate them into submission. The peacock can help you realize this.

Power Animals for Protection

Buffalo

The buffalo is one of the special power animals you feel a deep resonance with. You are essentially an embodiment of the buffalo spirit; strong, self-assured, determined to succeed, disciplined, self-controlled, sensual, down-to-earth, and willful. At the highest vibration, the buffalo symbolizes abundance, financial wealth and security, and prosperity, things you strive for in everyday waking life. Every word described for the buffalo spirit describes your true nature, Capricorn. Explore the buffalo's spirit in depth, further seeking new ways to integrate and embody its energy. You might want to use the visualization exercise given (pages 141- 2) on a daily basis or at least until you feel you are playing to your strengths. Do not underestimate the power of the qualities and attributes described (*page 103 for reference*), as they are your saving grace in the realms of love, finances, domestic and home life, family connections that stand the test of time, romance, friendship, and both societal and community circles.

Wasp

The wasp is often overlooked and seen as inferior to the beautiful bee, for example. The wasp represents the ability to work hard and stay focused on an end goal, determination, patience, and a long journey towards the end result; success, abundance, and fertility. The wasp is essential in our earth's ecosystems- without the wasp, the planet would not function the way it does, therefore homeostasis and the great equilibrium of life wouldn't be possible. This is your secret superpower, Capricorn… Like the wasp, you work hard and diligently behind the scenes, until you make your mark and come out into the spotlight. It can take years upon years for you to find the success and accomplishment you're seeking, whether it's qualifications, talent acquisition, social status and success, or abundance and wealth. The key is that you eventually achieve this, just like the wasp! You show conscientiousness in your work and duties, further being committed to service to others, society, and your local or greater communities. Some people fear the wasp too, and this signifies the secondary meaning of your personal power animal. The way you strive towards professional and personal victory can intimidate a lot of people. Even when you're not focused on competition or anyone else- only focused on your own talents, abilities, and qualifications or accomplishments, there are people watching you. People know you are one to watch out for, a power-house with unwavering determination and tenacity. It's a real gift. There is a reason why the wasp is feared, perhaps irrationally, but feared all the same; it's because you know how to stand your ground and put up boundaries when your security, livelihood, or well-being are threatened. Just like yourself, wasps are not one to sting *unless* there is a threat. There's a fabulous lesson here.

Observe how the wasp works peacefully towards their end goals. Reflect on how it remains unbothered by others around it, specifically humongous humans in size comparison, and causes no harm or bother to anyone. This is the key to your success. Whatever your vision, long-term plans, goals, dreams, or aspirations are, you should work in the same manner as the wasp. You do not need to "sting" someone simply for existing around or near you- a metaphor symbolic of your shadow traits; being oppressive, bullyish, and intimidating verging on combative. The wasp can help you transcend these. You don't need to stop your soul plan or path to accommodate or appease others either; if people want to fear you for no rational or apparent reason, let them! It shouldn't get in the way of your ambitions or aspirations. This is the dual meaning of the wasp and further how you can attain victory, abundance, fortune, fame, social status, peace of mind, happiness, self-respect, and inner balance, or any other intention you're manifesting. There's a lightness to the wasp spirit just as there is a strong level of self-protection. Apply this wisdom and message for ultimate living and wish fulfillment.

Animals You Should Work With for Integration

Based on the qualities you lack, you should work with the following spirit animals to integrate more balance, harmony, and unification of opposite (or dualistic) forces in your life.

Cat

The cat is here to remind you of the importance and power of your *sensuality*. Choosing a career or vocation as a manager, CEO, boss, business specialist, and so forth can disconnect you from your innate sensuality. Yet, many Capricorns- the ones who take a less traditional route, become dance teachers, yoga therapists, and even tantra practitioners! The point is, there are so many different dimensions and frequencies to tune into, so the cat is here when you've lost touch with your sensual and instinctive self. The cat spirit represents psychic powers, potent instincts, evolved intuition, and the desire to travel, wander, roam, and be free. Adventure is a keyword associated with the cat spirit. Call on the cat when you need to increase these attributes. Secondly, the cat teaches the true meaning of independence Vs codependency or healthy attachment. One moment the cat will be craving attention and affection like there's no tomorrow, and the next s/he will apparently lose all interest in physical affection, contact, and intimacy. This represents your true nature, Capricorn. You're a bit of a contradiction in terms, at times. You alternate between being this amazing lover, friend, and family person, to going straight back into business and work mode. It can create a lot of confusion, also making people apprehensive to be their true selves around you. Over time, this leads your closest supporters (friends, family, your partner..) to hold back, solely out of not knowing how they should act around you. When it gets too far, they may even become scared of your sporadic and alternating moods, and cut the connection altogether. Work with the cat for enhanced affection, deeper connection, and intimacy. Or call on the cat when you need to let loose from your responsibilities and duties and embody more fun, play, and travel or adventure. The cat spirit aims to serve your highest self so you don't push away essential supporters, kindred spirits, partnerships, bonds, and lovers.

Dolphin *and* Lizard

Community and play coupled with the importance of balancing work, rest, and play are available for integration with the dolphin spirit. You have a very difficult time relaxing, letting go, and disconnecting from your real-world commitments and practicalities. So, the dolphin is here when you need a reminder of the importance of play, laughter, and social and community bonds. In addition, the lizard can help you access a less explored aspect of you. This is your capacity to dream, enter the multidimensional and dream spaces for astral insights, astral projection, and lucid dreaming, and regularly receive guidance and wisdom from the subconscious planes. Check out the lizard symbolism to see what you might be lacking or missing; you may not choose to get too deep with this area of consciousness and self-exploration, but you can at least be aware of the possibilities available to you.

Chapter 18: Aquarius

I am Aquarius, the idealist and practical dreamer,
I take action, also excelling as a confident speaker and teacher.
I wish for unity, teamwork, and world peace-
I am generous, upbeat, and friendly, moreover help others in need.
As a great humanitarian with many unique gifts,
I'm intelligent, bright, logical, and creative.
I am also intuitive, imaginative, and artistic with clear vision,
I may be analytical and rational, but I certainly don't lack instincts.
Others see me as quirky, colorful, and extremely witty;
Uranus is my ruler, so I possess strong gifts in originality.
Despite being a go-getter who thrives in community projects,
I can be emotionally aloof, detached, and chaotic.
I need to learn how to open up to others with emotional honesty and vulnerability,
only then will I take my rightful place as a global change-maker and visionary.
But, I am wise, intellectual, passionate, expressive, and open-minded,
I thrive in both practical and imaginative pursuits, my glyph is the Water-Bearer.
This keeps my mind rooted in higher things, pursuits that can heal the world…
I am independent, philosophical, ambitious, and an excellent communicator;
represented by the 'Star' (in Tarot), I am the perfect inventor & collaborator.

What's my shadow, do I have any lessons?
I am emotionally detached and aloof, struggling to welcome deeper connection.
I focus so much on the intellectual planes that I become isolated, also lacking depth;
I become a rebel without consciousness, intention, directed focus, or purpose.

Key Animals: *Your Personal Animal Guides & Spirits*

Crocodile

As an intellectual and psychological air sign, emotions are one of your trickiest areas. You certainly possess emotional intelligence- this is a key quality of Aquarius, yet depth and vulnerability are the two things you need help with. The crocodile symbolizes sensitivity, emotional wisdom, depth, empathy, and the realm of emotions and feelings in general. But, the crocodile is also a deeply primal animal, it's instinctive and associated with the Root chakra. Themes of security, survival, libido, sexuality, and primal needs and urges come into the crocodile's realm. The crocodile is therefore perfect for you to explore your emotions and inner world sensations, because it's coupled with acceptance of your sexuality. Aquarius is a very upbeat, optimistic, and psychological star sign, which equally signifies having a strong libido. Exploring your emotional needs and responses *in harmony with* your primal self, libido, and physical needs helps you transcend the need to be a rebel. One of your worst traits is being a rebel just for the sake of rebellion, it's one of your main shadow personality traits! With the crocodile, you can explore your feelings within the realm of your needs for intimacy, romance, and passion, which is what's needed for your self-development. We all have a sexuality, but, as a masculine sign, your libido is stronger than a lot of others (it's a trait shared by fire and air signs specifically, in addition to super-sexual Scorpio…). The crocodile is here when you want to work on self-mastery of your emotions and the more trickier sensations and feelings, without feeling judged. For example, the animals from the 'Emotionally Intelligent' category would also benefit you, and they are very useful to work with and call upon, however the crocodile offers an extra dimension; emotions and intimacy exploration within the parameters of your sexually liberated and passionate self.

Further, the crocodile is not solely about love and lust, but represents family values. Despite being a free-spirit rebel who thrives in independence and originality, you are an amazing family person, Aquarius. You are fiercely protective, loyal, and dependable, just like the crocodile, and provide for those you love. With caring and nurturing qualities coupled with primal & physical instincts, the crocodile is perfect for when you wish to explore your emotional body, in a way that works for you. Sensitivity is available without going too deep! (Such as with the dove or swan, which emphasize peace, or the turtle, which also symbolizes emotional intelligence but in unison with introspection and retreat.)

Dolphin

You embody the spirit of the dolphin for many reasons. Firstly, you are extremely intelligent. Secondly, you are emotionally intelligent, while being capable of real empathy and kindness- you possess many altruistic values. Thirdly, you are a big believer in community, moreover love to play! This is the main symbolism of the dolphin. Emotional intelligence, empathy, and sensitivity to the needs of others can be balanced and harmonized with mental or psychological intelligence. You're intellectual, logical, and incredibly analytical and observant, yet you're just as intuitive and imaginative. Like the dolphin, you seem to have a balanced left and right brain, drawing from many different skills and abilities. The dolphin is therefore excellent for fine-tuning, strengthening, and mastering these yin-yang characteristics. Furthermore, you can be a bit of a loner or "lone wolf," choosing to dance away to the beat of your own drum, at least in youth before you're ready to join society; or start a family. The dolphin helps you to overcome an excessive need for solitude or introspection, further reminding you of the power and importance of social bonds and connections. Ironically, you are actually very social, you just sometimes/often go into long chapters of isolation for self-study, music or art talent acquisition, learning new things, and so forth. The problem is that this can become a comfort zone, which can then be difficult to transcend. So, the dolphin can be called one when you need assistance remembering the joys of connections and socializing, moreover the significance of *community*.

Monkey

The monkey represents your brilliantly innovative and curious mind. In fact, you are so alike the monkey on a mental and psychological level that this spirit animal can almost be seen as your 'alter-ego.' You're witty, intelligent, incredibly innovative and inventive, original, open-minded, bright, playful, and inquisitive. You're logical, analytical, perceptive, observant, and intellectual, while excelling in higher reasoning and problem-solving. You're intuitive, instinctive, imaginative, artistically gifted, and philosophical too. All of these mental traits resemble the energy of the monkey. Quite simply, you can read up on the monkey spirit to understand how your mind works better. This is an excellent spirit animal for psychological analysis and learning, in addition to developing gifts of the mind. Both your light or positive and dark or negative traits can be seen in the monkey spirit, making it an ideal power animal for shadow healing & integration. Accepting your shadow is the first step to finding wholeness and enlightenment. Vice versa; if you wish to become the best version of yourself, you will need to accept and heal your shadow. Remember that you're an air sign, as this will help you to make sense of your shine and shadow in the monkey spirit. In addition, your planetary ruler is Uranus, the planet of innovation, change, technology, scientific revolution, and original ideas that can change the world. You're very altruistic, empathic, and charitable, moreover concerned with humanitarian values, with a selfless side as well. Turn towards the monkey when you need help with coming terms of your gifts and strengths within your community or social circle. The monkey teaches total acceptance, self-love, and authenticity…

Bear, Stag *and* Bat

These three animals can all help provide the grounding element that you need. As a quirky, upbeat, and mental air sign, you tend to go with flow, being mastered in the realm of positivity and eccentricity. You're usually in high spirits and love to travel, explore, go on adventures, experiment with music and arts, and connect with others. Yet, this can make you lack the grounding element, the focus, concentration, and purpose. Many Aquarians don't choose a path until much later in life. You may choose to reside in immaturity or impulsiveness until at least your 30s, or even beyond, and often lack practical and monetary awareness. Wisdom comes with age and experience, least to mention maturity and shadow healing/work. The beat and stag are perfect for grounding, as well as developing strong foundations and a need for security. They can help you increase abundance, stability, and prosperity in your life through the wisdom and earthly connection they bring. The bat assists in channeling your strong libido, your sex drive, upwards into your higher energy centers. This enables you to see things from a more holistic and integrated mindset. Instead of wanting many lovers or to party lots, you instead direct your time and energy into creating a stable home life, gathering resources, or fine-tuning your career, service, or profession. There are lots of positive implications of not getting stuck or immersed in your root and sacral, your lower chakras (energy portals/centers). Working with these three grounding animals can create powerful changes in love, business, communication, the way you earn and spend money, core belief systems, health and well-being, domestic life, family bonds, friendships and social circles, and everything else you can think of. Don't underestimate the power of grounding and stabilizing forces in your life, Aquarius. You may be positive and friendly, loved by many for your expressive and outgoing nature, yet there is some immaturity, impulsiveness, and impracticalities left to heal around this. Everything has its duality.

Hawk

The hawk symbolizes clear sight, intuition, higher perspectives, vision, psychic gifts, and foresight. As the Water-Bearer, you are a natural in all of these things. The hawk can therefore strengthen these abilities. Your glyph, the Water-Bearer, is depicted by the *Star* in tarot, which represents a connection to the celestial and spiritual planes- the heavens, and our planet simultaneously. This is why you have innate humanitarian and altruistic tendencies, further believing in selfless service, working towards a more harmonious world, and healing (humanity's consciousness, core belief systems, ecosystems, etc.). Like the hawk, you are perceptive, amazingly observant, wise, philosophical, and analytical. You possess strong gifts in problem-solving, higher reasoning, and finding creative solutions to all things. You're a deeply original, creative, and inventive thinker, in fact, so the hawk is perfect for accessing higher mental *and* spiritual abilities. Intuition can be developed, as can visionary and idealistic gifts. One of your greatest strengths is being able to tune into the collective consciousness energy field to benefit the whole. You are able to tune into the ether, astral realm and planes, and spiritual dimensions where profound imagination and higher revelations are available, and then birthed them into the material plane. This is literally what the Water-Bearer signifies; taking ideas and information and channeling them into something physical.

The dual aspect of your astrological glyph is picking up on feelings, emotions, and subtle sensations, and then alchemizing them into higher mental reasoning, including ideologies, beliefs, thoughts, concepts, and rational perspectives. In other words, emotional intelligence leads to powerful psychological and mental currents and pathways that serve a number of purposes. Thus, destiny and purpose can be discovered through this gift combined with the medicine of the hawk.

Crow

Another Higher Self spirit animal, the crow expands magic, divination, and your connection to higher consciousness in your life. Some people equate the Aquarius sign with intellect, psychological gifts, and everything related to the mind and air, while others see Aquarius as the free-spirited earth-wandering hippy, the bohemian musician, artist, and dreamer who has little care for material thing or societal structures. Both are true! The crow specifically connects to your metaphysical, mystical, and spiritual side. If you're looking to explore the mystical powers of the universe, including the quantum field, metaphysics, and esotericism, call upon the crow.

Universe laws as well as sacred energy and divine ancient wisdom can be learned with the crow. The crow is excellent for if you've chosen an artistic, healing, musical, or creative path, just as it is for spiritual pursuits. There are many other qualities that can be acquired through the crow that are explained on page 80. Use the guided visualization meditation given to Gemini on pages 141-2 for self-development and self-mastery. As one of your personal spirit birds, the crow assists you in coming to terms with your own magic, without becoming uncentered or ungrounded. Your shadow traits of seeking control over others, in addition to becoming aggressive and impulsive when you've lost control of yourself, can equally be overcome and transcended. The crow applies to your Higher Self and is all about transcendence.

Lizard

As the practical dreamer, (coupled with Pisces, the actual dreamer of the Zodiac; the sign next to you and 'Old Soul,' the final sign), your list wouldn't be complete without the lizard. Despite being so intellectual and logical, you are blessed with a deep connection to the astral planes. Connecting to the ethereal, astral, and subtle dimensions and planes is something you can do. Not everyone can, you know. With help from your spirit animals, spiritual practices, and benevolent forces of the universe, like your spirit guides and ancestors, you can transcend the 3D limitations of the physical world. This signifies the ability to astral travel, lucid dream, and enter into deep states of transcendental awareness and enhanced consciousness through meditation, sound healing, etc. Also, to receive wisdom and insights from your subconscious mind. You are deeply connected to the subconscious realm, and your conscious and subconscious minds work in harmony with each other. There's a natural and organic "flow" with you, within and around. Energy flows- you're chilled, laid-back, and at ease. This opens you up to receiving guidance that people in a stressed or always busy mindset and frequency cannot attain. In waking life, the places before sleep, and during dreamtime, you are able to reach higher states of consciousness. The lizard helps to expand this in extraordinary ways. Quite simply, read up on the lizard spirit, understanding that you might be a cerebral air sign, but you're also strongly connected to the realms of spirit, emotions, the subconscious, and the invisible… This is where powerful revelations as well as your own and others' divinity can be found. Explore your dreams to take projects, partnerships, and unique gifts and talents to the next level.

Peacock

Your core personality is most symbolic of the peacock, when you're at your best and highest vibration. The peacock represents courage, confidence, self-expression, the ability to shine and stand in the spotlight, and a sense of devotion to your chosen path, career, vocation, or service. Peacock's medicine allows you to shine without fear and unapologetically, stepping into your glorious and radiant soul self. Light, color, creativity, innovation, originality, independence balanced with emotional intelligence, and self-leadership skills combined with potent intuition are all part of the peacock's symbolism. Seeking romance, beauty, and community bonds are also available to you. As a masculine sign ruled by Uranus, you possess a lot of confidence and courage without the peacock's assistance, but the peacock will help to bring this out and fine-tune it. You're assertive, friendly, outgoing, imaginative, inspirational, and a natural leader, once you reach a certain age and level of maturity. This spirit animal serves two main purposes.

Firstly, when you've been going through a certain period or chapters of isolation, loneliness, introspection, or soul-searching, you should work with the peacock to help bring you out of your protective bubble. Introspection to sociability is the name of the game with the peacock. Secondly, you should work with the peacock when you want to fine-tune and enhance your artistic and creative talents. This is the perfect power animal for speakers, performers, entertainers, musicians, artists, actors, teachers, and creative visionaries, directors, writers, and so forth. Essentially, anything that requires you to shine will get a boost and upgrade with the peacock spirit. You can also work with this spirit animal when you wish to increase integrity combined with reaching expert or master level in your field. It's the ideal spirit animal for taking your career to the next level, becoming a teacher, or stepping into new leadership positions. Coupled with getting serious about your service or profession and shining at the same time, the peacock enhances self-esteem, social charm and grace, charisma, a sense of glamor, and self-expression of all kinds.

The peacock can teach you how to shine without succumbing to ego. It will help keep in check your intentions for shining, such as not wanting to seek the spotlight for solely egotistical, vain, or self-centered reasons. You can sometimes take your need to appear positive and colorful too far, falling into superficiality or seeking the limelight without intent. This is where problems arise in both personal and professional relationships. You have such a big spirit, so work with the peacock's medicine when you want to release that spirit, while keeping your ego in check. The peacock has mastered this art!

Parrot

The parrot is another self-expression spirit animal for you. You are one of the most gifted star signs when it comes to communication, and the parrot represents the highest expression of communication possible. Similar to the peacock, the parrot's energy includes a colorful, innovative, creative, imaginative, and highly intuitive personality. But the parrot goes a step further and teaches you how to master your communication. Parrots are able to mimic sounds, speech, and songs, which signifies the abilities you have when you accept your emotional body. This is the key, further being what can be self-mastered through working with the parrot spirit. Psychological growth is not enough, you must also come to terms with your emotional needs and innermost sensations; your feelings. As the energy center relating to the water element, as well as sexuality, platonic and romantic intimacy, and emotions, the sacral chakra should be in focus. It's advised to work with your sacral chakra in harmony with your throat. These are two powerful energy centers that can cause havoc when blocked or unhealed and imbalance. Blocks in your sacral prevent you from speaking and communicating your truth. So, it's important to work on your emotions- your weakness and folly- to reach the top in communicative abilities. Life force energy flows from root to crown and vice versa, therefore your throat chakra (the center of communication combined with all aspects of self-expression) is not at its best when you haven't integrated the energy and wisdom of the lower chakras; specifically, in this case, the sacral. Read up on the parrot symbolism to discover more…

Buffalo *and* Giraffe

These are your two inspirational spirit animals that can lovingly assist you in work, service, family or home life, relationships, friendships, and love and romance. The buffalo brings abundance into your life the more you work with its energy, while the giraffe blesses you with the gifts of foresight and higher vision. Instead of repeating the energetic associations already written, here is a bit more insight into your personal astrology… You are a Fixed sign, meaning you possess a natural sense of stability, security, and need for physical structures. Physical environments that hold and nourish you are important to you, as are material comforts, luxuries, and possessions. Perhaps contrary to being ruled by the planet of innovation and change (Uranus), you have an inflexible side. Once you commit to a path or idea, or simultaneously create an ideology or belief that you know, from your own formed opinions and perspectives, to be true; it's extremely difficult to change your mind. Positively, this makes you loyal in love and very much committed to any person, project, or relationship you devote yourself to. Not so positively, and something you need to work on with the help of the buffalo and giraffe; you can become stagnant to taking things to the next level. In other words, once you've mastered something, become an expert, or reached a certain level in your profession or social status, you may feel it's enough, not realizing that you have an extraordinary mind. You can achieve more. You can master more subjects or talents. Why stop? Of course, I am not promoting constant doing, busyness to the point of burn-out or self-detriment, however the truth is you are a very gifted person. You have so much energy, optimism, originality, zest, and passion inside of you that it's quite easy for you to invent, perfect, or ascend in many things. Keep this in mind. The buffalo will provide you with the resources, abundance, and inner strength to elevate your life plan or purpose, and the giraffe will give you the vision, psychic gifts, and sensitivity necessary simultaneously.

Power Animals for Protection

Frog

The frog symbolizes purification and cleansing, something closely linked to your personal energy signature. As the 11th sign, you are very close to the karmic cycle of completion; soul growth and evolution at the highest level (seen in Pisces, the 12th sign). This implies that you have a certain level of duty and responsibility- to yourself, society, the planet, mankind, and your soul. Quite simply, the 11th house rules social and friendship groups in addition to community. It's how we leave our mark in the world, defined by the authentic and close bonds we make and keep. Thus, it's important to cleanse and recharge yourself regularly. Boundaries are significant for you, as is the ability to recognize your destiny or unique place in the world. Many Aquarians work towards a legacy, a lasting gift for mankind in which future generations can benefit from. Whether you're a teacher, visionary poet, successful musician, famous speaker, or humble eco-activist, you can make a big difference in this world. Working with the frog helps to keep your intentions pure, mind on point, and emotions & spirit body cleansed. The frog spirit aids in self-alignment, spiritual cleansing and growth, and emotional mastery, moreover the ability to perceive subtle energy for the best possible pathways. The frog protects you from harm while keeping you energized and cleared of anything toxic, destructive, or manipulative. Emotionally, physically, psychologically, and spiritually, the frog assists you in love and business (service, career, and vocation included). Further, the frog can protect you from your own toxic traits & behaviors, moreover any self-destructive or self-sabotaging habits, routines, or behaviors you might be repeating. The metaphor given earlier of the alchemy available with your glyph the Water-Bearer applies here as well. Overall, the frog keeps your spirit up, vibe high, and the whole energy system pure and cleansed.

Fox

The fox is your secret super-spirit animal in many life occasions! Everything described about the fox applies to your character, moreover your core personality and social identity. You can work with the fox in and for waking life and in your dreams. Foxes possess beautiful spirits, despite being so cunning and calculated, aka logical and intelligent. Consider how much of the fox's symbolism currently rings true- how much do you need to integrate, and are you already embodying the fox's strengths? Using the visualization exercise (pages 141- 2) consider which of your other spirit animals complement the fox. For example, which ones can you call on together for balance, wholeness, or harmony?! The fox's intellect and instincts complement a lot of your other animals. Begin in self-development practice including the fox spirit animal; take it seriously to see real changes in your life. Finally, you should know that in addition to Uranus, you also have an ancient planetary ruler, Saturn. Saturn symbolizes authority and structures, moreover rules, law and order, regulations, and so forth. The fox spirit helps to bring out your inner self-leader and self-autonomous side through an increase in intellectual powers. Similar to the coyote, there's a shamanic link to fox, as it represents a connection to the Moon as well as shapeshifting. Explore this with an open mind!

Animals You Should Work With for Integration

Based on the qualities you lack, you should work with the following spirit animals to integrate more balance, harmony, and unification of opposite (or dualistic) forces in your life.

Panther

The panther is one to work with when you want to develop a more feminine and romantic approach to sex. Sexually, you are more primal, upbeat, and energetic. This is fine if you only choose compatible partners, such as fellow air and fire signs. But earth and water in addition to someone with a lot of earth or water in their natal chart prefers a different approach. Feminine sexuality as well as divine sensuality- being in touch with your divine soul essence, feminine qualities, and nurturing and caring attributes, are symbolic of the panther spirit, and something you lack. You're less romantic and gentle in the bedroom, which can be improved. Emotional intelligence, depth, an appreciation of beauty, sensitivity, and feminine intuition can be enhanced with the panther's divine assistance. Regardless of your gender, feminine sexuality is needed to some degree. Consider working with the panther spirit in unison with Venus, the planet of love, romance, female sexuality, pleasure, wealth, and beauty. Venus is exalted in Pisces, which means it's at its best placement, and the panther is one of Pisces' personal power animals. Venus energy can be amplified and integrated with the help of the panther, which, in turn, improves your romantic, business, and platonic relationships. Astral insights and connection to the subconscious & subtle planes, including the spiritual dimensions, extrasensory gifts, and psychic abilities, are acquired through the panther. This is the perfect spirit animal to work with to increase depth,

inner beauty, majesty, sensitivity, and other feminine qualities in your life. Also, to become a better lover…

Swan

The swan is also ideal for enhancing beauty and sensuality in your life. Swans mate for life, they're monogamous creatures. This can help you overcome your shadow traits of being unfaithful and anti-commitment in youth. Deep emotions coupled with real intimacy scares you, certainly before you reach a reasonable age of maturity and adulthood. The swan therefore helps you to see that love is a beautiful thing. Romance, purity, passion, serenity, commitment, and loyalty are amplified in many magical ways. As the swan is connected to both water and the earth, this helps you to feel secure in your explorations of your sensual self. You are quite a practical person, if not a little emotionally aloof and avoidant. So, the swan reminds you that true intimacy is not born from (solely) primal desires or the need for physical pleasure, but from deeper and authentic connection. If you don't want to be a player or involved in multiple love affairs forever, start your own journey with deeper self-love and intimacy with the swan. Furthermore, this is the *perfect* power animal for if you wish to start your own family.

The ***Mouse*** is another one to work with, specifically for increasing work ethic and attention to detail. You're such an idealistic and visionary sign that it's sometimes hard to focus on the smaller details. This is because they seem insignificant to you. So, work with the mouse when you need help grounding, further for greater respect for your commitments, responsibilities, and the practical aspects of life.

Chapter 19: Pisces

I am Pisces, the Zodiac complete,
I allow spirit and higher awareness to be grounded through my feet.
It is my ancient soul that allows me to know,
to tune in and receive divine guidance from the spiritual world.
Highly intuitive and deeply aware,
I possess supernatural abilities with a gift like a seer.
Sensitive, deep, and receptive to dreams,
I can access wisdom from the subconscious, invisible realms, and the unseen.
I am the artist, the creative, the musician, and the dreamer-
the one with great imagination, and the psychic & natural healer.
I possess healing hands and am incredibly empathic,
I am clairvoyant, wise, and even telepathic!
Compassion, kindness, and selflessness define me,
I like to be of service and listen to those in need…
With a unique gift to know things without being told,
I am a natural intuitive who can perceive energy from the invisible world.
A symbol for unconditional love, plus an understanding of human nature most could only wish,
I am the sign that represents all 12, the Zodiac's Old Soul, the Fish.

What's my shadow, do I have any lessons?
I can be moody, withdrawn, hyperemotional, and prone to depression.
I exist in many realms, picking up infinite subtleties, which make me lack boundaries,
so I need to learn to balance psychic gifts with practicalities & grounded spirituality.

Key Animals: *Your Personal Animal Guides & Spirits*

Dove, Deer, Turtle, *and* Swan (All 'Emotionally Intelligent' ones!)

Like fellow 'sister sign' Cancer, you are an empath with evolved emotional sensitivity and intelligence. You're deep, empathic, kind, impressionable, compassionate, devoted, loyal, a giver, a lover, peace-loving, fair, just, and gracious. You can be hyper-emotional as well as super-sensitive, two of your shadow traits you must work on if you wish to find your true place in the world, but you are the sweetheart of the zodiac. Your sensitivity and ability to treat everyone with kindness coupled with unconditional love are two of your most admirable traits. So, spend sufficient time exploring all the animals under 'Emotionally Intelligent,' specifically the dove, deer, turtle, and swan. (The dolphin is one of your personal power animals for protection.). All of the qualities and attributes available for integration are where you excel- these animals reflect your core personality; your soul essence. Work with these animals for spiritual illumination and self-growth as well as shadow work and healing. Consider how far along on your personal evolution journey you are, and continue to return to these animals for upgrades, guidance, and support. They can all serve as your saving grace in key moments in waking life…

Elephant

Like the elephant, you are gentle, compassionate, empathic, self-aware, and wise, moreover sensitive, nurturing, and blessed with feminine wisdom. The elephant symbolizes your royal blood and DNA; you are a very royal person, due to your ancient planet Jupiter. In addition to philosophy and higher learning, Jupiter represents expansion, luck, and social justice- high morals and ethics too. Some of your core qualities include dignity, nobility, and standing up for truth, wisdom, higher values, and spiritual ideals. You're deeply wise and philosophical with evolved intuition. The elephant is a symbol for royalty and ancient wisdom- they are compassionate, sensitive, self-aware, empathic, and loyal creatures, qualities you can learn from and work towards perfecting. Elephants are further a symbol of matriarchy; the females tend to raise the young as a large family or community. The elephant is a powerful grounder and stabilizing presence in your life, further helping to energize innate qualities linked to feminine, emotional, and spiritual energy. Community, family, and loyalty values can be learned, while you can master the art of patience, commitment, and returning to your roots. These are qualities you need to embody. Like Sagittarius, a sign you share a planetary ruler with, you can be flighty, frivolous, and anti-commitment. You're also known for being very impractical, irresponsible, and ungrounded, yet the elephant is extremely grounded, moreover full of duty. This is the perfect spirit animal for enhancing the qualities you lack, while simultaneously strengthening the attributes you already possess. The elephant can help you with shadow work/integration, as well as self-mastery.

Cow

The cow is a faithful spirit animal helper and guide that serves your soul on a deep level.
The cow symbolizes higher consciousness, karmic cycles, and transcending toxic behaviors, mindsets, and belief systems. With the help of the cow, you can get deep and explore your wounds, shadow personality traits, and strengths. Universal compassion, self-love, self-care, unconditional love, kindness, sincerity, selflessness, and healing are key meanings of the cow. You are a sensitive soul who is genuinely concerned with the well-being of others. You're a natural healer and empath, you believe in charity and selfless service. You're definitely not selfish or self-righteous, quite the opposite. In fact, you have a problem with being too kind and giving, Pisces. One of your key sets of shadow traits include naivety, gullibility, and innocence, in addition to being conned, used, and taken advantage of. Some lost souls see your kindness and unconditional love and trust and see it as an opportunity to take. It's unfortunate, but it makes you stronger. Like the cow, you suffer at the hands of abusive, mean-spirited, and ugly personality takers- the people who have no respect for gentle and beautiful qualities. The cow is tortured, used, and abused verging on murdered, while you- until you are grown with years of wisdom and maturity integrated- are equally abused. Whether it's physical in terms of your assets and resources, emotional, spiritual, or psychological abuse; people see you as an easy target. Some people of this world are cold and don't appreciate nor respect and honor kindness, soul, and the angelic type of faith you display. You should find time to read up on the cow spirit, further seeking to work with it in waking life and real time to heal, grow, and prosper. The more you choose what and who you don't want with the cow's assistance, the more you will attract the people who are meant for you; your soul family, tribe, and true friends who share the same values, morals, and ethics as you do. Life involves challenges, trauma, and difficulties, so the cow teaches you patience and compassion combined with inner peace, acceptance, and the art of self-respect! Boundaries coupled with self-love can be learned with the cow spirit animal.

Bear

The bear is your ultimate grounding and dreaming spirit animal merged and combined. The bear represents dreams, introspection, rest, self-care, self-love, healing, and parenting instincts. The bear is caring, compassionate, nurturing, loyal, and extremely protective of loved ones, especially family and children. But the bear also symbolizes grounding, creating strong physical foundations, abundance, security, material stability, and respect for the material-earthly realm. This makes this spirit animal perfect for all of the above, however equally for when you want to find balance, attaining wholeness and becoming the best version of yourself. For example, any super-sensitive or spacey (dreamy, floating away with the fairies...) tendencies can be overcome with the bear. As a symbol for dream time as well as the astral, subconscious, and introspective realms, you will find your artistic, imaginative, and musical gifts expanding and soaring the more you work with the bear. Your healing gifts too! Many people with this power animal go on to become masters of the Healing Arts or teachers of esotericism, metaphysics, mysticism, etc. Well, these are ideal career choices for you. You live to be of service, help others, and heal others through your actual healing gifts as well as your profound and evolved wisdom. As the last sign, you are incredibly wise with access to the divine- divine insights and revelations, higher perspectives, spiritual and cosmic consciousness, and wisdom and information that can only be found in the invisible realms. Astral and subconscious guidance and hidden knowledge too. You should work with the bear to enhance all of these qualities, moreover achieve master, elder, guide, teacher, or expert level. Finally, the bear can help you in both waking life and in dreamtime, specifically for amplifying astral, psychic, spiritual, empathic, and clairvoyant/clairsentient/clairaudient gifts.

Squirrel

The squirrel represents your ability to work with the energies of Mother Earth, of Gaia, natural environments and the spirits of the earth or forests. Sacred energy is available to you with the squirrel spirit, despite it being such a small creature in comparison to most others. Regardless of its size, the squirrel lives close to the ground, uses the trees for shelter, and relies on the fertility of the earth for nourishment and sustenance. Thus, the squirrel teaches you the art of divine simplicity, in addition to using the earth, Mother Earth, for food, shelter, and resources. The message is that our planet is fertile, abundant, and benevolent; when you work in harmony with nature, also respecting her and engaging in daily practices that honor her and your own body, you open yourself up to fruitful rewards. You are not a materialistic sign, however it is useful to be *reminded* of your natural philosophies and belief systems towards life. One of your shadow attributes is a lack of boundaries coupled with being pulled into other people's "flows;" their manipulations, false stories, dramas, and so forth. So, you might temporarily forget that you are actually a deeply humble and gentle soul by trying to be like everyone else. Greed, money, fame, superficial things, accumulating big wealth just for the sake of being wealthy or rich- these things don't interest you. You stand for selflessness, authentic spirituality, community, deeper connection, intimate bonds, universal love, sisterhood and brotherhood, and divine simplicity. There is no-one quite as charitable or sincerely spiritual as you. The squirrel, therefore, helps to remind you of your core life values and morals, assisting you in remembering that you are humble, down-to-earth, and a genuine lover of the simple life. And there's nothing wrong with this… We all have our strengths, and yours, dear Pisces, is being as selfless and humanitarianly-minded as they come. You don't need to lower your standards or change your core frequency to fit in. Call on the squirrel when you want to return to innocence, Source, and a humble way of life that simultaneously enriches your soul, talents, and spirit.

Beetle

You are an ancient and deep spirit, Pisces. You're magical, multidimensional, and blessed with wisdom not comprehensible to most humans. You're ruled by planet Neptune, the planet of psychic instincts, spirituality, illusions, and mysticism. You're also the sign of the 12th house, the house of spirituality, completions, and returning to Source and unity consciousness; the essence of the soul. The beetle is a symbol for ancient wisdom, magic, manifestation, the law of attraction as well as other universal laws, and knowledge of both sacredness and the divine. Like the squirrel, the beetle lives close to the earth, making a key message and lesson the importance of honoring the earth and planet. But, the beetle provides the extra dimensions of extrasensory perception, telepathic and psychic gifts, enlightenment, spiritual and soul illumination, and self-knowledge linked to the ether, astral planes, and multidimensional worlds. The beetle is a personal guide and protector. It is an animal that is often overlooked, just like you. You can be shy, reserved, quiet, and too humble, your humility and selflessness being the two things that leave you undervalued for your talents. The truth is, you are one of the most talented star signs-you're multi-talented, gifted in many areas, and extremely emotionally mature, intelligent, and wise. The power of emotional intelligence and maturity shouldn't go overlooked. So why do you always take selflessness and humility too far? The answer lies in one of your less desirable traits: self-sacrifice. Self-sacrifice is one of your worst character traits, a shadow attribute that makes you lack self-worth and self-esteem because you're always "giving" without "receiving." You give away your time, talents, love, money, resources, energy, caring, attention, devotion, etc.

As a master alchemist and manifestor, you don't always realize how powerful your intentions and energy are, which signifies that you unconsciously "transfer" your amazing soul gifts and talents onto others. You've mastered the art of holding space for others, which is a beautiful thing, yet you take this too far. Spiritual self-development combined with shadow work can help you transcend this toxic trait. Self-sacrifice literally means sacrificing yourself… so keep this in mind.

Eagle, Hawk, *and* Raven

Quite simply, these three spirit birds resonate with your Higher Self. Intellectual, imaginative, spiritual, intuitive, and visionary abilities and attributes can be found, strengthened, and mastered with the help of these power animals. Read up on their symbolism carefully. Examine how you're currently embodying their qualities, or not. Do you feel connected to your higher mind? As an emotional and spiritual sign, you are less logical, intellectual, and calculated than most. It's not that you don't have a sharp or witty mind, you do. You're just not cold in a business type of way; you don't believe in obliterating competition, in other words. You would rather work towards peace, unity, and cooperation, so all humans can benefit. This is admirable as well as needed in this superficial and somewhat narcissistic world, yet it also creates problems in your personal life. You can lack boundaries for one, further losing yourself and thus losing touch with reality. A bit of higher reasoning, logic, and analytical thinking is good for you.

In addition to creative vision, artistic and imaginative gifts, and powerful intuition- these spirit birds symbolize problem-solving, cognitive abilities, inventiveness and innovation, and ambition that leads to self-autonomy. You can enhance personal power, authority, and financial self-sovereignty with the help of these Higher Self spirit animals. You should work with these animals when you need to outgrow disillusioned and naive or immature cycles from your past. Innocence can remain (your innocence is beautiful…), but naivety is not good for your growth and self-evolution. Practicalities, self-responsibility, and supporting yourself through accepting the physical and 3D aspects of life are essential to all aspects and areas of life. Try to integrate these missing qualities with the help of the eagle, hawk, and raven.

Chameleon

You are a Mutable sign, like Gemini, Virgo, and Sagittarius. This means that you have the midas touch! You are a master of many things Pisces, gifted in the realms of healing, the imagination, intuition, psychic and instinctive powers, music, art, poetry, creativity, listening, counseling, and being a loving guide and way-shower for others. You're naturally inspiring through your devoted nature and genuine desire to do good in the world alone. You're sometimes misperceived as ambitionless, however this is only because you're deeply compassionate, sweet, and nurturing, moreover sensitive, spiritual, and mystical. You prefer to work in the spirit and dream worlds or do your work behind the scenes, and you can be surprisingly private despite being so friendly and charming. Actually, you're the sort of open-hearted spirit who projects such potent positivity and charm that people confuse your optimism with extroversion. In other words, they believe you to be sociable and always up for a chat when you're actually just projecting peace and positivity. In other situations, you're the one strangers come up to to share their deepest and most vulnerable secrets, emotions, and stories with. People sense that they can trust you- you're incredibly trustworthy and unconditionally compassionate. This has its positives and setbacks. A lack of boundaries has already been mentioned, so this is something you must work on. Yet, being so adaptable, open-minded, and pure-spirited opens a world of opportunities for you. Also, your adaptability enables you to be seen as many different things to many different people. Call on the chameleon spirit when you wish to be your liberated, free, intellectual, imaginative, quirky, positive, colorful, and wonderful self. Here's a hint: You often get so caught up in the emotional and spiritual realms that you forget how intelligent, independent, and colorful you are! You have an infectious smile, upbeat personality, and childlike naivety and innocence that guides you on your path… Never lose touch with your high-spirited and adventurous self, as it's the key to new connections, opportunities, and miracles in your life.

Lizard

As a symbol for dreams, astral visions and insights, and the multidimensional & spiritual planes, the lizard is an animal you share a close affinity and resonance with. This spirit animal could have easily gone in your personal 'power animals for protection' ensemble. Quite simply, get familiar with the lizard's meaning and energetic associations. Meditate often and work with the lizard spirit in visualization and dreamwork, as well as on the astral planes before sleep. Explore how this unique creature can open you up to cosmic portals of higher consciousness, self-awareness, and wisdom. Remember to say thank you, sending gratitude out into the ether… Be receptive too. Nothing is too strange, impossible, or unattainable with the multidimensional magic of the lizard.

Peacock *and* Parrot

Both of these animals help you become communicative. Direct communication is not your strength. You are passive, magnetic as opposed to electric, receptive, and selfless verging on self-sacrificial. You have a problem with speaking up, asserting your needs, and even honoring your own feelings. You're always putting other people's feelings and desires above your own, therefore direct, blunt, and assertive communication is a real issue for you, at least until later in life. You can be emotionally aloof, avoidant, and passive to the point of remaining in apparent perpetual silence. It doesn't help that others around you aren't as psychic as you, or don't understand that there are some truly selfless and passive souls; astrology isn't taught in mainstream education, for instance. You feel shy and reserved in youth, so you can work with these two spirit animals to shine more (specifically the peacock) and use your voice (the parrot). Come out of your shell. Embrace your talents, even if your voice shakes a little or you feel minor anxiety. Resistance is a sign that fear is soon to be released. When you feel fear taking over, it means a breakthrough is in divine order. Be bold, courageous, and self-empowered; know that you have a lot to share with the world, and suppressing yourself is hindering other people's growth as well as your own. This knowledge can help you. Because you're so concerned with the well-being of others, becoming aware that not speaking or shining your light prevents others from growing, evolving, or finding their own spiritual gifts and/or creative talents is a catalyst to you coming out of your bubble. Apply the philosophy of oneness, *we are all one*, to being assertive, communicative, and expressive. You definitely don't lack passion- you just need a reminder coupled with some assistance that it's ok to be a little loud, direct, or even blunt and forceful. Dominance and boldness are two masculine traits you can learn from both the peacock and parrot.

Rabbit

All aspects of creative, imaginative, and artistic expression come under the rabbit's realm. Sel-knowledge expands with the rabbit's medicine, as does wisdom of the seasons, natural cycles of nature, and abundance and fertility available to you. Every creative gift, service, hobby, professional pathway, or talent you possess and further want to develop can be accomplished with the rabbit. Your ideas, creativity, and originality, moreover innovation come alive. The rabbit is traditionally associated with Spring, the time you were born, Pisces. This means the rabbit is symbolic of your organic gifts and abilities. You're musical, creative, passionate, fertile- as a feminine sign, receptive, and gifted. You have skills in poetry, writing, performing, acting, and bringing others together; your body alone is a channel or conduit for higher consciousness energies to flow through. You genuinely believe in unity consciousness and spirituality that can heal the world. Working with the spirit of the rabbit will introduce synchronicity, the magic of co-creation, connectivity, deeper intimacy and soul bonds, and enhanced self-expression into your life. Any creative project or venture will get a boost with the rabbit's help, so don't be shy.

Power Animals for Protection

Panther

The panther is the perfect spirit animal for you, Pisces. You are deep, majestic, full of soul, graceful, elegant, and sophisticated. You radiate warmth, kindness, caring, compassion, sensitivity, and so forth, moreover you are sensual and spiritually sexy. Even when you think you're being sweet or simply sensitive and selfless, a lot of people see you as a sex magnet! This is because your heart is pure and therefore makes you physically attractive, while your true character is magnetic and submissive. You don't seek attention too, which makes you irresistible to a lot of people, especially the people who prefer a modest and graceful, humble, person. Well, the panther symbolizes divine sexuality, sensuality, soul, depth, and a number of spiritual powers Psychic gifts, potent instincts, eye glances that can penetrate the soul, and the power of invisibility- blending into the background while being the opposite of attention-seeking, are key meanings and attributes of the panther spirit. You already possess these, so working with the panther will sharpen and strengthen them. The panther is linked to astral guidance, ancient wisdom, and the subtle planes; the ether, spiritual consciousness, and primordial feminine energy.. As the Old Soul, you have an affinity with the panther spirit animal in a way only sister sign Scorpio shares, and this is because Scorpio is the sign of the shaman. Many Pisces' become shamans, spiritual healers and teachers, practitioners of herbal medicine, astrologers, psychics, etc.

The panther protects your feminine side. All of your beautiful qualities that make you unique are protected, seen, and cherished with the panther's assistance. We live in a world of duality, which means some people will see you and others won't. Some people see your kind and selfless nature as a weakness, even an opportunity to take from you; others see it as a blessing and something to nurture, admire, and cherish. The truth is, you are a diamond, and I'm not being biased. (Remember I am a Pisces Sun with my Venus in Pisces too…) We are the 12th and final sign, which implies we embody qualities and strengths from all 12 signs- we're the sign of completion, evolution of the soul, and spiritual enlightenment and illumination. Quite simply, you're a gem, a rare diamond, and as pure and selfless as they come. Like the panther, it's important that you stay sensual, down-to-earth, and somewhat hidden. Panther's exist in the subtle and astral realms, they don't just show themselves to anyone nor do they make themselves available to just anyone. The panther is here to show you how to honor your sacred essence, your divine sensuality, your sacred and divine sexuality, and your boundaries. Trust me, this is something you need help with, even if you're not yet conscious of it! Read up on the panther symbolism, as this spirit animal symbolizes your core nature. Then, seek to expand or embody the qualities, asking for this amazing animal's guidance. The panther is here to assist you in both waking life and the dreamworlds and planes.

Dolphin

You are the dolphin, Pisces! Emotionally intelligent, playful, kind, a lover of community, and even telepathic; you share a real resonance with the dolphin spirit, and this has two main meanings. Firstly, all of the panther's energy and medicine is reflected in your belief systems, personality, and innermost character. You naturally embody the qualities of the dolphin, so make sure you spend time working with this animal closely to expand all areas of your life. Secondly, there is a widespread belief that dolphins are linked to the star system Sirius, the Sirians believed to be an ancient civilization who were connected to ancient technologies and healing gifts; their consciousness was evolved and elevated. Sirians had extraordinary powers, powers currently possessed by you, Pisces. There are various advocations around the star system Sirius and our subsequent 'star seed' souls, but one popular one is that dolphins are these advanced souls, incarnated here to show us humans the power of telepathy, community, and advanced emotional intelligence. (The other notion is how Sirius is linked to Atlantis, the rise and fall of Atlantis being symbolic or an analogy for the rise and fall of our consciousness…) If you have your Sun, Moon, Venus, or Rising signs in Pisces, you most likely exhibit some of these rare gifts. Psychic gifts, premonition, mind-reading born from powerful empathy, super-foresight and cognition, unexplainable spiritual abilities, advanced imagination, the ability to travel the dreamspaces- the ability to astral travel and project, or lucid dream; these are all symbolic of Pisces' gifts.

Quite simply, you can and should work with the dolphin when you need to enhance and amplify your natural powers. Also, work with the dolphin when you need help remembering who you are. I Am presence and consciousness can be discovered with the dolphin spirit, as well as guidance for Higher self alignment and your soul's plan, life's purpose, and true north or destiny.

Furthermore, the dolphin is ideal for when you've become a bit serious or withdrawn due to feeling everything so deeply and intensely; the dolphin helps to restore your love of play, in addition to bringing out your inner child.

Animals You Should Work With for Integration

Based on the qualities you lack, you should work with the following spirit animals to integrate more balance, harmony, and unification of opposite (or dualistic) forces in your life.

Cat *and* Dog

Cat Vs dog energy: Pisces is a dual sign, always swimming with the tides and changing direction. These two animals could have easily made your personal spirit animal list, and you should still keep this in mind and therefore call on them for guidance and healing or protection. You have your own inner cat and inner dog within. In fact, as a dual sign who swims with the tides and flows with the currents, different people see you as different things. You're not fake, but you are highly adaptable, which signifies a number of people will have created a different personality or character for you altogether. To some people you embody a cat spirit, fiercely independent and clearly intuitive and instinctive. To others, you radiate a warmth and loyalty that is symbolic of the dog spirit. The truth is you are both, therefore these two animals which are so close to humanity can be seen as your 'inner yin and yang' animals. The cat represents your "lone wolf," incredibly independent, and freedom loving side. The dog is your sweet, nurturing, supremely kind, caring, and devoted one. Everyone knows you are a sweetheart, a sincere friend, lover, and kindred spirit to have. You're a soul sister or brother to a lot of people! Ruled by the glyph of the fish, you tend to swim in opposite directions as already expressed. One moment, you will be entwined in emotional and spiritual bonds, deeply dependent on the people in your life; in the next moment, you will apparently lose interest, wanting to instead wander off and dance away to the beat of your own drum. This latter energy is due to your ancient ruling planet, Jupiter. Jupiter now rules Sagittarius, so a lot of Sag's personality traits can be seen to be reflected in your own soul and psyche. You love freedom, adventure, community bonds, cultural learning opportunities and activity, and travel. You can also be frivolous, flighty, and both non-committal and impractical, especially in youth. These are the strengths and weaknesses of Sagittarius.

So, remember how the cat and dog represent your inner dual nature. Work with the dog when you've become too independent and free-spirited, and call on the energy of the cat when you need help remembering that it's ok to be your loving, open-hearted, loyal, and deep self… even if it means suffering a little. Why suffering? Because as a sensitive soul you feel things very deeply, further becoming sensitive and super-empathic once you've found your place in the world. Connections, friendships, and so forth make you a better person, but they also remind you of your own shadow personality traits. I.e. you can be self-sacrificing, somewhat codependent, and overly emotional and kind, caring, and generous with your time and love, just like the dog spirit.

Monkey *and* Coyote

The monkey and coyote are both perfect for intellectual and mental gifts. You now know that you are an emotional and sensitive sign- you're empathic, compassionate, dreamy, spiritually inclined, and submissive. You're also a giver and a lover, not a taker or a fighter. This makes you lack rationality, reasoning, and logic at times. You prefer to feel than think, tuning into subtle undercurrents of a situation or relationship. This is fine, but balance and harmony are essential for wholeness, so call on the monkey for ingenuity, higher reasoning, and logical and intellectual expansion, and the coyote when you need to detach emotionally. Both of these "mental" spirit animals can help you be more intellectual, psychological, and detached in a way that serves business acumen, financial savviness, and your ability to support yourself. The practical aspects of life are important, Pisces. Further, at a lower vibration, you are one of the signs most likely to be an earth-wandering hippy for the rest of your days... or live off of your parents! This may be ok in youth, but it's not a lifestyle choice once you reach adulthood. Thus, work with these two intellectual power animals to help you find your feet, become more self-sovereign and self-autonomous, and find comfort and acceptance in the 3D world of money, finances and practicalities.

Finally, if you wish to increase your primal desires and drive, call upon the **Crocodile** and **Horse** spirits. As the 12th sign, you are a symbol for spirituality and soul. You are the most unconditionally loving and universally compassionate zodiac sign, further having many gifts in the psychic, clairvoyant, and emotionally empathic and mature realms. Yet, you rule and are ruled by the 12th house, which can make you very spacey and also cut off from your body, the material world, and physical reality. Aries is the 1st house, which symbolizes personal identity and superficial things (from your spiritual eyes!); the 1st and 12th houses are very far apart... This signifies that you lack physical vitality, passion, and sexual drive or life force, at least compared to most others. In other words, you're so focused on the spiritual, astral, ethereal, subtle, and imaginative aspects of life that you forget the importance of physical well-being, strength, stamina, and so forth. You can therefore work with the crocodile and horse to amplify missing gifts.

Chapter 20: Universal Spirit Animals (All Signs!)

These are the animals that tend to be inherent within all of our psyches. They are usually reflected through the subconscious mind, accessed or shown through glimpses and insights in dreams; or presented in the form of signs and synchronicities (in waking life). Being open to the spiritual universe and subtle, ethereal, astral, quantum, and cosmic energies and forces allows you to receive animal wisdom. Spirit animals are always around us, as suggested in chapter 1. The following spirit animals can be considered *universal* because they resonate with the shared human collective soul, thus not being limited or exclusive to any one star sign.

You can call on any and all of these spirit animals to work with for your healing, spiritual, and self-development work. It's important you do.

Spider

The spider is a magnificent spirit animal representing the web of life, including creativity and interconnectedness. Synchronicity can be learned through the spider spirit. We are one with nature and the ethereal-invisible threads that weave us together in this divine orchestration. This is why the spider is a universal spirit animal. It helps us to see how one we are with each other and the world as a whole. Working with the spider can assist you in fine-tuning creative, artistic, and imaginative gifts. This is a potent power animal for recognizing your dreams, living up to your highest potential, and finding self-actualization. Self-realization coupled with multiple epiphanies come with the spider spirit. You can travel and delve into the depths of the mystical and spiritual universe, finding yourself and deeper truths in the process. Genius creativity and originality can be found, further life force and soul essence increased. The spider reminds you of ancient and primordial power, deep wisdom and higher awareness buried deep within. It's through the astral and ethereal planes where profound insights and inspiration flow to us. The universe is here to support you, it's all about co-creation and tuning into magnetic and electric power and energies, further co-creating with the energies of the universe for ultimate goal and wish fulfillment. We each have a soulprint, a unique soul blueprint. This is the ideal frequency or vibration that can guide us towards our highest joy. Living life with ultimate passion and purpose, in alignment with our life plan and path, is part of the spider's medicine. Your destiny can be discovered. Like the threads of the spider's web, you can unravel the mysteries of your deepest self and of the greater universe. Miracles can be found. Becoming present and having patience with yourself and time cycles are further main meanings. Presence allows you to tune into the subtle energies and vibrations of the astral, spiritual, and ethereal planes…

Ultimately, the spider is a cosmic unraveller of truth, astral wisdom and knowledge, ancient energy, and unity consciousness. Source energy is available to tune into, as well as spiritual, psychic, and intuitive gifts. Harmonious energy for your visions expand, while innate dormant imaginative and artistic ideas, memories, and plans come to full light! You are a force of nature with the spider by your side. Vision, subtle perception, dream knowledge, and access to the subconscious realms are enhanced. The spider is great for music, journaling, writing, painting, gardening, cooking, channeling, visionary art, or even academic studying. Spiritual insight, illumination, and connection with divine higher energies. Subtle energy flows through you and everything in the universe. The spider at the highest vibration represents dreaming weaving; working with your dreams, including your guides and ancestors, for healing and inspiration. Patience, receptivity, feminine energy, creativity, and embracing our fate are further associations. Coming to terms with your own shadow self, your darker psyche, and the darkness of life in general can be seen and understood from fresh and higher eyes. When we see with a spiritual lens, it opens us up to a world of fearlessness and bravery, boldness and courage to live our truth and joys with heart, passion, and soul. Cosmic perspectives coupled with multidimensionality are available. Creative directors, visionaries, artists, and performers best benefit from the spirit of the spider. If you're prone to the multidimensional and dream worlds, you may even get a visit or two from the spider through the astral planes, as I have many, many times… The spider is a symbol of the divine feminine energy, the Great Mother, and Gaia. This spirit animal is a weaver of divine destinies, all linked to a higher power. Finally, the spider is here to show you the true meaning and power of synchronicity. Pay close attention to the subconscious messages and clues you receive, as synchronicities are the key to community and self-evolution. Shadow traits include becoming too immersed in creativity, artistry, and the astral and subconscious planes as well as dream worlds. Take inspiration from these places, but be mindful of an excessive need for solitude, introspection, or isolation.

Snake

The snake is the ultimate kundalini awakening spirit animal perfect for healing all aspects of your sexuality, on all dimensions. The snake represents wisdom, sensuality, sexuality, psychic gifts, intuition, instincts, and your "rainbow body." This is your 7 chakra system that results in an active and healed kundalini. Your kundalini is your life force, which, when in a constant state of flow, leads to longevity and the gifts mentioned; psychic gifts, sensuality, etc. Also, creative life force and evolved imaginative as well as artistic gifts. Working with the snake spirit stimulates kundalini energy and potent life force, which manifests as wholeness, healing, and integrating on the spiritual, emotional, mental, physical, and astral planes. All of these dimensions and bodies can be healed and balanced with the snake's medicine. When energy is free to flow through the chakras, you can reach heightened states of consciousness, further healing your wounds. Lower and higher self can be healed and merged for wholeness, in addition to unity consciousness. Past pains, wounds, traumas, and memories that keep you stuck in limiting and self-destructive cycles can be explored. The snake helps you get to the root. Issues on a core, soul, and moreover deep level can be looked at honestly and addressed. Potent life force is increased with the snake's help. Working with the energies of the earth are advised- both earthly and ancestral powers, and heavenly celestial ones. The snake helps you to connect with the divine linked to the kingdom of heaven, God, the celestial and ethereal planes, just as it can entwine you with sensual, primal, and primordial powers and abilities. People with this spirit animal tend to be very sensual, enjoying frequent dance, self-care, love-making, physical passion, exercise, movement, and surrendering to divine flow and will.

The Snake is the animal of the Shaman, alongside the Owl. While the owl represents feminine and astral wisdom, intuition, and potent instincts, the snake symbolizes masculine sexuality, which, when healed, leads to enlightenment. Like the owl the snake is a shapeshifter. The snake is very significant in many religious and spiritual texts and schools of thought, moreover teachings. This special animal sparks life force and heals past life traumas. Personal and collective karma can be healed through taking a deep dive into your own soul, in addition to your subtle energy bodies. The snake teaches we are holistic beings, mind, body, and spirit, and also with multiple layers. Wholeness can be achieved, as well as self-realization of your unique gifts, moreover your shadows self and light self, enlightenment and the darker parts you may want to repress. The second main message of the snake relates to your healing abilities. The snake spirit reminds you that you have healing hands, healing presence, and natural healing gifts. Every human is a natural healer- some of us just choose to unravel the layers of conditioning, programming, and fear timelines, to embrace our healing gifts. Divine will, ancient wisdom, sacred knowledge, awareness of universal and sacred laws, rebirth, and alchemy are part of the snake's symbolism. The snake is the ultimate 'I Am a healer!' power animal to work with.

Primal instincts and passions come alive the more you work with the snake spirit animal. Unconscious driving forces can be brought to light. The more you come to terms with your own sexuality, shadow self, and desires, the ones that are usually denied, rejected, or dismissed, the more unconscious patterns of thinking, doing, and behavior can be transcended. Questions like, 'how do I use my energy?' 'What's my idea of fun?' (Dance, creative expression, heart-to-heart communications, drama, gossip, t.v. video games…?) 'what are my views and beliefs around love and sex?' 'Do I see platonic intimacy with the opposite sex as acceptable?' 'Is romance only exclusive to sexual partners?' 'Do I live my life consciously, with full awareness and mindfulness?!' 'Do I still have/are there toxic cycles to let go of, remove, and transcend?' Pay attention to inner world sensations that arise when working with the snake in your meditation and self-development practices. Furthermore, sexual and sensual energy usually has its roots somewhere, such as your Root, Sacral, Solar Plexus, Heart, Throat, Third Eye, or Crown. Become mindful of which chakra your sexual desires, thoughts, and fantasies arise from. This can teach a huge deal about yourself, moreover your needs, motivations, and deepest impulses.

Finally, in Greek mythology, Asesclepius, the God of Medicine, is depicted as two snakes climbing up a rod, a symbol that is further known today as Caduceus. The snake symbolizes important life changes and transitions, rebirth, transformation, awakening, spiritual development, protection from harm and negative energies, and self-empowerment! Negative themes to be careful of if you feel drawn to the snake are: temptation, deception, betrayal, repressed desires- usually around intimacy and sexuality, and potentially dangerous situations or people. The snake warns us against weak boundaries, letting in harmful people and vibrations that cause harm emotionally, spiritually, psychologically, or physically. In the Bible, the snake represents original sin. You don't have to be religious to understand the teaching in this. As a perfect symbol for the kundalini and therefore healing gifts, higher wisdom, and awakened consciousness, the metaphor signifies how the snake enticed Adam and Eve to eat an apple, which became the starting point of sin. The apple represents our basic human needs and desires for survival; food, security, shelter, and longevity. This is synonymous with the root chakra. From eating the apple this holy couple were believed to become disconnected from the divine, which is a truth actually rooted in the journey of the kundalini, the *serpent-energy* that flows from root to crown, and then spirals back around on itself. We must eat food to sustain us, also energizing our roots and lower chakras. This naturally prevents us from living solely in our crowns and higher chakras, the energy centers symbolizing divinity, spiritual perception, and enlightenment. Thus, the kundalini represents wholeness, moreover we find wisdom when acknowledging and paying respect to all 7 main chakras- the kundalini, in essence.

I am the Snake, a symbol for immortality,
Many consider me evil yet they fear my special abilities.
It is my serpent energy that people often despise,
yet in truth they are misguided, they're not seeing from the higher eye.
Intensely powerful with immense creative energy,

you may be a natural healer if you relate to me.

On the mental plane I represent intelligence, intellect and intuition;
on the emotional plane your dreams and a sense of healthy ambition.
On the spiritual plane I am understanding, inner knowing, and wholeness,
The physical plane provides me the strength and power to truly show this.

Transmutation, alchemy, and ascension define me,
I represent rebirth and evolution with an ability to communicate telepathically.
I do not possess ears for the bones in my head conduct sound;
I hear a range of frequencies and sense vibrations through the ground.
With a healing presence and deep understanding of the eternal nature of life,
for those that recognise my true nature, you will see that all is light.

Owl

The owl is a spirit animal spiritual seekers and those destined for a shamanic path come to know on a deep level. The owl is one of the shaman's special animal guides. Holistically, the owl symbolizes vision, insight, evolved intuition, psychic gifts, access to subconscious wisdom and the subtle realms, and potent instincts. The owl is a feminine animal because it allows us to access the shadow realms, i.e. darkness. Darkness isn't seen as something to fear in those with this spirit animal, as we recognize that darkness is where deep wisdom and self-knowledge can be discovered. The owl connects us to the astral planes. Astral projection, lucid dreaming, and conscious dreamwork can be amplified to new levels with the owl. The owl can see in the dark and through hidden deception, BS, and manipulation. This is why the owl is known as the messenger and discoverer of secrets. Clear sight, higher perspectives, multidimensionality, pearls of wisdom and guidance through the ether and astral planes, spiritual ideals, self-realization, and potent instincts are the key themes. Also, clairvoyance, prophecy, higher level cognition, advanced imaginative gifts, and creative genius. The owl teaches us how to make peace with our shadow selves, further coming to terms with the darker places of the human psyche. Individual/personal and collective/planetary consciousness gets a boost with this majestic bird. Illumination as well as enlightenment are core to the owl's medicine. Through coming to terms with your own darkness, you can see through and into the darkness and manipulations of others. The shadow self is integral to finding the light, so call on the owl to make peace with your shadow. This is the only way to self-realization, enlightenment, and authentic integrated living. Getting to the root of truth, moreover seeing beyond and through the veil of illusion, can bring much darkness to light.

In addition to secrets, the owl helps in attaining soul connection, divine alignment, and depth. Powerful psychic, intuitive, and instinctive senses are available, which allow for a number of magical frequencies and vibrations to come through. Extrasensory perception, telepathy, finding solace in darkness and your own shadow self, and acquiring knowledge and inspiration at night…. The owl's magic is strongest at night. As one of the shaman's spirit animals, the owl is further a shapeshifter. Those with this power animal strongly integrated can shapeshift between multiple realms, frequencies, and dimensions. Navigating the ethereal, subtle, subconscious, shadow, astral, spiritual, and multidimensional realms is a gift not everyone can manage. We may only receive glimpses into prophetic vision and divine gifts, but, with the owl, you can fine-tune these. Super-empaths, clairsentients, clairvoyants, healers, and seers often have the owl as a close spirit animal companion, at both night and during waking hours. The owl aims to serve the Higher Self. It can expand healing gifts and presence, for example the ability to see into another person's health, past, future, inner self, etc. The owl spirit is here to help you read auras and heal and expand your own auric field, if you should so choose. Hidden emotions, belief systems, energies, karmic exchanges, weaknesses, strengths, feelings, and subtle sensations can all be seen clearly with the owl's assistance. Further, feminine qualities are increased, profoundly magnetism, receptivity, caring, compassion, nurturance, kindness, gentleness, humility, selflessness, empathy, grace, motherly love, female instincts, and sacred wisdom. Moon magic-lunar energy- is deeply connected to the owl, and sensitivity is seen as a superpower. The message is: always trust your intuition, as there is more to life than meets the eye; life is a multidimensional experience with many hidden and subtle realms and layers. Shadow traits to be mindful of include deception, manipulation, extreme secrecy or isolation, hypersensitivity, and getting lost in the spiritual and astral planes.

I am the wise Owl,
I can see everything around.
Being highly intuitive, an ability to know things without being told,
I thrive in darkness and receive my wisdom from the unknown.
The Moon is my friend as I feel strongly connected to her light,
I am mysterious and a messenger of secrets,
traveling swiftly through the night.

Wolf

The wolf is another shamanic power animal. Have you noticed the pattern? These universal spirit animals cannot be included in chapters 2- 8, because they would all be assigned to virtually everyone of you. They are a part of our core programming, our collective human soul, psyche, and Higher Self. So, like the Snake and Owl, the Wolf represents our inner shaman. Key themes and meanings include powerful instincts, physical vitality, evolved intuition, extrasensory gifts and powers, and protection. Fierce self-protection coupled with protection for loved ones, in fact. In addition to these qualities, the wolf is here to show us the significance of healthy attachment Vs independence, family bonds Vs introspection, and community Vs solitude. It's all about balance, a balance and harmony of the close relationships in our lives with sufficient time for introspective and solo activities. It's in isolation where we recharge and rejuvenate. The wolf is one of the best animals for recognizing your inner animal merged with your spiritual self. Instincts meet higher awareness, primality merges with spiritual perception, and you can discover the true meaning of 'human having a spiritual experience.' Basic instincts, needs for security, family and friendship bonds that transcend all time and space, and physical vitality coupled with life force are part of the wolf's medicine. The bond they share with others in their pack is extraordinary, which is a message in the rare type of telepathy that can exist between kin. Loyalty, protection, the desire to defend and serve, friendship, kindness, sincerity, depth, intensity, and authentic communication can be increased and developed. The wolf guides you to trust in your inner voice, moreover your gut feelings.

Sensations of the flesh, i.e. bodily wisdom and instincts, are linked to the Higher Self and higher mind, which is where intuition arises and flows. Instincts (body, emotions, raw and primal sensations of the lower self)... and intuition (higher mind, Higher Self, and spiritual vibrations, awareness, and perception) can be unified, strengthened, and harmonized with the wolf's assistance. You can learn how to accept your primal and therefore lower self. In doing so, you let life force energy flow as it should, opening yourself as a channel for it to reach the higher chakras. Even one authentic moment of self-acceptance of your shadow can spark higher consciousness as well as self-awareness. It's repressing the darker and less desirable aspects of the self that lead to extremes, also preventing us from moving energy from our lower centers to our higher ones. It's not about getting lost in the shadow traits or behaviors, nor is it about becoming so reliant on the root chakra that we're unable to transcend comfort zones. One of the main meanings of the wolf spirit is attachment and community & family bonds Vs independence and solitude, therefore the message is to embrace and surrender to yourself to let go and transcend. Let energy keep flowing, changing, and moving. Similar to the fox, the wolf symbolizes agility, flexibility, and adaptability. Telepathic communication, fine-tuned empathy, and advanced extrasensory gifts are available when you work with the wolf's medicine. You can learn the true meaning of living life in both your conscious mind and with a deep connection to subconscious wisdom. Subtle energy and deep ancestral knowledge are available. Telepathy is a type of spiritual power and psychic gift built off of advanced intuitive combined with clairvoyance, clairsentience, and clairaudience. Wolves are very sensitive to external energy, environmental factors and influences, and other people, as well as their own internal needs and desires. Sensitivity, empathy, and self-awareness are three key gifts you can learn with the wolf.

Furthermore, you can access dreams, finding guidance, wisdom, and inspiration in the dreamworlds and planes. The wolf lives a solitary life, meaning they are content in their own company. This signifies the importance of introspection, solitude, soul-searching, and disconnecting from the drama, chaos, and unnecessary distractions of the world. People who identify very strongly with the wolf spirit animal tend to spend a lot of time learning, studying, and finding themselves, to then integrate their new found wisdom in their community. They gather a lifetime of expertise, self-knowledge, resources, experience, gifts, abilities, and inner strength cultivated through self-study coupled with soul-searching/introspection, and then step into a self-leadership position. Master teachers, wayshowers, healers, shamans, and energy workers tend to have the wolf as a close spirit companion and guide. Positive karma is encouraged through the intimate and honest connections you form, so keep this in mind when choosing your lover, partner, friendship group, or social circle. Soul family is the aim of the game with the wolf, once you've integrated your darker attributes with your light self and then found the perfect balance between finding peace, pleasure, and solace in your solitude with community, social, and family relationships. The wolf can teach you the ultimate test of loyalty, in addition to finding self-respect and honoring your boundaries. The final message is to be very cautious and conscious with who you give your energy to. Not everyone is for you, and that's ok! Some people are not part of your soul family or tribe, while others will cherish, love, honor, support, and admire you unconditionally. In addition, mystic energy is strong, such as the ability to travel dimensions, moreover shapeshift. You should learn from mentors and elders to acquire your own self-mastered knowledge and expertise, and, finally, gather the resources and physical strength, vitality, and stamina to see lifelong goals, dreams, and ambitions, as well as plans that honor your soul's purpose, through to completion.

The wolf is symbolic of the pathfinder who shows you the way to your soul's innermost desires. It's an excellent power animal to work with for aligning with your destiny and discovering your soul's plan, purpose, and hidden talents. Sharp intelligence, self-protection, courage, resilience, determination, inner wisdom and vision, and an appetite for freedom are final meanings that haven't yet been mentioned. All of these can be embodied and enhanced with the wolf's assistance. Shadow traits to watch out for include deception, misusing hidden knowledge, and altering between the extremes of "lone wolf" syndrome- loving your quiet time too much, and family or community play, bonding, and expression. Be careful of isolation, dishonesty, losing trust and faith in yourself and/or others, and domination and control tactics. Connection, intimacy, and companionship are always favored over control.

Whale

The whale symbolizes ancient memory, the power of sound, song, music, and vibration, and the mystery of life itself… The whale is one of the most deep and ancient memory sparking spirit animals of them all. The whale is here to show us the power and significance of song, sound, and music. Everything in life is vibration, everything produces its own unique frequency, a melody or specific vibratory frequency. Song, dance, music, creativity, poetry, writing, speaking, performance, and self-expression… The Whale is here to fine-tune and strengthen any creative activity you perform. It is specifically wonderful for singers, musicians, and sound practitioners, or for those who work with subtle energy, such as Reiki Masters, Holistic therapists, Shamanic healers, etc. This spirit animal is perfect for unraveling life's deeper mysteries and truths, further getting to the root and core of illusions. You can find real wisdom, awareness of sacred laws, and inspiration with the whale's assistance. The whale teaches that all wisdom, experience, and memory is available to tune into; it's available in the cells of your body… each drop of the ocean… and in the subtle and astral planes. The ether is connected to it all, so detaching from the mind games, stories, illusions, drama, and made-up BS often associated with the material 3D realm, naturally helps you align with the ether and Great Spirit. The divine realms are where real peace, joy, higher wisdom, fresh perspectives, ultimate truths, inspiration, and unity consciousness are found. The whale is very content being alone or with others. They walk their path gracefully, in tune with their surroundings and with their needs. Sensitivity, grace, gentleness, empathy, nurturance, depth, soul, and selflessness are key themes available for integration.

The beginning of time, the original primordial sound of creation, and memory of the entire planet's herstory ('history' is based on a patriarchal view of the world, and is very biased and limited) can be found in the whale's call. It's an ancient echo that sparks memory and higher consciousness on a deep, deep level. This spirit animal is not for the cowardly or faint-hearted. It takes considerable strength t o explore the depth of your soul, desires, wants, needs, and beliefs. Every sound, emotion, event witnessed, observation, and sensory experience has shaped you into the being you are now. The whale helps to awaken dormant gifts as well as ancient memories. Ancestral and celestial wisdom shines through when you work with the whale spirit. You may start to remember past lives, significant soulmate or karmic connections, or the power that comes with seeing everyone as family, with discernment and boundaries, of course. Past lives and karmic contracts, as well as soulmate bonds, are very significant to the whale spirit animal. Remembrance is sparked. You will start to leave behind toxic relationships and cycles, and only be interested in people who spark your soul. Soulmates come in all forms, from animals to blood family and lovers to friends. When you unravel the mysterious depths of your own primal self, psyche, and heart, you begin to see the same qualities in others. This isn't about living in naivety and gullibility, but about positive reflection while recognizing our shared humanity and divinity. Working with the whale can help you to strengthen sensitivity, feminine-nurturing qualities, etc., so you can then find others on your wavelength.

Secrets of creation can be uncovered. Invisible frequencies come to light, while seeing through and beyond the veil of illusion. Learning the laws of time and space, understanding metaphysical principles, and finding solace in the ethereal, subtle, and subconscious planes are part of the whale's medicine. Call on the whale if you wish to learn the secrets of the universe, moreover heal past pains and wounds. Emotional healing and the maturity, wisdom, and intelligence that comes with it are in store. In fact, cleansing and healing emotional pain, as well as sexual trauma, are integral to the positive effects of the whale spirit animal. Devotion, fluid and empathic communication, vulnerability, deep awareness, and lyrical and musical skills can be learned. People with this spirit animal tend to be excellent communicators and masters in the realm of emotions, sensitivity, and deep awareness, because emotional and spiritual rebirth are a norm. Life is cyclic, so these in addition to cleansing, detoxification, soul alignment, healing, and clearing away the past can all be enhanced and practiced on a regular basis. Intuitive and psychic abilities can also be expanded, while evolved empathy coupled with imaginative gifts flow to and through you. The message is that there is more to life than material reality, thus this is one of the best spirit animals for poets, artists, musicians, dreamers, astrologers, psychics, tarot readers, healers, seers, and visionaries. Mysticism, knowledge of your own and others' healing powers, and extrasensory and psychic gifts are all expanded with the whale. Further meanings include finding your authentic voice, DNA activation, and accessing the higher spiritual planes, such as the quantum field. Connection with your Akashic Records, the cosmic omniscient library, can be accessed with this super-empathic spirit animal. Be mindful of depression, isolation, and loneliness, however, as shadow traits include super-sensitivity, disconnection from others and society, and fear of intimacy.

I am the Whale, the record keeper for eternity,
in the ocean's deep waters are stored long lost memory.
I can travel through time to the beginning where it all began-
memories and secret knowledge are stored in music, song, and sound.
Creative gifts and inspiration can be awakened through my magic,
I have the ability to communicate on a wave that is telepathic.
I have seen it all, around since the start of time and roots;
I can hear the voice of all life's creatures, in my call is echoed truth...

Ladybird

The ladybird is a spirit animal of good luck, blessings, and abundance. Being so close to Mother Nature brings the energy of prosperity and abundance through healing, spiritual development, and honoring nature's cycles. The message is to embrace change while getting in tune with natural cycles, such as the cycle of your body as well as the cycles of nature and the universe. The ladybird signifies ancient energy, including soulmate bonds. You can call on the ladybird spirit to help with rebirth, personal alchemy, and transformation, moreover metamorphosis, for example, transitioning from one significant life chapter, emotional state, or belief system to another. It inspires positivity, courage, determination, steadfastness, sensitivity, and patience. Pursuing pleasure is included in this spirit animal's healing abilities. You can find your deepest joys and passions coupled with what brings you most peace with the ladybird. Aa a symbol of good luck; blessings, fortune, and wealth increase in your life the more you embrace your passions and further act on your greatest joys. Paying respect to the ladybird can bring you abundance in significant measures! Keep a pure heart, live with integrity, and commit to a spiritual or healing path. Grace, modesty, and humility are powerful attributes that increase with the ladybird's medicine. In the pursuit of pleasure, try to embrace a guilt-free approach and mindset. But, don't fall into greed, hedonistic tendencies, excess, extremes, or over-indulgence. Moderation is important to attract new wealth, love, luck, opportunities, and anything else you consider a blessing.

Light-heartedness comes with the ladybird, while staying grounded. Balance is the name of the game, meaning you should always stay mindful of the following. Be upbeat, positive, and optimistic without becoming superficial or narcissistic. Be playful, fun-loving, and spontaneous without succumbing to impulsive and ungrounded. Finally, be practical, grounded, and disciplined without forgetting the importance of laughter, community, and positive vibrations! The ladybird represents balance and harmony in many life areas. Affectionate loving relationships expand with the ladybird's assistance. Working with the ladybird amplifies loyalty, friendship, romance, sensitivity, beauty and harmony within a relationship, platonic intimacy, and deeper connection. The ladybird is excellent to work with for making changes in your love life, career and work situation, and home, family, or living environment. Both sexual and platonic partnerships get a boost from the ladybird spirit's energy and medicine. This power animal is a guardian of sacred, nurturing, and loving relationships, so be mindful of the importance of beauty, depth, soul, and sensitivity in your life. Also, the ladybird brings a unique type of grace and humility when dealing with conflict, disagreements, and so forth. If there's been tension in a relationship, or if there's a difficult conversation upcoming that you know could be a little chaotic, ambiguous, drama-infused, call on the ladybird's support. Empathic communication coupled with compassion are increased and available for embodiment. The ladybird is your ally that can assist you in connecting to ethereal and subtle energy for spiritual insights, higher perspectives, subconscious wisdom, and deep revelations into the energy currents and exchanges of a situation.

Representing potent change, and transformation, this power animal asks you to listen to your inner voice, moreover your intuition. This allows you to get to the root of events, relationships, karmic bonds and exchanges, life choices and challenges, and everything above, below, and in between. This animal represents soul evolution coupled with having supreme patience and wisdom with the transformation process. Innocence, naivety, and a fresh child-like perspective also come with the ladybird's medicine. Inner beauty, compassion, and emotional intelligence can be cultivated. Further, you can learn the true art of accomplishing things while remaining humble, modest, and down-to-earth. Also, rest, rejuvenation, and recharging your energies are highly significant, in addition to open-mindedness, exploring spiritual belief systems, and new philosophies. The shadow attributes of the ladybird include fear of change, being too passive and self-sacrificial, too much humility and modesty so your gifts and talents get overlooked, and a lack of focus and direction.

Bee

The bee symbolizes community, the soul, karmic cycles, completion, and self-evolution. The bee is an intrinsic member of a thriving ecosystem, which teaches us the power of community, unity, and solidarity; working together towards a common goal and cause. Understanding your roots in your community, as well as the importance of stewardship, are integral to the bee spirit. You can learn the art of teamwork, cooperation, and creating sustainable systems that will benefit more than the individual. Magic and synchronicity can be acquired and increased. The bee reminds us of the divine, spiritual, and interconnected universe where magic and miracles are possible. Working consciously with nature and creative life force produces fruitful rewards, as does working hard with soul. Creativity, joy, laughter as a medicine, optimism, courage, and devotion are powerful associations. The bee spirit teaches that following your highest joy coupled with living with soul are the keys to ultimate wish fulfillment. You can call on the bee to master patience, determination, practicality, organization, creating order and strong foundations, and energizing long-term plans and goals. Dreams and aspirations can be realized! There's a visionary aspect to this humble little creature, so a healthy sense of idealism, artistic and imaginative gifts, and advanced creative life force can be accessed as well as expanded. Similar to the butterfly, the bee helps you to make sense of the past, presnet, and future, including the experiences that have shaped you. While the butterfly, as we explore next, is specific to the psyche and soul for personal transformation, the bee represents how your psyche and soul urges show up *within a community or social scene*. You can explore your desires, personality traits, social identity, and inner realm (psyche, soul, feelings, emotional undercurrents, belief systems, etc.) in the context of how others perceive you, how and why you choose to show yourself, and how you choose your conscious waking life interactions. As you can observe from a bee hive, every member works together, with the Queen Bee holding it altogether.

So, the secondary meaning of the bee is the significance of feminine energy. Ancient royalty and memory, moreover recognizing how special your DNA and its health is, on a spiritual level, are included in the bee's wisdom. Emotional depth, sensitivity, wisdom, awareness, and empathy can be learned, while unlimited potential and the opportunities that follow increase the more you listen to your inner voice, choose joy and love, and trust in the universe. The bee works closely with Gaia, Mother Earth, and the ecosystems that sustain us, which signifies the importance of respecting the earth, your body, and your sensuality. Respect for your divine vessel, in addition to the sacredness of life and the earth herself (the earth is a feminine principle), and further engaging in regular acts of kindness and service to both your body and the earth, are called for. Sensual expressions such as through healthy creative cooking, gardening, dance, self-care, and other routines that honor your self-worth and inner glow are also on the cards. The more you honor your body, physical well-being, emotional health, and psychological & spiritual well-being, the more you find your soul talents, true path, and authentic purpose. Daily acts of self-care are essential to align with your tribe or community, or simply find yourself in the world.

In addition to embracing your sensuality through self-love, working directly with the earth is equally part of the bee's medicine. Permaculture, working with herbs and essential oils, studying or training to become a herbalist, organic farming, volunteering or working in an eco project or seed bank, or even becoming a plant, tree, or botanical specialist may be part of your unique path if you strongly resonate with the bee. Fruitful blessings come when you pay close attention to the signs of Mother Earth, and then work in harmony with her. When you give back, you receive. The bee teaches that there's a natural exchange and flow of energy. Honoring your soul calling tied into the work you do in your local or greater communities is entwined with the level of prosperity, wealth, and synchronicity you receive. Further, the bee asks for conscious living and communication, such as speaking, acting, and living with grace, integrity, mindfulness, empathic awareness, and honest and transparent speech. Additionally, having a powerful work ethic coupled with determination, high productivity levels, commitment, evolved responsibility, and a sense of duty can be developed and integrated. The bee helps you to balance work, rest, and play, having both the best family and domestic life and professional life simultaneously. Teamwork, networking, authentic relating, problem-solving, finding solutions to all life's challenges, courage, devotion, self-discipline, and willfulness combined with sensitivity are in store. Fairness, equality, and social justice are also potent themes for self-development. Shadow traits to be mindful of include all work and no rest and play, as well as the inability to unwind, relax, or surrender to the flow and will of things. Too much planning, prep, organization, and order, moreover focus on routines and security, are things you need to watch out for.

Butterfly

The butterfly is a symbol of transformation of the soul. This beautiful spirit animal that is part of our shared collective psyche and consciousness represents soul growth, self-evolution, personal transformation, awakening, and transcending toxic cycles and behaviors. Anything can be toxic- a mindset, behavior, belief system, relationship, job, social or friendship circle, daily habit, living environment… Toxicity implies that we are not living up to our fullest potential, we're still operating from "lower" cycles that aim to serve our lower selves, or self-destructive, self-limiting, and self-sabotaging cycles. Healing and deep soul worth can be acquired with the butterfly's assistance, but this doesn't mean that healing or shadow work has to be heavy. The butterfly also brings the medicine of the spirit of joy, positivity, and lightness. You can find your freedom, independence, and liberation with the butterfly's assistance, moreover self-autonomy and self-sovereignty. The butterfly teaches the power of learning through life's struggles, hardships, and challenges, and then taking the life experience and wisdom to shine. You can live with soul and a strong sense of personal integrity, in addition to majesty, nobility, higher self-awareness, humility, and grace. Alchemy can be practiced and embodied. Positive alchemy is recognizing you have certain shadow traits to transcend, or toxic and limiting cycles to outgrow, and then working towards change. Enlightenment is literally becoming the light, first seeing and finding the light within and around, and then making positive steps to move away from darkness. Further, the butterfly can help if you have a tricky time coming to terms with your shadow self, for example if you're someone who wants to deny, reject, or dismiss your shadow altogether. Integration and wholeness are possible with the butterfly spirit animal

If you resonate with this power animal, you may have a very powerful desire for freedom, change, and liberation from oppressive or restricting structures. Limitless possibilities coupled with unlimited potential are in store. Breakthrough is a key word associated with the butterfly spirit. Committing to a path of light, service, community, brotherhood or sisterhood, helping heal the earth, environmentalism, authentic spirituality, and other pathways that aim to serve a pathway of light instead of fear are core themes. There are two main timelines, fear or love. Choosing fear keeps us stuck in limiting and self-destructive cycles and chapters, life experiences that don't serve our souls or higher selves, further perpetuates darkness. Unhealed wounds, traumas, fears, insecurities, and projected shadow traits come into the category of 'fear.' Oce you set your mind on a better way, a more harmonious way, as well as a timeline that serves your Higher Self, you start to realize the amazing magic available. This is what the butterfly brings! Magic, synchronicity, co-creation, complete freedom and liberation (from oppressive structures, etc.), and passions that honor your soul growth. A desire to be free and live with heart and soul can steer you onto new horizons. Limitation, stagnation, and self-sabotage are three things the butterfly works strongly against; transformation requires growing pains, breakthroughs that can be difficult, and total accountability. So, responsibility, practicalities, duties, determination, willpower and courage to succeed, and positive rebirth and renewal of internal energy systems are amplified. Also, soul talents, innate gifts, and unique abilities that lead to manifestation. Natural beauty within and around can be realized. Cherishing, respecting, and honoring your own body as well as the earth are key to the lessons of the butterfly spirit. You are a sacred, divine, and sensual being… The butterfly asks you how your daily actions and habits reflect this.

Start to see the magic and beauty everywhere, as it is all around you and inside. When you make changes to your inner world, such as your mindset, belief systems, emotions, feelings, and reflections, you begin to change your outer world. When you start to make healthy choices and changes in your outer world, your inner world shifts for the better. The universe is reflected in your eyes. Self-mastery can be attained. Self-realization leads to self-actualization too, so daily epiphanies are possible. Don't underestimate the power of one small shift. Even minor changes can serve as the catalyst for big breakthroughs. Furthermore, the butterfly is here to show you how to surrender, in addition to going with the flow. Subtle and psychic instincts, intuition, and higher wisdom and awareness can be embodied. Vision is increased, as is your ability to see through illusions and false Matrix or 3D fear timelines. Enhanced vision and psychic sensitivities allow you to get to the root of truth, seeing through BS and manipulations, and uncovering metaphysical secrets. Finally, acceptance of change comes with the butterfly spirit. This power animal can help you overcome resistance to significant shifts that need to take place. Potent manifestation abilities are available as well. Negative or shadow attributes to be mindful of include getting lost in addictions, repetitive toxic cycles, pessimistic thinking, a lack of spiritual perception and spiritual/soul disconnection, and a lack of emotional intelligence. All of these can be countered by working with the butterfly spirit.

I am the Butterfly, free to flutter by…
From caterpillar to flying free,
I transform through growing wings you see.
I know I am beautiful, a delicate design of life;
I value all of nature and find beauty in every eye.
Trapped in my cocoon for some time in the beginning,
I am a symbol of evolution, transformation, and learning.
I love my freedom and find joy in spirit,
if you relate to me- you may be highly creative.

Did you know my eye consists of thousands of individual lenses,
or that I can see colors outside of your visible spectrum?
If you wish to learn my soulful secrets and see like my eye,
it's quite simple really- observe me fluttering around outside!

I am the Dragonfly, traveling swiftly on wings of change,
I have mastered movement through the air and treat life like it's a game.
For my first two years I live in water and the rest of time in air-
this reflects my true nature; I balance thoughts with emotional care.
I can twist, turn, move up or down;
change directions in a heartbeat, fly backwards or hover around...
My movement mastery is greater than any bird,
with a deep love of light and color
I travel freely through the spirit world.

Dragonfly

The dragonfly symbolizes seeing through the veil of illusion. Everything related to higher truth, wisdom, spiritual ideals and mindsets, philosophy, and transcending illusions come into the dragonfly's medicine. If this is your power animal, you are on a quest of ultimate truth! You like to find wisdom in every life experience and situation, and know how to turn negatives into positives. Even the most challenging and difficult times can be perceived as a portal for growth. The dragonfly represents powerful positive alchemy, transformation, and rebirth. Higher perspectives coupled with profound wisdom as well as highly evolved intuition are available for development and integration. The dragonfly teaches that there are multiple realms, dimensions, timelines, and different states of being. We are multidimensional, so rising above the 3D and material reality, which often keeps us bound, is essential for integral and blissful living. Joy and lightness of being comes into the mix. There is certainly great depth and grace available with this majestic spirit animal, but being "deep" shouldn't be equated with being depressed, mellow, or down. In fact, depth is what leads to sensitivity, self-awareness, and higher wisdom. These in turn lead to pursuing the path of highest pleasure, following your highest joys, and living your ultimate life. Joy, pleasure, passion, laughter, free-spiritedness, an upbeat and optimistic persona, and emitting positive vibes are essential. This spirit animal encourages you to leave negative behind, moreover act on the ideas and sensations that bring you happiness.

Change and transformation are key meanings. Also, adaptability; the ability to change plans or direction from gut feelings, intuitive inner guidance, psychic impressions, etc. This may sound normal, but it's a rare gift! Many of us value routine and logic or rationality too much. To be able to be so flexible and open-minded, least to mention intuitive, that you can listen to the subtle messages of the universe and change your plans to be better in alignment with your soul or Higher Self, is a powerful ability. People with this spirit animal excel in the realm of emotions and feelings. So, you can call on the dragonfly to help with increasing your openness to depth, sensitivity, gentleness, empathy, nurturance, emotional intelligence, soul, and grace. To be able to navigate your feelings and the emotions of others is a gift- sensitivity is a superpower, not a weakness. You can master feeling comfort in the realm of emotions, feelings, and subtle sensations. Psychic gifts are enhanced, while intuition, instincts, and spiritual perception are also increased. Emotional intelligence coupled with seeing through BS and deception is one of the main gifts of the dragonfly meaning and symbolism. You can become a BS and manipulation detector, or you already are one if you've felt a resonance with the dragonfly for a long time. In addition, the dragonfly symbolism includes a strong connection with the fairy realm, nature spirits, and elemental queen/kingdom. Further, linked to this is the wisdom that truth is subjective. There are so many realities, frequencies, and personal and collective stories occurring simultaneously, that varying truths can be present simultaneously. Ultimate truth is truths rooted in natural laws and sacred & universal cycles, which are also available for discovery and embodiment. The dragon represents wisdom and truth at the highest level, while fresh perspectives, new belief systems and ideologies, and philosophical awareness are in store.

If you observe the dragonfly, you will see how it reflects light and energy through its wings and body. This teaches us the significance and power of self-reflection, as well as seeing everyone as a mirror or reflection of us. We reflect what we see inside, and this is why embodying emotional intelligence and other feminine qualities are so important. They help to expand inner beauty and loving, kind, and harmonious thoughts, so we can then consciously mirror, or project, these qualities out to others. Introspection, contemplation, and silent or transcendental meditation are called for with the dragonfly. Sound therapy is equally on the cards when working with this spirit animal. The more you increase multidimensional awareness, the better you are able to integrate psychic, instinctive, telepathic, clairvoyant, and intuitive abilities. Everybody is a mirror. Transcending our own judgements, negativities, and toxic characteristics allow us to realize that we hold considerable power in creating our realties. We can either see the light along with many positive qualities in others, or we can mirror, project, or reflect less desirable traits. We essentially create our outer worlds based on our inner worlds. Thus, raising your vibration is inherent with the dragonfly spirit. Divine revelations and spiritual illumination & enlightenment are core to the dragonfly's message and meaning. Other key associations include hope, rebirth, spiritual maturity, ancient knowledge of the Self and sacred law, divine order, and higher consciousness, and exploring new realms and dimensions. The message is to trust in your Higher Self, connect to Source energy, practice mindfulness and self-alignment (centering; putting up healthy boundaries whilst radiating love, joy, and light), and developing inner knowing. Finally, subconscious wisdom, imaginative abilities, and a deep connection to the subtle, dream, and subconscious realms and worlds are integral to the dragonfly spirit. Divine feminine and divine masculine attributes can be strengthened and embodied, because the dragonfly is connected to both the emotional and spiritual waters of divinity- water and feminine energy, and the air realm, which is masculine by nature.

Things to be mindful of include being resistant to change, getting lost in false stories or other people's illusions, and being a victim to manipulation, deception, emotional or psychological abuse, and gaslighting tactics. Psychic attack is common to people with this spirit animal, in addition to weak or under-developed boundaries.

Hummingbird

The hummingbird symbolizes a deep connection with the emotional and spiritual planes. The message is: there is beauty and sweetness all around you. Time is ultimately timeless, eternal, and infinite, and there are infinite possibilities in store. There's so much magic, connection, and synchronicity to be found. Joy, lightness of spirit, subtle depth and self-awareness, sensitivity, and empathy are core to the hummingbird's wisdom and energy. The hummingbird teaches the true meaning of presence, of 'be here now.' You are an eternal and limitless being, which can only be fully realized when you return to Source, inner stillness, and presence. Always being on the go can pick up a lot of illusions, which disconnects you from your true joy. As humans, we get pulled into the chaos, drama, and ignorance of others, so, over time, we become completely closed off to ultimate joy and pleasure. The hummingbird is all about joy, but not "false joys" rooted in 3D timeliness and distractions. For example, if you think joy and pleasure are symbolic of death metal, video games that kill people, binge-watching endless series and movies while eating crap, and watching porn, you are largely mistaken. This is the message of the hummingbird. True joy is found in authentic connection, heart-centered intimacy whether it's platonic or romantic, community, music, art, nature, and finding shared human soul essence and resonance with others. Without stillness, silence, and presence, living in the moment and thus coming back to full consciousness, we mistake "joy" and "pleasure" for distractions, drama, and things that dull our soul shine. The hummingbird represents the highest vibration of soul joy, love, light, glow, shine, and expression! Self-expression, imagination, artistic gifts, creativity, poetry, and collaborations that serve the soul and Higher Self are part of this power animal's magic.

A connection to the realms of spirit enhances divine feminine and divine masculine qualities simultaneously. Like the dragonfly, the hummingbird is connected to the emotional feminine realms of spirit just as it is to the logical and imaginative masculine realms of air. Balance, harmony, and unification of opposites are therefore available. The hummingbird is a messenger of love as well. Good luck, agility, open-mindedness, fresh perspectives, love, and compassion come with this spirit animal helper. Playfulness and resilience are both required for ultimate joy and living, in addition to independence, self-autonomy, and self-reliance. Finding a balance between playfulness and determination to complete long term goals are available for integration. The hummingbird is able to travel great distances very quickly, which is where the agility symbolism arises. As for swiftness of communication, you can learn how to respond quickly and with wit, moreover with elegance, class, and a sense of sophistication. Hummingbirds are able to move their small wings at an unbelievably fast pace, from 10 to a record 80+ times per second. This is due to developed muscle power, which also brings the message of the importance of physical health and vitality, as well as physical strength, stamina, and courage to continue on our paths. Sophisticated, swift, and conscious communication leads to manifestation powers, advanced soul growth, and deeper connections. Mindful and empathic communication too. Good luck, inner beauty, healing, sweetness, kindness, and choosing vibration raising activities are further associations. Divinity can be found in the most simplest things, which brings the lesson of appreciating the simple things in life. Divine simplicity coupled with small joys that lead to your happiness are key here. Spirit flows through all things, so seek to be more mindful and present to attract your rightful blessings. Divine 'I Am presence' can be realized.

Follies to keep in mind when working with the hummingbird include getting caught up in distractions and false stories or vices of others, lowering your vibration to appease people who don't wish to change, and forgetting to slow down and center to redirect your energy. Try not to take on so many things that you come out of alignment, also becoming ignorant to real joy, love, unity, happiness, and pleasure. *Hint*: these are not rooted in the material or superficial world!

I am the hummingbird, a symbol of sheer joy and happiness,
I fly into the smallest places and have supreme levels of endurance.
Did you know I can use light from my mouth to help me heal,
or that my gift to stop completely still in mid-air is not a myth, but tangibly real?
Allow me to teach you the joys of simply being just from my movement and sound,
for I am the bird that represents infinity- my cyclic nature spirals round.

Sometimes we become stuck in time and forget the rhythmic nature of reality;
To let go of the past means to keep moving forward, distancing ourselves from states
of separation and hostility.
True joy cannot be realized when we're still playing out toxic cycles, you see,
I am here to show you there are endless possibilities… multiple vibrations and
frequencies.

I am the Tiger, many seem to fear my natural fire,
yet they do not realize my strength comes from passion, self-protection, & desire.
I represent the most primal parts, the deepest and most raw essence of Self;
the aspects that many still attempt to repress.
The shadow- the darkness, the subconscious suppressed
are allowed full release with me, as I survive nature's tests.

I am the hunter that may see as fearsome, this much is true,
yet I also long for affection just like you do.
My instincts and primal nature allow me to thrive,
My coat is pure beauty; my inner strength and courage are divine.
I am the wildness within demanding expression that's free,
Your inner animal and ultimate passion… sacred sexuality.

Tiger

The tiger is the best spirit animal for exploring and integrating your wild, primal, and inner animal essence. The tiger represents your lower self and more primal needs; desire, sexuality, self-protection, security, and survival. Tiger's are bold, courageous, and supremely confident creatures who face challenge and adversity like a boss. They are fiercely protective of their homes and kin- their children and family, and aren't afraid to show their "violent' side. This is not advocating violence of any kind, but, as a spirit animal, it's important to recognize that the human journey may involve aggression. Aggression to defend and protect is the message, not violence, intimidation, or bullyish behavior simply to show power and strength. In saying this, the tiger symbolizes immense courage, devotion, strength, power, and physical instincts as well as vitality. Tiger's are independent, self-autonomous, and majestic. They're sensual and down-to-earth too, also having a deeply caring side. All of this best signifies the symbolism of the tiger available for integration. Devotion, social charm and grace, generosity, kindness, a deeper connection with your own sensuality, and the power of stillness- finding strength in solitude and silence, can be expanded with the tiger spirit. Loyalty too. The tiger not only teaches the power of force and passion, but of learning to love our solitude. It's in solitude where wisdom and enhanced instincts coupled with powerful intuition arise, because we are able to find inner stillness, peace, and serenity, moreover silence. Silence is the first "sound," if you will, the original sound of creation from which all other sounds arise. Without silence there would be no sound nor music, and this is what the tiger's medicine brings; knowledge of our divine selves through slowing down and connecting with the cores of who we are.

Primarily, the tiger spirit represents determination, action, self-confidence, self-esteem, perseverance, and willpower. Working with the tiger spirit animal will give you a healthy dose of these, further assisting you in overcoming blocks to motivation, inspiration, and conscious forward movement. The tiger also symbolizes curiosity, raw emotions, and sexuality. This is very important to be aware of. People who resonate strongly with the tiger likely have a strong libido, powerful sex drive, and passionate emotions. They tackle life with courage and aren't afraid of expressing their sexual desires, fantasies, and needs. All of these themes can be embodied. Another main meaning is independence. You can regain self-sovereignty and self-autonomy, while overcoming fears and insecurities to inner wholeness. Vitality, energy, and physical stamina coupled with good luck, health, and well-being make the tiger a well sought-after spirit animal. Primal sexuality merged and harmonized with sensuality that serves the soul and spirit are key themes. As a symbol of good luck, the tiger spirit animal increases fortune, as well as wealth manifestation. You can find an abundant love life in addition to increased income, clients, job opportunities, gifts, and finances the more you work with the tiger. Confidence to go after what and who you want is available. Focus, concentration, and creating long-term plans and goals that serve your greatest aspirations are part of the tiger's symbolism. With persistence and determination you can succeed! This is the message of the tiger. Whatever your dreams are, you can accomplish a great deal when you believe in yourself and apply spiritual and emotional, as well as psychological and physical, strength. The tiger spirit is seen as lucky in many cultures, which creates possibilities for manifestation, prosperity, and positive energy flow.

Stay optimistic, be positive, and remember that assertiveness combined with sensitivity goes a long way. The tiger asks you to remain humble and compassionate without becoming a pushover, people-pleaser, or an emotional dumping ground or doormat. The tiger knows how to put up healthy boundaries and stand their ground! This is an excellent spirit animal to call on for actual competition, such as in sports, business, or anything that requires a bold and competitive attitude. Further, if you're currently facing conflict or know you are about to go into court p legal proceedings, or similar, and need to stand your ground; seek to embody the strength and ferocity of the tiger, however combined with a more peace-loving and diplomatic power animal, such as the deer or swan. Remember that you can work with different spirit animals for the perfect blend of energies. Patience is a virtue, another key quality associated with this spirit animal. Observant, intelligent, instinctive, charismatic, and highly independent, those with the tiger power animal make fierce friends, partners, and companions. A natural form of camouflage is available, which signifies blending into the background or appearing timid or shy in a crowd. Of course, the tiger is not shy at all, but to be able to appear invisible or unseen is a gift. This gives you the power of adaptability, flexibility, and being a social chameleon. Finally, masculine sexuality is a main theme linked to the tiger. Just like the panther symbolizes divine feminine sexuality, the tiger is the divine masculine counterpart. It's the perfect power animal for healing sexual trauma and wounds, therefore. Blocks, issues, or fears surrounding intimacy and sex can be overcome with the tiger spirit, if you're looking to embody more strength and fire, as opposed to something more romantic and gentle.

Be careful of procrastination, erratic behavior, aggression, impulsiveness, volatile temperaments, and being overly zealous or excitable. What you may perceive as enthusiasm and strength or assertiveness can be taken as a threat, danger warning, or sheer aggression to another. A shadow trait to watch out for is being so excitable or optimistic that you forget some people are naturally passive, submissive, or peace-loving, thus getting (unconsciously) dragged into explosive reactions and responses through misunderstanding and disagreement.

Moth (Wild Card…)

The moth is so often overlooked and treated as insignificant, so that's why I chose to call this the 'Wild Card' animal. Moths are small and less appreciated in the society we find ourselves in. We are attracted to butterflies, because they are colorful with pretty patterns. We notice the more visually appealing and beautiful animals, large or small, because we live in a superficial and somewhat narcissistic society. This is why I felt to include the moth. From experience, I've witnessed how many people observe moths and just dismiss them, overlooking their existence or even treating them as inferior creatures. Yet if you *slow down*, become aware of the more ethereal and spiritual, subtle, energy permeating our physical existence; you will see just how beautiful moths are. Some would even say they resemble fairies or fairy-like entities from another dimension… Moths symbolize the journey one takes to reach the light. Many of us see moths as insignificant or even ugly because we are denying a part of our own selves and souls. We can see how true this is when we observe the symbolism. Moths often "take themselves out" through trying to reach the light. They are so attracted to light, or the light when thinking metaphorically, and ruled by such an intense and instinctive desire to merge with this light source, that they end up taking their own life. The moth spirit therefore shows us the beautiful, yet dark human journey. Our essence, motivations, hidden desires, strength, and inner qualities are reflected in the moth. Our fundamental nature is very similar to the moth spirit, in fact. We spend a lifetime trying to find the light to then leave this realm.

So, death and rebirth, as well as the cyclic nature of the human journey are reflected in the moth spirit. Are you able to surrender to the journey, the divine will, your destiny, and the plan laid out for you? This is what the moth teaches- the art of surrender and flow, moreover the importance of destiny. Enlightenment. Soul evolution. Spiritual illumination. Divine inspiration. Surrender. Flow. Time cycles. Karmic cycles. Each of these key themes hold many important lessons. The moth represents what and who you direct your precious energy to. Time is precious, as is energy. Your resources, love, and light in addition to the way you use them come into the moth's realm. This means there's a strong karmic influence. Karmic cycles must come to a completion unless you want to die attached to your toxic energies and attributes. This is a universal or ultimate truth that many people find it hard to accept, it's not subjective truth. Being in tune with your Higher Self and the Great Spirit, the source of creation; Source energy, cosmic consciousness, the divine… means that you recognize certain truths as ultimate and others as subjective. Subjective ones are specific to our unique individual journeys, opinions, reflections, judgements, etc. Ultimate truth, such as the existence of time cycles and the soul, can help you find ultimate wish fulfillment on your journey. The soul needs expression, and there are certain things that limit us. Karmic cycles and relationships must be transcended, therefore transcendence is a key theme with the moth spirit. If we don't- if we continue to play out toxicity and repeat negative karmas? Well, we bring them into the next life.

A soul can repeat lifetime after lifetime being presented the same experience, if it repetitively fails to learn wisdom and teaching. The universe is benevolent, yet there is darkness inherent within ourselves and the cosmos itself. As you can see from the moth who repetitively touches the light to the point of self-destruction, we too keep attaining to find enlightenment. Death should not be taken literally, but metaphorically. For instance, rebirth and renewal can occur multiple times throughout life, at many different stages, and both unexpectedly and planned. With one of the main themes, 'surrender,' your aim is to unify surrendering to divine will and flow- either your own or from the messages you receive from the universe, with a conscious plan of action. Long term dreams, hopes, and aspirations are key associations. Also, listening and paying attention to psychic, instinctive, and intuitive messages within and around. Regarding karmic cycles, the moth helps you to find wisdom in repeating life situations and events. Ask yourself, does this truly bring me joy, comfort, love, security, and soul alignment? Or do I keep hoping and wishing for change, for things to get better, as well as relying too much on my comfort zones? The moth is here to assist you in transcending comfort zones that don't truly serve your Higher Self. Self-love, self-care, and living with integrity are other key meanings. Further, finding higher awareness and beauty in the challenges, hardships, and setbacks. We may get "burned" temporarily, but, hopefully, we learn from our mistakes, therefore stop repeating the self-destructive behaviors. Self-sabotage can be overcome with the moth spirit animal.

Furthermore, a dual meaning of the moth is to recognize when we might be destroying ourselves in the search for enlightenment. Self-realization is one thing, however what happens when you seek the light- the ultimate goal and highest manifestation of the soul, so much that we take yourself out? In this respect, the moth not only teaches us how to ascend and evolve, but how to find peace in our shadow selves, human selves, and earthly bodies. Similar to the snake, the moth assists us in accepting our Roots, the root chakra being the key to security, survival, self-preservation, longevity, life force, and primal physical needs. Kundalini energy and awareness is linked here. If we were to reside solely in the crown chakra, we may "destroy" (kill) ourselves through extreme periods of fasting. This is an extreme example, yet is a possibility. From root to crown and the other way round, a universal principle lies in acceptance of both our physical forms and divine spiritual essence. Both must be honored and respected for survival, soul growth, and longevity. Living life in balance, moderation, and both peace and pleasure are the main messages of the moth.

Watch out for codependency, toxicity, past wounds and trauma yet to heal, unwillingness to change, heal, and grow, unwillingness to accept your physical body and needs, and stagnation through resistance and ignorance. Blocks to growth come in many shapes and forms. Addictions, escapism, abusive relationships, repeated karmic cycles, trauma bonding, negative family and societal influences, and failure to embrace our soul talents and life purpose are integral to the shadow side of the moth power animal. Letting go is the key.

253

Life spirals round, we are multidimensional creatures,
Toxic patterns need to be transcended if we wish to move from student to teacher.
Karma is real, its an exchange of energy that affects us all;
It can either keep us blocked and stuck, stagnated, and trapped, or open new doors.
Just like me, you're always searching for something better, even if you're not sure.
Light is the way to wisdom, self-knowledge, realization, and the possibility of
more…

We each have a Higher Self, a best version of our souls,
So if you want to attain spiritual illumination and enlightenment, remember the
power of *letting go*.

Chapter 21: Self-Evolution & Completion…

Transcending Karmic Cycles

Spirit animals teach us a lot about our emotional, psychological and mental, physical, and spiritual needs. In Reiki, a sacred lineage that aims to restore health and harmony, as well as connect us with our soul selves, our core essence; it is taught that we each have a perfect vibratory frequency inherent within our DNA. This state of being and consciousness is the ideal manifestation of our souls- the highest blueprint. I personally have found this to be true, having only recently experienced my Saturn Return (age 29- 30) while beginning and completing this book. It's interesting, as during the writing process throughout 2022, I remembered many astral visions and encounters I had received since 2012 and during my twenties. Essentially, we may receive glimpses of higher insight and guidance from Spirit, from our souls, and Higher Selves, but we may not be quite ready to integrate the lesson or wisdom. During my Reiki Masters ceremony-initiation, for example, my Shamanic Reiki Master had a powerful vision of me desperately clinging onto an old dirty toy. I was so stubborn! I wanted to hold onto this old toy, yet it needed to be released. From my perspective, I had floated away somewhere, leaving this 3D earthly plane to go elsewhere for healing; I remember coming back into my physical body by throwing my right arm out. My right arm quite literally, in actuality, flew out just before awakening back into this realm… I was trying to let go of something; my body was forcing me to release something and 'throw' it away.

This is quite amazing considering the vision my Reiki Master received. Subtle energy is real. The astral, spiritual, and multidimensional planes and dimensions are real. Furthermore, she told me that she saw the toy as representing my adult body, the real world of practicalities, earning my living, supporting myself financially, and embracing my divine 'Golden Goddess' sexuality. This is fascinating considering these are the only things I was missing. It wasn't until my Saturn Return in 2022, where I turned 30, that I fully realized the healing blessing and message in this. It took me a while to fully integrate these things; practical responsibility and maturity, becoming financially self-sovereign, and embodying my sexually liberated and mature, divine, and golden-goddess sexuality. There was a vision for my future self at age 22, when I received my Reiki Masters ceremony, that didn't fully manifest and integrate in "real time" until I became an adult, at age 30. The point is, karmic cycles will keep repeating until we learn the lesson. There are multiple realms, dimensions, and subtle frequencies trying to assist us, and this is where profound wisdom, spiritual guidance, and divine insight are available. Not everything can be understood or explained with the rational mind nor with logic, scientific reasoning, or left-brain thinking. This is a very limited world-view. And this is where spirit animals come in.

Like in practices such as Reiki, Shamanic healing, and other systems that work directly with subtle and spiritual energy, spirit animals *want* to help us. They are able to transmit messages through the subtle planes and realms, and they do so for our benefit. I didn't happen to receive an animal visitation during my Reiki Masters, at least not consciously, however I frequently communicate with my personal animal guides. I do so both in waking life and during sleep, when the Higher Mind/Self is lit up. Spirit animals are here to help us outgrow old cycles, the repeat life experiences that hinder our growth and keep us stuck in self-sabotage. A cycle becomes karmic when we repeatedly fail to learn the message. Not all toxic traits, behaviors, or relationships lead to negative karma, yet being shown messages from Spirit as well as wisdom from our spirit animals, and failing to listen, change, or act on the guidance given, does lead to karmic repercussions. For example, say you have a friend or spirit animal (I am using both humans working in this dimension and spirit animals as examples, as each of our journeys are unique… we're all at different stages) who continuously tried to help you; offer you free guidance, compassionate advice, gentle loving words of wisdom and inspiration, or support that could align you with your best self, your Higher Self, and true path... But instead of accepting the love and guidance, or even appreciating it and saying thank you, giving respect from the higher wisdom from Spirit, as both humans and power animals are messengers of Spirit, channels for a higher consciousness; you choose to insult, ridicule, slander, or turn against that messenger. 'Grace is a fake shaman, she's delusional- there's no such thing as astral planes.' 'Screw the owl, what good can it do?' 'This is ridiculous… subtle energy doesn't exist!' *Exactly*. Turning against the people, spirits, and animals that are trying to help you leave your karmic cycles behind is one of the most powerful acts of "anti-self-love" and "anti-spiritual growth" you could do. Perhaps doing it once or twice is natural, it's normal for humans to experience resistance. Yet, to do it to the point of making it into a belief system, further lowering your vibration to accommodate your toxic behaviors, addictions, and mindsets more than the tool (messenger spirit) that can help you find soul-evolution and illumination? This then becomes a karmic cycle, especially if you choose to cut cords with the human helper or animal and instead turn towards your vice as a distraction.

A karmic cycle can last a year, 12 years, or a lifetime. It all depends on the individual and the lessons, moreover experiences, your soul has chosen to participate in. We each have a Higher Self, a version of ourselves that resonates with a shamanic, soulful, or spiritual path. Spirit animals help you heal whatever wounds, blocks, and traumas, in addition to pain and unconsciously accumulated karma, you have yet to overcome. Individual, family, collective, personal, and ancestral karma and wounds can be released and transcended with the assistance of your power animals. Spirit animal guides and helpers, just like shamans, healers, and spiritual teachers and elders, are catalysts to clearing karmic exchanges that have accumulated in your energy field. They inspire us, also creating internal shifts for us to transcend, evolve, and reach higher states of consciousness. Self-love, deep ancestral healing, self-alignment, soul talents, hidden gifts, awareness of your shadow self, memories pushed to your subconscious mind, and integration can all be sparked. Our conscious minds cannot pick up on everything- a huge portion of reality remains in the unseen, invisible, and subconscious, astral, and spiritual realms. This is where spirit animals work their magic! As the bridge or cord- a channel- it's your job to stay open, as well as receptive and appreciative of the healing gifts and messages in store.

Dreams, the Astral Planes, and Spirit Animals

As a qualified Dream therapist, in addition to someone who's been working consciously with dreams since as young as 14- 16, I am overjoyed to share this knowledge with you. In addition to waking life, you can work with your chosen spirit animals on the astral planes and in the dreamworlds (in dreams). Our subconscious minds and higher selves come alive during sleep, and we are further able to receive powerful wisdom, guidance, and insight in the dreamspace.

There are three main techniques or areas for self-development you can engage in to increase your susceptibility to dreams, as well as receive visitations from spirit animal guides and helpers.

1. Crystals to raise your vibration and enhance consciousness

Crystals are conscious entities that have their own electromagnetic energy field. Each crystal species has its own set of unique qualities and healing properties, just like the spirit animals have their own energetic associations and frequencies we can embody. Through meditation, holding your crystals with intent, and sleeping with them next to, on top of, or by your pillow, you can absorb the healing properties of the crystal. There are three specific ones that are incredibly effective for the purpose of receiving astral insights and visitations from your spirit animals.

Amethyst is incredibly powerful for the Third Eye chakra, sparking the Higher Self and increasing spiritual perception. Amethyst promotes peace of mind, clear vision, and mental clarity, so you can receive wisdom and guidance from the ether. Enhanced cognition, subconscious wisdom, access to dream states, psychic gifts, spiritual wisdom & illumination, and profound intuition are all part of amethyst's healing properties. Dream recall coupled with having vivid dreams too. Telepathy and clairvoyance, clairsentience, and clairaudience amplify, making Amethyst one of the most powerful dream and astral connection gemstones.

Equally as powerful is ***Lapis Lazuli***. Lapis Lazuli was revered by Ancient Egyptians as a dreaming stone, where they had actual dream temples people in the community would go to dream together. Ancient Egyptians alongside many other ancient cultures recognized that dream abilities, astral insights, and the capacity to receive higher, divine, and spiritual guidance increased when humans shared space. There's a collective consciousness energy field- a collective human psyche…. Lapis Lazuli is a special stone for lucid dreaming, astral projection, and dream recall. It promotes memory, truth, wisdom, higher power, intuition, manifestation abilities, and purification. It cleanses and purifies while energizing and activating simultaneously. Lapis Lazuli is for both the Throat and Third Eye chakras, enhancing psychic gifts coupled with spiritual perception just as much as self-expression and communication. This crystal can shield you from psychic attack, negative energy, and harmful vibrations being sent, thus opening you up to a world of possibilities after protecting you. It blocks harmful energy while enabling receptivity to spirit contact and communication. It's one of the best gemstones for everything linked to the multidimensional and dream realms and planes.

Clear Quartz is one of the most holistic and all-encompassing crystals. It is associated with the Third Eye and Crown chakras, but also related to kundalini energy and awakening. Clear Quartz stimulates inspirational, telepathic, psychic, spiritual, astral, creative, artistic, imaginative, sexual (life force, kundalini), divine, and healing energies. It is a catalyst for healing and self-development, further sparking and amplifying any intention you set. Clear Quartz is a powerful protector and energizing crystal, which means you can use it as a dreamstone or use it to charge and activate other crystals. Further, you can place this gemstone on any chakra. For example, your Root if you're wanting to attract the spirit of the tiger or lion; your Third Eye if you hope to receive communication from the owl, eagle, or hawk, and so forth. It's one of the best crystals to use for astral work like astral projection or astral travel, lucid dreaming, and spirit communication. Additionally, you can "program" Clear Quartz with your intentions for your dreaming or astral work. Hold a cleansed (in water) and charged (in sunlight) crystal in your left hand with your palm flat. Hover your right hand over the top, 1- 2 inches away. Visualize pure healing light and energy flowing through your right palm and into the crystal. Project your intentions, as they're powerful.

2. Herbal supplements for lucid dreaming + vivid dream recall & enhancement

Herbal supplements are the best things you can add to your daily self-care and spiritual development routine if you want to get serious with spirit animal communication. Instead of writing out available information, I'm going to give you some key ones to research, in your own time. Make sure you do sufficient research before purchasing and consuming any; there's a lot of different articles and sources online. I can personally confirm I've tried *all* of these and have had no problems, but I don't take pharmaceuticals, recreational drugs, or anything similar. My body is a pure channel, in other words, therefore there have been no side effects.

1. Mugwort
2. Silene Capensis (African Dream Root)
3. 5-HTP
4. Calea Zacatechichi
5. Passion flower
6. Valerian
7. Lemon Balm
8. Chamomile tea

3. Conscious fasts and detoxing combined with sound healing are two of the most effective routes to all shamanic and spirit animal contact and connection. There are a number of sound frequencies and tools you can explore, from the 432 hz 'Gaia' frequency to Tibetan singing bowls, OM chanting, binaural beats, shamanic drumming, and nature sounds. Do your research! Everyone's journey is unique, so what may resonate for someone else may not resonate for you...

Working With Your Animal Guides for Soul Expression

Congratulations! You have completed your soul's journey to find your individual and collective spirit animals and personal power animals, and how to integrate their messages and wisdom for the best possible realities and timelines. If you need any further assistance, I am always available for contact.

My email address is: **gracegabriella33@gmail.com**

Alternatively you can visit my Website or Youtube channel. I have a range of FREE educational and consciousness-expanding videos available, from wisdom sharing audios on a number of topics, to spoken word poetry.

https://gracegabriella33.wixsite.com/grace

https://www.youtube.com/@TheDreamSpiritWeaver

Printed in Great Britain
by Amazon